MW00438891

Voices of OLD TESTAMENT PROPHETS

Sidney B. Sperry

Other volumes in the Sperry Symposium Series from Deseret Book Company:

The Doctrine and Covenants, a Book of Answers

Nurturing Faith through the Book of Mormon

The Apostle Paul: His Life and His Testimony

Thy People Shall Be My People

The Heavens Are Open

Doctrines of the Book of Mormon

The Lord of the Gospels

A Witness of Jesus Christ

Doctrines for Exaltation

Voices of OLD TESTAMENT PROPHETS

The 26th Annual
Sidney B. Sperry Symposium

Deseret Book Company
Salt Lake City, Utah

Library of Congress Cataloging-in-Publication Data

Sperry Symposium (26th : 1997)
Voices of Old Testament prophets : the 26th annual Sidney B. Sperry Symposium.
p. cm.
Compilation of articles presented at the 1997 Sperry Symposium on the Old Testament.
Includes bibliographical references and index.
ISBN 1-57345-360-9
1. Prophets—Congresses. 2. Prophets (Mormon theology)—Congresses. I. Title.
BS1505.2.S64 1997
221.6—dc21 97-32982
CIP

Printed in the United States of America 72082

10 9 8 7 6 5 4 3 2 1

Contents

Preface

Joshua once approached Moses, concerned when two men began to prophesy by the Lord's Spirit in the Israelite camp. Moses' classic response was this: "Would that all the Lord's people were prophets and that the Lord would put his spirit upon them" (Numbers 11:29).

The Lord's people have rarely achieved this ideal. Yet the Lord Jehovah has in all dispensations worked with his people through prophets, whose teachings and examples are timeless. Living prophets conveyed the voice and will of the Lord to their contemporaries. The example of their lives and much of what they taught is still relevant for the Saints in this dispensation.

The Old Testament is the focus of the 1997 Sperry Symposium. The symposium theme, "Voices of Old Testament Prophets," is reminiscent of Brother Sidney B. Sperry's volume *The Voice of Israel's Prophets: A Latter-day Saint Interpretation of the Major and Minor Prophets of the Old Testament* (Salt Lake City: Deseret Book, 1965). It provides a welcome opportunity to reflect on significant prophetic voices of the past and their value for the present.

Neither the papers in this volume nor the symposium from which they were drawn can adequately cover all the prophets and their teachings in the Old Testament. Thus, we have selected papers for this compilation that we hope will provide greater insight into various aspects of Old Testament prophets and prophecy. Some papers are traditional studies of doctrine or prophecy but with a sharpened focus or new perspective; others demonstrate the value of sensitivity to the biblical text or to an understanding of the cultural context in which past prophets lived. All have been written by faithful Latter-day Saints who have strong testimonies of the Savior and the Restoration; however, the views presented are those of the respective authors and do not necessarily represent the views of the Sperry Symposium committee, Brigham Young University, The Church of Jesus Christ of Latter-day Saints, or Deseret Book Company.

We hope that this study of Old Testament prophets and their teachings will be valuable to Latter-day Saints and will encourage them to listen to modern prophetic counsel. Surely, as declared by Amos nearly twenty-seven hundred years ago, the Lord will do nothing unless he reveals his will to his people through his prophets (see Amos 3:7; see also JST Amos 3:7).

Dennis A. Wright
Craig J. Ostler
Dana M. Pike
Dee R. Darling
Patty A. Smith

The 1997 Sidney B. Sperry
Symposium Committee

CHAPTER ONE

Remnants Gathered, Covenants Fulfilled

RUSSELL M. NELSON

To be invited to give the keynote address at the twenty-sixth annual Sidney B. Sperry Symposium is an honor for which I am deeply grateful.

Dr. Sperry was educated in Old Testament studies and ancient languages at the University of Chicago before he joined the faculty of Brigham Young University in 1932. Author of many works, Dr. Sperry was a distinguished scholar. His personal life was equally exemplary. I join with you in paying a well-deserved tribute to Dr. Sidney B. Sperry.

I bring love and greetings from the First Presidency and the Quorum of the Twelve Apostles. We appreciate your faith. We are thankful for your companions and your families, who sustain you. Your work is very important. Your students will bear great responsibilities in the Church in the exciting years of the future. We commend you; we appreciate you; and we pray for you in all of your righteous endeavors.

Someone once said that you should survey large fields and cultivate small ones.[1] The theme of this symposium, "Voices of Old Testament Prophets," suggests that you will have large fields to survey—from Genesis to Malachi—and many small ones to cultivate as well. But you will have to

Elder Russell M. Nelson is a member of the Quorum of the Twelve Apostles of The Church of Jesus Christ of Latter-day Saints.

work at it. You can't plow fields by turning them over in your minds.

The title of my message is "Remnants Gathered, Covenants Fulfilled." It comes from the Book of Mormon. There the Lord speaks of fulfilling "the covenant which the Father hath made unto his people," the house of Israel. "Then," he continues, "shall the remnants, which shall be scattered abroad upon the face of the earth, be gathered in from the east and from the west, and from the south and from the north; and they shall be brought to the knowledge of the Lord their God, who hath redeemed them" (3 Nephi 20:12–13).

The gathering of those remnants and the fulfilling of that divine covenant are occurring in our day. Yet this big picture is obscure to the eye of many who focus upon bargains at supermarkets and rankings of favorite football teams. Let us examine our place in God's plan for his children and for The Church of Jesus Christ of Latter-day Saints. We are part of a destiny known by relatively few people upon the earth.[2]

During the year 1997, attention across the world has been attracted to the history of the Church. Its pioneers arrived at the valley of the Great Salt Lake 150 years ago. Replications of handcarts have been featured from Siberia to Swaziland, from Scandinavia and South America to the isles of the South Pacific. Through theater and stage, printed and electronic media, stories of early converts to the Church have been told.

Generally, writers of these accounts have done well in reporting what these pioneers did. But only a few have captured the reasons why. Even fewer have understood that history in context of the voices of prophets of the Old Testament that link with the great latter-day work that is now being accomplished.

Connections with the New Testament would be no surprise to any who understand the deep commitment to Jesus Christ held by members of this Church that bears his holy name. Its stalwart pioneers opened the period of the

Restoration of all things—the promised dispensation of the fulness of times—as prophesied by Peter and Paul (see Acts 3:21; Ephesians 1:10). Those apostolic records and other scriptures of the New Testament are an integral part of the legacy of the restored Church. Its name describes members as Latter-day Saints, to distinguish them from those of the Church in the meridian of time. Members were then called *saints,* as they are now. Paul addressed an epistle "to the saints which are at Ephesus, and to the faithful in Christ Jesus" (Ephesians 1:1).[3] To recent converts of that time and place, Paul said, "Now therefore ye are no more strangers and foreigners, but fellowcitizens with the saints, and of the household of God" (Ephesians 2:19; see also 3:17–19).

In that epistle Paul used the word *saint* at least once in every chapter! The term *saint* does not connote beatification or perfection in this life. It simply describes each member of the Church as a believer in Jesus the Christ. It means that members are committed to love God and their neighbor. They are to sacrifice, to serve, and to build the Church as directed by its inspired leaders.

But the connection between the Church and the Old Testament is less apparent. This symposium, which focuses on the voices of the prophets in the Old Testament, is an opportune time to speak of the strong and significant links between ancient and modern Israel.

As I speak to this theme, you will doubtless think of additional connections. You will also recognize that much more could be said on each segment that I will discuss. That is good. You can explore these interrelationships later without the limitations of time and talent that press upon me now. I would like to limit my discussion to five major links that are of immense importance.

The Link of Joseph

The first link I shall label as the link of Joseph. This link applies both to Joseph who was sold into Egypt and to the Prophet Joseph Smith. Few men in the Old Testament are of greater importance to Latter-day Saints than is Joseph of

Egypt. Many Bible commentators have described him as a type, or shadow, for the Savior. But we also know him as a specific type for the Prophet Joseph Smith and a generic type for all members of The Church of Jesus Christ of Latter-day Saints. Many of the Church's members claim descent from Joseph through his sons, Ephraim or Manasseh.

The importance of Joseph in the book of Genesis is signified by the fact that he figures prominently in sixteen of its fifty chapters (see Genesis 30; 33; 35; 37; 39–50). Joseph's life span from cradle to grave[4] represents only 4 percent of the twenty-seven hundred years covered by the book of Genesis. Yet his life is reported in nearly one-third of its chapters.[5]

In the King James Version, Genesis 50 ends with verse 26, which records the death of Joseph. In the Joseph Smith Translation, that chapter not only adds important information to verses 24 through 26 but provides twelve additional verses that enrich our knowledge of the link of Joseph (see JST Genesis 50:27–38). Those additions include the following insights, which I paraphrase:

1. A righteous branch would be raised up later out of Joseph's loins (see JST Genesis 50:24).

2. Israel would be scattered. A branch would be broken off and carried into a far country (see JST Genesis 50:25).

3. A choice seer would be raised up from Joseph's loins to do work for the fruit of his loins (see JST Genesis 50:26–29).

4. Writings from the fruit of Joseph's loins would grow together with writings from the fruit of Judah's loins to bring knowledge of their fathers and of everlasting covenants. That knowledge would come in the last days (see JST Genesis 50:30–32).

5. The promised seer would be called Joseph, after the name of his father, and he would be like unto Joseph, son of Jacob, bringing salvation to the children of the Lord (see JST Genesis 50:33).

These additions are good examples of "plain and

precious" truths that have been restored through the Prophet Joseph Smith (see 1 Nephi 13:40).

He and the ancient Joseph had much in common, as shown by other scriptures that I will cite. From the Book of Mormon we read: "A part of the remnant of the coat of Joseph was preserved and had not decayed. . . .Even as this remnant of garment . . . hath been preserved, so shall a remnant of [Joseph's] seed . . . be preserved by the hand of God" (Alma 46:24).

We are remnants of that precious seed. Joseph Smith had been chosen by the Lord to take up the labors of the tribe of Joseph, son of Jacob. Centuries ago that same Joseph had prophesied of Joseph Smith and described their linkage. Again I quote from the Book of Mormon:

"Yea, Joseph truly said: Thus saith the Lord unto me: A choice seer will I raise up out of the fruit of thy loins; and he shall be esteemed highly among the fruit of thy loins. And unto him will I give commandment that he shall do a work for the fruit of thy loins, his brethren, which shall be of great worth unto them, even to the bringing of them to the knowledge of the covenants which I have made with thy fathers.

"And I will give unto him a commandment that he shall do none other work, save the work which I shall command him. And I will make him great in mine eyes; for he shall do my work" (2 Nephi 3:7–8).

The link of Joseph applied not only to Joseph Smith Jr. but to his father as well. Again I quote from Joseph who was sold into Egypt:

"Behold, that seer [Joseph Smith] will the Lord bless; . . . for this promise, which I have obtained of the Lord, of the fruit of my loins, shall be fulfilled. . . .

"And his name shall be called after me; and it shall be after the name of his father. And he shall be like unto me; for the thing, which the Lord shall bring forth by his hand, by the power of the Lord shall bring my people unto salvation" (2 Nephi 3:14–15).

Joseph and Joseph Smith had more in common than

their lineage-linking. At age seventeen, Joseph, son of Jacob, was informed of his great destiny (see Genesis 37:2). At that same age, Joseph Smith was informed of his destiny regarding the Book of Mormon: He was seventeen when first visited by the angel Moroni, who told the boy prophet that "God had a work for [him] to do." He was to translate a book written upon golden plates containing the fulness of the everlasting gospel. His "name should be had for good and evil among all nations, kindreds, and tongues" (Joseph Smith–History 1:33; see also 1:34–41).

Both Josephs were persecuted. Joseph in Egypt was falsely accused of a crime he did not commit and was put into prison.[6] Joseph Smith was incarcerated on trumped-up charges and false accusations.[7]

Joseph's coat of many colors was taken from him by his brothers in a cruel attempt to convince their father that Joseph had been killed (see Genesis 37:2–33). Joseph Smith's life was taken from him, largely because of betrayals by false brethren.

Anciently, "when all the land of Egypt was famished, the people cried to Pharaoh for bread: and Pharaoh said unto all the Egyptians, Go unto Joseph; what he saith to you, do" (Genesis 41:55). In the latter days, people starving for nourishment that only the gospel can provide are again to be fed—by Joseph. The Lord declared that "this generation shall have my word through [Joseph Smith]" (D&C 5:10). Today we "feast upon the words of Christ" because of Joseph Smith (2 Nephi 32:3).

This link of Joseph is summarized in lines from the book of Ether:

"The Lord brought a remnant of the seed of Joseph out of the land of Jerusalem, that he might be merciful unto the seed of Joseph that they should perish not. . . .

"Wherefore, the remnant of the house of Joseph shall be built upon this land [of America]; and it shall be a land of their inheritance; and they shall build up a holy city unto the Lord, like unto the Jerusalem of old. . . .

". . . and blessed are they who dwell therein, for it is they whose garments are white through the blood of the Lamb; and they are they who are numbered among the remnant of the seed of Joseph, who were of the house of Israel.

". . . and they are they who were scattered and gathered in from the four quarters of the earth, and from the north countries, and are partakers of the fulfilling of the covenant which God made with their father, Abraham" (Ether 13:7–8, 10–11).

The Link of the Book of Mormon

Link number two I shall identify as the link of the Book of Mormon. In September 1997 I had the extraordinary privilege of seeing portions of the original manuscript and virtually all of the printer's manuscript of the Book of Mormon.[8] That was an incredible experience!

Voices of prophets in the Old Testament foretold of this great book. You are familiar with the prophecy of Isaiah:

"Thou shalt be brought down, and shalt speak out of the ground, and thy speech shall be low out of the dust, and thy voice shall be, as of one that hath a familiar spirit, out of the ground, and thy speech shall whisper out of the dust" (Isaiah 29:4).

Could any words have been more descriptive of the Book of Mormon, coming as it did "out of the ground" to "whisper out of the dust" to people of our day?

Other Old Testament passages foretold the Book of Mormon. One such came to mind last January when I attended a prayer breakfast at the White House in Washington, D.C., hosted by President Bill Clinton. During an informal reception that preceded the breakfast, I was chatting with a distinguished and scholarly Jewish rabbi from New York. Our conversation was interrupted by another rabbi who asked his colleague from New York if he could recall the scriptural reference to the stick of Judah and the stick of Joseph that would come together one day. My friend paused for a moment, stroked his chin pensively, and then replied, "I think you will find that in the book of Ezekiel."

I could not restrain myself. "You might look in the thirty-seventh chapter of Ezekiel," I interjected. "There you will find the scriptures that you seek."

My rabbi friend was surprised. "How did *you* know that?"

"This doctrine," I said, "is very important in our theology."

Indeed it is. You know it, and I know it. I would like to read it:

"Moreover, thou son of man, take thee one stick, and write upon it, For Judah, and for the children of Israel his companions: then take another stick, and write upon it, For Joseph, the stick of Ephraim, and for all the house of Israel his companions:

"And join them one to another into one stick; and they shall become one in thine hand" (Ezekiel 37:16–17).

Saints of modern Israel in 160 nations across the world are blessed to hold the Bible and the Book of Mormon as one in their hands. The worth of this privilege must never be underestimated.

Keys of authority for the Book of Mormon—the stick of Ephraim—were held by the angel Moroni (see D&C 27:5). The Book of Mormon is the great amplifying, clarifying, and converting scripture. It is indeed "Another Testament of Jesus Christ" (Book of Mormon, title page).

Children of the Lord have ever been admonished to "search the scriptures" (John 5:39; Alma 14:1; 33:2; 3 Nephi 10:14). In addition, we of modern Israel have been specifically commanded to study one particular voice and prophet of the Old Testament. Which one? Isaiah! (see 3 Nephi 20:11; 23:1). The importance of that commandment is underlined by the fact that 433 verses of Isaiah appear in the Book of Mormon. Studying them is not repetitious. Sidney B. Sperry reported that 234 of those verses differ from their biblical counterparts.[9] In addition, the Doctrine and Covenants has more than seventy quotations from or paraphrases of Isaiah.[10] Study the words of Isaiah! Do *we* get the message?

Other prophets of the Old Testament were quoted to our

modern prophets. Malachi's teachings have been repeated.[11] Elijah,[12] Moses,[13] and others have taught people of both ancient and modern Israel.[14]

Isaiah described the spirit of the Book of Mormon as "familiar." It resonates with people who know the Old Testament, especially with those who are conversant with its Hebrew language. The Book of Mormon is filled with Hebraisms—traditions, symbolisms, idioms, and literary forms. It is familiar because more than 80 percent of its pages come from Old Testament times.[15]

The Link of the House of Israel

Link number three I shall designate as the link of the house of Israel. It includes doctrines of the Abrahamic covenant and of the scattering and gathering of Israel.

About four thousand years ago, Abraham received a promise from the Lord that blessings would be offered to all of his mortal posterity.[16] Included were promises that the Son of God would come through Abraham's lineage, that certain lands would be inherited by his posterity, that nations and kindreds of the earth would be blessed through his seed, and more. Knowledge of and reaffirmations of this covenant are evident in scriptures of the Old Testament.[17] Although certain aspects of that covenant have already been fulfilled, many have not. The Book of Mormon teaches that we of modern Israel are among the covenant people of the Lord.[18] And, most remarkably, it teaches that the Abrahamic covenant will be fulfilled only in these latter days.[19] The Lord bestowed this Abrahamic covenant upon the Prophet Joseph Smith for the blessing of him and posterity after him.[20] Did you know that Abraham is mentioned in more verses of modern revelation than in all the verses of the Old Testament?[21] Abraham—this great patriarch of the Old Testament—is inextricably linked to all who join The Church of Jesus Christ of Latter-day Saints.[22]

Doctrines relating to the scattering and gathering of the house of Israel were also among the earliest lessons taught in the Book of Mormon. I quote from the first book of Nephi:

"After the house of Israel should be scattered they should be gathered together again; . . . the natural branches of the olive-tree, or the remnants of the house of Israel, should be grafted in, or come to the knowledge of the true Messiah, their Lord and their Redeemer" (1 Nephi 10:14).

The Old Testament is replete with prophecies that relate to the scattering of Israel. May I cite one from the book of First Kings:

"For the Lord shall smite Israel, as a reed is shaken in the water, and he shall root up Israel out of this good land, which he gave to their fathers, and shall scatter them" (1 Kings 14:15).

In this citation, the word "scatter" was translated from the Hebrew verb *zarah,* which means "to scatter, cast away, winnow, or disperse." The richness of the Hebrew language provides other verbs to describe similar actions. For example, from the book of First Kings we also read:

"I saw all Israel scattered upon the hills, as sheep that have not a shepherd" (1 Kings 22:17).

In this instance, "scattered" was translated from the Hebrew verb *puwts,* which also means "to scatter" or "be dispersed."

Isaiah used yet another verb in this prophecy:

"He shall set up an ensign for the nations, and shall assemble the outcasts of Israel, and gather together the *dispersed* of Judah from the four corners of the earth" (Isaiah 11:12; emphasis added).

In this case "dispersed" was translated from the Hebrew verb *naphats,* which means "to shatter, break, dash, or beat in pieces."

References to the scattering were also recorded in the New Testament. For example, the book of James begins with these words:

"James, a servant of God and of the Lord Jesus Christ, to the twelve tribes which are scattered abroad, greeting" (James 1:1).

In this reference, "scattered" was translated from the Greek feminine noun *diaspora,* which means "dispersed" or "scattered." You may wish to look up the word *diaspora* in the Bible Dictionary.[23] There the scattering of the house of Israel is succinctly summarized.

Saints of modern Israel know that Peter, James, and John were sent by the Lord with "the keys of [his] kingdom, and a dispensation of the gospel for the last times; and for the fulness of times," in which he would "gather together in one all things, both which are in heaven, and which are on earth" (D&C 27:13).[24]

The travels and travail of our pioneers were of eternal consequence. Their mission was not limited to an international immigration or a transcontinental migration with wagons and handcarts. They were to lay the foundation of an endless work that would "fill the world."[25] They were essential to Jeremiah's prophecy:

"Hear the word of the Lord, O ye nations, and declare it in the isles afar off, and say, He that scattered Israel will gather him, and keep him, as a shepherd doth his flock" (Jeremiah 31:10).[26]

They got the message. Missionaries were sent very early to "the isles afar off" to commence the work of the Lord. As a result, the Church was established in the British Isles and in the islands of French Polynesia years before the pioneers entered the valley of the Great Salt Lake. It has been my privilege to participate in sesquicentennial celebrations in the British Isles in 1987 and in French Polynesia in 1994. Now in 1997, I celebrate this one with you in Utah.

Another aspect of the gathering of Israel reflects back to our first link regarding Joseph. The word *Joseph* comes from the Hebrew masculine personal noun *Yowceph,* the literal meaning of which is "Jehovah has added." *Joseph* also relates to the Hebrew root *yasaph,* which means "to add," and "to *asaph,*" which means both "to take away" and "to gather."[27]

The Hebrew verbs *yacaph* and *acaph*[28] are used in the Hebrew text of the Old Testament 186 and 180 times respectively. Both words were usually translated into English as "gather" in one of its several forms. For example, in the verse, "David *gathered* together all the chosen men of Israel" (2 Samuel 6:1),[29] the Hebrew verb *yacaph* was used.

Another scripture from Genesis deserves special comment. It reports the naming of Jacob and Rachel's firstborn son: "She called his name *Joseph;* and said, The Lord shall *add* to me another son" (Genesis 30:24).[30] In that verse both the words "Joseph" and "add" were derived from the Hebrew root *yacaph.*

The lineage of Joseph—through Ephraim and Manasseh—is the seed appointed to lead in the gathering of Israel.[31] The pioneers knew—through their patriarchal blessings and from doctrines of the Old Testament, amplified by scriptures and revelations of the Restoration—that the long-awaited gathering of Israel was to commence with them.

The Link of the Exodus

The fourth link connecting ancient and modern Israel I shall name the link of the Exodus. At a Church Educational System fireside satellite broadcast in September 1997, I spoke to the subject of "The Exodus Repeated." Then I spoke of some connections between ancient and modern Israel that will also be relevant to a more comprehensive coverage of the topic, "Remnants Gathered, Covenants Fulfilled." Fascinating are the many parallels between the exodus from Egypt of the Israelites under Moses and the exodus from the United States of the pioneers under Brigham Young.

Both peoples were oppressed by their governments. The ancient Israelites were "bondmen" in Egypt.[32] The Latter-day Saints were persecuted by their own government.[33]

Moses had been prepared in the courts of Egypt and had gained much experience in military and other responsibilities (see Hebrews 11:24, 27). Brigham Young was likewise prepared for his leadership role. In the march of Zion's Camp, he observed the leadership of the Prophet Joseph Smith under difficult conditions.[34] Brigham Young aided in the removal of the Saints from Kirtland and directed the move of the persecuted Saints from Missouri to Nauvoo.[35]

God preserved ancient Israel from plagues that he sent upon Egypt (see Exodus 15:26). God preserved the Saints from the plague of the United States Civil War that caused more American deaths due to war than any other war.

Both groups had to leave their homes and earthly possessions. Both had to learn to rely wholly upon the Lord and be sustained by him during their travels. Both traversed deserts, mountains, and valleys of untamed wilderness. Ancient Israelites left Egypt via the waters of the Red Sea "as by dry land" (Hebrews 11:29). Some pioneers left the United States by crossing the wide waters of the Mississippi River—frozen to become a highway of ice.[36] Both groups endured trials of their faith during which the weak were winnowed away and the strong were empowered to endure to the end (see Ether 12:6; D&C 101:4–5; 105:19).

The children of ancient Israel had a portable tabernacle wherein covenants were made and ordinances were performed to strengthen them on their journey.[37] Originally the tabernacle was intended to be a portable temple, before the Israelites lost the higher law (see D&C 84:23–26; 124:38; JST Exodus 34:1–2). Similarly, many Latter-day Saints were endowed in the Nauvoo Temple before their trek.

The journey from Egypt to Mount Sinai took about three months.[38] The journey from Winter Quarters to the valley of the Great Salt Lake also took about three months.[39]

The promised land for each group also bore similarities. That of ancient Israel had an inland sea of salt water, the inlet to which was the River Jordan. That for the pioneers also had an inland sea of salt water, fed by the Jordan River. The destination of each group was described by the Lord as a land "flowing with milk and honey."[40] The pioneers turned their wilderness into a fruitful field[41] and made the desert blossom as a rose[42]—precisely as prophesied by Isaiah.

For both the Israelites and the Saints, civil and ecclesiastical law were unified under one head. Moses bore that responsibility for the early Israelites.[43] Brigham Young—a modern Moses[44]—led the Latter-day Saints' movement west, with the Lord's blessing.[45] Moses and Brigham Young followed parallel patterns of governance.[46] And each of them endured dissension from their close associates.[47] Nevertheless, that same unified pattern of government will again prevail when the Lord shall be "King over all the earth,"[48] and he shall govern from Zion and Jerusalem.[49]

The Israelites celebrated their exodus from Egypt. The Latter-day Saints commemorated their exodus with the establishment of the world headquarters of the restored Church in the tops of the mountains. Both celebrations acclaimed their miraculous deliverance by God.[50] The link of the exodus reminds us of an Old Testament scripture of gratitude:

"Moses said unto the people, Remember this day, in which ye came out from Egypt, out of the house of bondage; for by strength of hand the Lord brought you out from this place" (Exodus 13:3).

The Link of the Timeless Truths of the Gospel

The fifth connection between ancient and modern Israel I shall denote as the link of the timeless truths of the gospel. Those truths are included in the unending priesthood order of Melchizedek, though he is mentioned but twice in the Old Testament.[51] The Melchizedek Priesthood was removed from ancient Israel shortly after the exodus from Egypt.[52] Thereafter, ancient Israel functioned under the Levitical Priesthood and the law of carnal commandments.[53]

Timeless truths and principles of the gospel were and are important to people of ancient and modern Israel. The Sabbath day, for example, was honored for different reasons through the generations. From the time of Adam to Moses, the Sabbath was observed as a day of rest from the labor of Creation.[54] From the time of Moses to the resurrection of the Lord, the Sabbath also commemorated the liberation of the Israelites from their bondage in Egypt.[55] In latter days, Saints keep the Sabbath day holy in memory of the atonement of Jesus Christ.[56]

The restoration of the priesthood rejuvenated the principle of tithing, linking to the Old Testament teachings of Genesis and Malachi.[57] Saints of modern Israel know how to calculate their own tithing from this simple instruction:

"Those who have thus been tithed shall pay one-tenth of all their interest annually; and this shall be a standing law unto them forever, for my holy priesthood, saith the Lord" (D&C 119:4).

In contrast, have you ever amused yourself with the thought, on or about April 15th each year, that the filing of income tax returns is a bit more complicated? I'll confess that I have.

Turning our attention again to the timeless truths of the gospel, none are more vital than those associated with temple worship. They compose another link between ancient and modern Israel. The Bible Dictionary states that "whenever the Lord has had a people on the earth who will obey his word, they have been commanded to build temples in which the ordinances of the gospel and other spiritual manifestations that pertain to exaltation and eternal life may be administered."[58]

The best known temple of ancient Israel was Solomon's temple. Its baptismal font[59] and dedicatory prayer[60] provide patterns that are employed for temples today.[61] Old Testament scriptures refer to special clothing[62] and ordinances[63] that are associated with temples.[64] How thankful we are that the Lord chose to restore the highest blessings of the priesthood to his faithful sons and daughters! He said:

"For I deign to reveal unto my church things which have been kept hid from before the foundation of the world, things that pertain to the dispensation of the fulness of times" (D&C 124:41).

Revealed truth that we know as the Word of Wisdom came to the Prophet Joseph Smith in 1833. Every Latter-day Saint is familiar with it as one of the visible hallmarks of our faith. The final verse of that revelation forges another link back to ancient Israel:

"And I, the Lord, give unto them a promise, that the destroying angel shall pass by them, as the children of Israel, and not slay them"(D&C 89:21).

This reference to the Passover shows that the Lord wanted obedient Saints of modern Israel to receive physical and spiritual protection just as he had provided for his faithful followers centuries before.

Summary

Ancient Israel and modern Israel are linked arm in arm. In our day, many Old Testament prophecies are being fulfilled. Isaiah foretold:

"And it shall come to pass in the last days, that the mountain of the Lord's house shall be established in the top of the mountains, and shall be exalted above the hills; and all nations shall flow unto it" (Isaiah 2:2).[65]

During the past year, visitors from more than one hundred nations have come to visit world headquarters of The Church of Jesus Christ of Latter-day Saints.[66]

Ancient and modern Israel subscribe to an ageless message of the Old Testament:

"Know therefore that the Lord thy God . . . keepeth covenant and mercy with them that love him and keep his commandments to a thousand generations" (Deuteronomy 7:9).[67]

All faithful members of the Church will receive their just reward:

"All things are theirs, whether life or death, or things present, or things to come, all are theirs and they are Christ's, and Christ is God's" (D&C 76:59).

I would like to bear my testimony as one with you, my

beloved brothers and sisters. We love our Heavenly Father. We love the Lord Jesus Christ. We are his people. We have taken his holy name upon us. We are his remnants now being gathered and gleaned into his eternal garners.[68] We are fulfilling "the covenant which the Father hath made unto his people" (3 Nephi 20:12). We are being brought to the knowledge of our Lord who has redeemed us.[69] We are "children of the covenant" (3 Nephi 20:26),[70] destined to be as was ancient Israel—"a kingdom of priests, and an holy nation" (Exodus 19:6).[71] We know that Joseph Smith is the great prophet of the Restoration and that President Gordon B. Hinckley is the prophet of the Lord today.

My testimony, my love, and my blessing, I leave with you, in the name of Jesus Christ, amen.

Notes

1. Also quoted by Franklin D. Richards, in Conference Report, October 1964, 77.

2. Ten million members of the Church compose 0.0017 of a world population of 5.8 billion.

3. The term *saints* appears in sixty-two verses of the New Testament.

4. Joseph died at the age of 110 years (see Gen. 50:26).

5. Sixteen of fifty chapters equals 32 percent.

6. See Genesis 39:11–20.

7. See J. Reuben Clark Jr., *On the Way to Immortality and Eternal Life* (Salt Lake City: Deseret Book, 1949), 133; Ezra Taft Benson, in Conference Report, April 1954, 58.

8. About 25 percent of the original manuscript is in the historical archives of the Church. The printer's manuscript is owned by the Reorganized LDS Church and was on loan to The Church of Jesus Christ of Latter-day Saints. It is reported to be complete except for two lines of the title page.

9. *Improvement Era,* October 1939, 594.

10. Monte S. Nyman, in *Encyclopedia of Mormonism,* ed. Daniel H. Ludlow, 4 vols. (New York: Macmillan, 1992), 2:702. Another is mentioned in Joseph Smith–History 1:40.

11. 3 Nephi 24:1; D&C 110:14; 128:17; 133:64; 138:46; Joseph Smith–History 1:36.

12. See 3 Nephi 25:5; D&C 2:1; 27:9; 35:4; 110:13, 14; 128:17; 133:55; 138:46, 47; Joseph Smith–History 1:38.

13. Moses is mentioned in 1300 verses of scripture, 515 (40 percent) of which are in modern revelation.

14. See D&C 27:5–13.

15. Personal communication from Elder Jeffrey R. Holland, June 1997.

16. See D&C 132:29–50; Abraham 2:6–11.

17. See Genesis 26:1–4, 24; 28; 35:9–13; 48:3–4.

18. See 1 Nephi 14:14; 15:14; 2 Nephi 30:2; Mosiah 24:13; 3 Nephi 29:3; Mormon 8:15.

19. See 1 Nephi 15:12–18.

20. See D&C 124:56–59.

21. Abraham is mentioned in 506 verses of scripture, 289 of which are in modern revelation.

22. The covenant may also be received by adoption. See Matthew 3:9; Luke 3:8; Galatians 3:27–29; 4:5–7.

23. See LDS edition of the King James Version of the Bible, Bible Dictionary, s.v. "Diaspora," 657.

24. Compare with Paul's prophecy of the Restoration in Ephesians 1:10.

25. Joseph Smith, quoted in Wilford Woodruff, *The Discourses of Wilford Woodruff,* sel. G. Homer Durham (Salt Lake City: Bookcraft, 1946), 39.

26. *Gather* is used to translate the Hebrew verb *qabats,* which means "to gather, assemble."

27. See LDS edition of the King James Bible, Genesis 30:24, footnote *a.*

28. Spellings in James Strong, *The Exhaustive Concordance of the Bible* (1890; reprint, New York: Abingdon, 1965), "Hebrew and Chaldee Dictionary," 50, 15.

29. Emphasis added.

30. Emphasis added. Joseph was "added" to Rachel's family because her handmaid, Bilhah, had given birth to Dan and Naphtali previously (see Genesis 30:5–8). See also Deuteronomy 33:16–17, which refers to the people of Joseph being pushed together "to the ends of the earth: and they are the ten thousands of Ephraim, and they are the thousands of Manasseh." JST Genesis 50:34 also affirms that Joseph's seed would be preserved forever.

31. See Erastus Snow, in *Journal of Discourses,* 26 vols. (London: Latter-day Saints' Book Depot, 1854–86), 23:183–84.

32. See Deuteronomy 6:21.

33. The pioneers were forced out of Missouri under threat of an order signed by Missouri's governor directing that the "Mormons must be treated as enemies and must be exterminated or driven from the state" (Joseph Smith, *History of The Church of Jesus Christ of Latter-day Saints,* ed. B. H. Roberts, 2d ed. rev., 7 vols. [Salt Lake City: The Church of Jesus Christ of Latter-day Saints, 1952–51], 3:175). In 1887, the Congress of the United States of America took the unprecedented step of eliminating the Church's legal existence by revoking its corporate charter and authorizing federal receivers to assume ownership of virtually all of the Church's property and other assets, including its most sacred houses of worship—temples in Logan, Manti, St. George, and Salt Lake City (see *The Late Corporation of The Church of Jesus Christ of Latter-Day Saints v. United States,* 136 U.S. 1[1890]). Yet the Saints knew that they were Abraham's seed and heirs to promises and protection from the Lord (see D&C 103:17–20).

34. See Smith, *History of the Church,* 2:6–12, 185; Leonard J. Arrington, *Brigham Young: American Moses* (New York: Knopf, 1985), 58.

35. See Smith, *History of the Church,* 2:529; 3:252, 261; Preston Nibley, *The Presidents of the Church* (Salt Lake City: Deseret Book, 1974), 41.

36. See Orson Pratt, in *Journal of Discourses,* 21:275–77, 20 June 1880.

37. Ordinances and covenants of ancient Israel are referenced in 1 Corinthians 10:1–3; for modern Israel, see D&C 84:26–27.

38. See Exodus 12:2, 3, 6, 18; 13:4; 19:1.

39. One hundred and eleven days.

40. For the people of ancient Israel, see Exodus 3:8; 17; 13:5; 33:3; Leviticus 20:24; Numbers 13:27; 14:8; 16:13, 14; Deuteronomy 6:3; 11:9; 26:9, 15; 27:3; 31:20; Joshua 5:6; Jeremiah 11:5; 32:22; Ezekiel 20:6, 15; JST Exodus 33:1. For the pioneers, see D&C 38:18–19.

41. See Isaiah 32:15–16.

42. See Isaiah 35:1.

43. See Joseph Smith, *Teachings of the Prophet Joseph Smith,* sel. Joseph Fielding Smith (Salt Lake City: Deseret Book, 1938), 252.

44. See D&C 103:16. President Spencer W. Kimball wrote of Brigham Young's role in that exodus: "Since Adam there have been many exoduses and promised lands: Abraham, Jared, Moses, Lehi, and others led groups. How easy it is to accept those distant in time as directed by the Lord, yet the ones near at hand as human calculations and decisions. Let us consider for a moment the great trek of the Mormon refugees from Illinois to Salt Lake Valley. Few, if any, great movements equal it. We frequently hear that Brigham Young

led the people to make new tracks in a desert and to climb over mountains seldom scaled and to ford and wade unbridged rivers and to traverse a hostile Indian country; and while Brigham Young was the instrument of the Lord, it was not he but the Lord of heaven who led modern Israel across the plains to their promised land" (*Faith Precedes the Miracle* [Salt Lake City: Deseret Book, 1972], 28).

45. See D&C 136:1–42.

46. See Exodus 18:17–21; D&C 136:1–4.

47. See Numbers 12:1–11 (Aaron and Miriam); for latter-day examples, see Smith, *History of the Church,* 1:104–5 (Oliver Cowdery); and 1:226 (William E. McLellin).

48. Psalm 47:2; Zechariah 14:9.

49. See Isaiah 2:1–4.

50. See Jeremiah 16:15; 23:7. Other miracles were shared, such as food provided by the "miracle of the quails." (For ancient Israel, see Exodus 16:13; Psalm 105:40; for the pioneers, see Stanley B. Kimball, "Nauvoo West: The Mormons of the Iowa Shore," *BYU Studies* 18 [winter 1978]: 142.) Protection was provided for ancient Israel by the Lord, who "went before them by day in a pillar of a cloud, to lead them the way; and by night in a pillar of fire" (Exodus 13:21; see also 22; Numbers 14:14; Deuteronomy 1:33; Nehemiah 9:19). Similar care has been noted for the pioneers (see Smith, *History of the Church,* 3:34; Thomas S. Monson, in Conference Report, April 1967, 56).

51. See Genesis 14:18; Psalm 110:4.

52. See JST Exodus 34:1–2; D&C 84:23–25.

53. See D&C 84:27.

54. See Exodus 20:8–11; 31:13–17; Mosiah 13:16–19.

55. See Deuteronomy 5:12–15; Isaiah 58:13; Ezekiel 20:20–22; 44:24.

56. See D&C 20:40, 75–79; 59:9–19; see also Matthew 26:26–28; Mark 14:22–24; Luke 22:19–20; Acts 20:7; 1 Corinthians 16:2; Revelation 1:10.

57. See Genesis 14:20; Malachi 3:8–12.

58. LDS edition of the King James Bible, Bible Dictionary, s.v. "Temple," 781.

59. See 2 Chronicles 4:15.

60. See 2 Chronicles 6:12–42.

61. See D&C 109:1–80.

62. For examples, see Exodus 28:4; 29:5–9; Leviticus 8:7–9; 1 Samuel 18:3–4.

63. For examples, see Exodus 19:10; 14; 2 Samuel 12:20; Ezekiel 16:9.

64. See D&C 124:37–40.

65. See also 2 Nephi 12:2; JST Isaiah 2:2.

66. Estimate provided by the Temple Square Mission.

67. See also Deuteronomy 11:1, 27; 19:9; 30:16; Joshua 22:5; 1 John 5:2–3; Mosiah 2:4. Other Old Testament scriptures refer to rewards for those obedient to God's commandments through a "thousand generations" (see 1 Chronicles 16:15; Psalm 105:8.)

68. See Alma 26:5.

69. See 3 Nephi 20:12–13.

70. See also Acts 3:25; 3 Nephi 20:25.

71. See also D&C 76:56–57.

CHAPTER TWO

Jethro, Prophet and Priest of Midian

ANTHONY RIVERA JR.

The significance of Jethro's calling and ministry is often overshadowed by the more extensive prophetic narratives of Abraham and Moses. Nevertheless, Jethro is a key link in the line of priesthood authority between these two prophets and is worthy of a place among the great early prophets of the Old Testament. Although the narrative mentioning Jethro is limited to a few chapters in the book of Exodus, these chapters provide significant information on the ministry and priesthood of this man. His influence in teaching Moses about Jehovah/Yahweh, the God of his ancestors, affects generations to come. (It is not clear from the Bible how much Moses knew about Jehovah prior to leaving Egypt.)

Jethro is called the priest of Midian, which name implies that he had priestly duties at a shrine, a temple, or a mountain altar in the land of Midian. Jethro fills prominent roles as a father, priest, and mentor in the book of Exodus. As a father, Jethro becomes Moses' father-in-law after Moses marries one of Jethro's seven daughters. As a priest, Jethro descends from a long line of Melchizedek Priesthood holders and appears to have ministered over a desert region that included the mountain of God (Sinai). Finally, as a mentor,

---

Anthony Rivera Jr. is a doctoral candidate in the Department of Near Eastern Languages and Cultures at the University of California–Los Angeles.

Jethro instructs Moses in some important duties of the priesthood and trains him to be a caring shepherd of people and a faithful follower of God.

Jethro as Father

Jethro is first introduced by the name *Reuel* in Exodus 2:16. He is the father of seven daughters, the oldest of whom may have been Zipporah (although this is never explicitly stated), who help tend the family's flock of sheep. After a skirmish with some troublesome shepherds as they are watering their sheep, the daughters return to report to "Reuel their father" how Moses, who had apparently just arrived in Midian, single-handedly "stood up and helped" them (Exodus 2:17–19). Some important points emerge from these passages which illustrate Jethro's fatherly role. First, although Jethro is introduced initially as "the priest of Midian" (Exodus 2:16), his primary role is that of a father. Second, Reuel may have been Jethro's clan name. If so, then Jethro is not only a father to his own family but also the patriarch of an entire clan.[1]

In their rush to inform their father of the altercation at the watering hole, the daughters of Jethro neglect their valiant deliverer. Once Jethro sees that all his daughters are accounted for, he inquires about their lack of hospitality by asking: "And where is he? why is it that ye have left the man?" (Exodus 2:20). He instructs his daughters to go back and summon Moses to his tent for a meal. The hospitality of this Midianite family makes Moses feel "content to dwell with the man," and because of Moses' valor and service, Jethro "gave Moses Zipporah his daughter" to be his wife (Exodus 2:21). Through this union between Moses (an Israelite) and Zipporah (a Midianite), Jethro's family begins to increase with the birth of his grandsons Gershom (Exodus 2:22) and Eliezer (Exodus 18:4).

The next time Jethro appears in his fatherly role is after Moses and the tribes of Israel are liberated from Egyptian bondage. Moses takes his wife and sons with him as he follows the Lord's instructions to return to Egypt (Exodus 4:20).

The text does not specify why or when Moses sends his wife and sons back to Jethro in Midian, but the reason probably relates to the severity and potential danger of Moses' mission in Egypt (Exodus 18:2). While Moses is in Egypt helping deliver the Israelites, Jethro, his daughter Zipporah, and his grandsons Gershom and Eliezer are probably waiting anxiously for word of Moses' welfare and safety. Finally, back in Midian, Jethro receives word of "all that God had done for Moses, and for Israel his people, and that the Lord had brought Israel out of Egypt" (Exodus 18:1). As soon as Jethro hears that the Lord has delivered Moses and Israel from Egypt, he sends a message back to Moses saying: "I thy father in law Jethro am come unto thee, and thy wife, and her two sons with her" (Exodus 18:6). Upon Jethro's entrance into the camp of Israel, Moses "went out to meet his father in law, and did obeisance, and kissed him; and they asked each other of their welfare" (Exodus 18:7). It is interesting that no mention is made of Moses' reunion with his wife or sons, only with his father-in-law, Jethro. Moses, the author of the book of Exodus, may have done this consciously to emphasize the patriarchal role of Jethro and their close relationship. Jethro's family was his new family, and Midian had been his new home until the Lord called him back to Egypt to deliver his people.

Jethro as Priest

Jethro is first mentioned as the "priest of Midian" in Exodus 2:16. The sudden appearance of this priest within the Exodus narrative raises these questions: For whom was he a priest? From whom did he receive his priesthood? It is clear that Jethro is the priest of the God whose mountain was in the land of Midian and who later revealed himself to Moses as I AM or Jehovah (Exodus 3:1, 14).[2] Yet the Exodus account is silent concerning from whom Jethro received his priesthood authority. Because of this lack of information, non-Latter-day Saint scholars traditionally view Jethro as a pagan priest of desert gods.[3] Latter-day Saints are fortunate, however, to have further information on the priesthood authority of Jethro through modern revelation and prophetic exposition.

The Lord revealed to the Prophet Joseph Smith that Moses received the Melchizedek Priesthood from Jethro. After the Lord addresses the topic of the temple in Doctrine and Covenants 84, he immediately reveals the complete priesthood lineage from Moses back to Adam: "And the sons of Moses, according to the Holy Priesthood which he received under the hand of his father-in-law, Jethro; and Jethro received it under the hand of Caleb; and Caleb received it under the hand of Elihu; and Elihu under the hand of Jeremy; and Jeremy under the hand of Gad; and Gad under the hand of Esaias; and Esaias received it under the hand of God. Esaias also lived in the days of Abraham, and was blessed of him—which Abraham received the priesthood from Melchizedek, who received it through the lineage of his fathers, even till Noah; and from Noah till Enoch, through the lineage of their fathers; and from Enoch to Abel, who was slain by the conspiracy of his brother, who received the priesthood by the commandments of God, by the hand of his father Adam, who was the first man" (D&C 84:6–16).

Significant for this discussion are the unfamiliar names of the priesthood bearers between Jethro and Abraham. The Lord does not provide any detail about the relationship of Caleb, Elihu, Jeremy, Gad, and Esaias to Jethro or Abraham. It is not clear from the revelation whether these men are Midianite ancestors of Jethro or simply righteous men with no direct relation to the Midianites; however, Church leaders have had a great deal to say on this matter. Regarding the priesthood line of Jethro, Joseph Fielding Smith stated that "some of them, at least, we may presume were descendants of Abraham and of Midian."[4] If we are to understand that there was a direct line of Midianite priests with "Jethro being fifth in regular descent from Midian"[5] the son of Abraham, then how do we explain the ordination of Esaias? Doctrine and Covenants 84:12 states that Esaias received the priesthood "under the hand of God." We are also told in the following verse that Esaias lived "in the days of Abraham" and that he was "blessed of him." Professor Sidney Sperry explained that "obviously this would not be the pre-existent Savior, but His Father or some authorized representative. If the latter, it would probably be Abraham."[6] Esaias' ordination by "the hand of God" may have been similar to that of Edward Partridge. The Lord told him that "I will lay my hand upon you by the hand of my servant Sidney Rigdon" (D&C 36:2; see also v. 5). Regarding the ordination of the Prophet Joseph Smith to the Melchizedek Priesthood, the Lord revealed that it was "Peter, and James, and John, whom I have sent unto you, by whom I have ordained you" (D&C 27:12). The language in these revelations may lead us to concur with Professor Sperry's suggestion that God the Father probably ordained Esaias by the hand of Abraham. If so, Jethro's line of priesthood authority went directly back to Abraham, his ancestor, and eventually to Adam. Furthermore, this indicates that the gospel and the priesthood were not restricted to the Israelites, who were then in Egypt, but were among at least one other group of people not directly associated with the Israelites.

Although the priesthood holders listed in Doctrine and Covenants 84 who lived between the time of Abraham and that of Jethro are not attested in the Old Testament, the names they bore are familiar. Other individuals mentioned in the Bible bore the same names, and many of them have some association with Midianite tradition and lineage.[7] Nevertheless, linking them in some way to the Midianites does not necessarily mean they were ancestors of Jethro. Although the exact identity of the men mentioned in Doctrine and Covenants 84 is a mystery to us, they are known to the Lord, who has graciously revealed their priesthood lineage and their association with Jethro.

Jethro as Mentor

The book of Exodus indicates that Jethro helped train Moses to better lead, serve, and judge the Israelites. Thus,

Jethro can be considered a mentor to the younger prophet. We first see Jethro in this role after Moses rescues Jethro's daughters and sheep from the shepherds at the well (Exodus 2:17). The next scene depicts Moses tending Jethro's flock! (Exodus 3:1). That may seem a petty job for such a hero as Moses. Surely Jethro has children and servants to tend the animals. In Exodus 2:20, Jethro questions his daughters' treatment of their deliverer and orders them to summon Moses respectfully to his tent. Why, then, was Moses made shepherd of Jethro's flock rather than guardian of his house or leader of a Midianite caravan? (see Genesis 37:28). The answer may be that Jethro wanted to help Moses learn the essential qualities of a shepherd of a flock—namely, humility, care, and leadership.

As the priest of Midian, Jethro presumably also instructed Moses in the nature of Jehovah, his God, during the many years Moses dwelt with him, thus qualifying and preparing Moses for his own revelations from God and for his critical, prophetic mission to Egypt. Exodus 3:1 not only informs us that Moses was the shepherd of a flock but tells us that he "led the flock to the backside of the desert, and came to the mountain of God." Moses was probably not wandering aimlessly in the desert but journeying purposefully toward the holy mountain of Jethro's God. Reading the account, one can sense Moses' awareness of the sacredness of the space he is approaching as well as his preparedness for the event that is about to take place. Upon the mountain, Moses witnessed the glory of God manifested in a great burning fire in a bush that was not consumed (Exodus 3:2; KJV reads "angel of the Lord;" JST reads "presence of the Lord"). The text informs us that Moses determines to see more of the great sight he is beholding: "And Moses said, I will now turn aside, and see this great sight" (Exodus 3:3). The Lord then calls him by name, and Moses answers in the traditional Hebrew idiom of readiness and preparedness, *hinneni,* or, "here am I."[8] God introduces himself to Moses (Exodus 3:6) and issues the calling to deliver Israel from Egypt (Exodus 3:10). Sometime later the marvelous revelations recorded in Moses 1–4 were bestowed upon Moses (Moses 1:17, 26 indicate that these revelations were given between the episode at the burning bush and Moses' return to Egypt).

The book of Exodus indicates that after the theophany at the burning bush, Moses "returned to Jethro his father in law, and said unto him, Let me go, I pray thee, and return unto my brethren which are in Egypt, and see whether they be yet alive. And Jethro said to Moses, Go in peace. And the Lord said unto Moses in Midian, Go, return into Egypt: for all the men are dead which sought thy life. And Moses took his wife and his sons, and set them upon an ass, and he returned to the land of Egypt: and Moses took the rod of God in his hand" (Exodus 4:18–20).

Moses is a spiritual giant by the time he departs from his mentor; however, his training is far from complete. Jethro's value as a mentor to Moses is next seen in Exodus 18, after Moses accomplishes the first part of his mission; that is, delivering the children of Israel from Egyptian bondage and bringing them to the land of Midian to the mountain of God. In this chapter, we read Jethro's additional counsel to Moses and his associates.

Exodus 18 begins, "When Jethro, the priest of Midian, Moses' father in law, heard of all that God had done for Moses, and for Israel his people" (Exodus 18:1). The lessons Moses learned by tending the flock of Jethro prepared him to lead a greater flock—all the tribes of Israel—to the mountain of God (Exodus 18:2–5). The Psalms capture this motif in two particular verses: "Thou leddest thy people like a flock by the hand of Moses and Aaron" (Psalm 77:20) and "[the Lord] made his own people to go forth like sheep, and guided them in the wilderness like a flock" (Psalm 78:52).

As Jethro approaches the camp of Israel, Moses goes forth to meet him. When they meet, Moses, who had challenged Pharaoh and parted the Red Sea, bows himself down and kisses him (Exodus 18:7). Whether he kissed Jethro's feet or arose and kissed his face is not clear from the text. Although this greeting is the traditional, formal, ancient

Near Eastern custom, it may also display Moses' great personal respect for his father-in-law's authority and their previous relationship. Jethro is now the guest in Moses' camp, although Moses has returned to Midian and Jethro's territory. Within his tent, which would represent the local seat of the tribal leader,[9] Moses reports to Jethro the wonderful works the Lord has performed by his hand (Exodus 18:8). As a result, "Jethro rejoiced for all the goodness which the Lord had done to Israel" (Exodus 18:9). The elder, Midianite priest then blesses the Lord and testifies: "Now I know that the Lord [Jehovah] is greater than all gods" (Exodus 18:11). Employing words similar to the Lord's when he declared to Abraham, "Now I know that thou fearest God, seeing thou hast not withheld thy son, thine only son from me" (Genesis 22:12), Jethro utters a confirmation (not the original acquisition) of his testimony and a proclamation to all that Jehovah is the only true God.

In the next scene Jethro officiates over a burnt-offering sacrifice and sacred meal. "And Aaron came, and all the elders of Israel, to eat bread with Moses' father in law before God" (Exodus 18:12). It is Jethro, not Moses or Aaron, who presides over (and perhaps demonstrates?) the legitimate order of sacrifice in the desert. As a typical Near Eastern host, it would have been normal for Moses to provide a sacrificial meal in honor of his guest, just as Jethro had done earlier for Moses (Exodus 2:20), as Jacob had done for Laban (Genesis 31:54–55), as Joseph had done for his brothers in Egypt (Genesis 43:25), as Job had done for his relatives (Job 42:11), and as the woman of Shunem later did for the prophet Elisha (2 Kings 4:8). Yet in this case, it is Moses' respected guest who presides, conducts, and officiates before God at the sacrifice and meal. Moses' deference to Jethro suggests that Moses still sees Jethro as the presiding priest of the region.

Concerning Jethro's role as mentor, President J. Reuben Clark Jr. observed that "great as was Moses' training in the royal courts of Pharaoh, it was not enough for his new duties. So Jethro, the priest of Midian and father-in-law of

Moses, having learned of God's dealing with Moses and his people, came to Israel's camp and instructed Moses in the rudiments of government for a people dwelling in tents and on the march. This revelation from a high priest of God did not come while Israel was yet in Egypt, as a matter of fitting them for their trek, but it came at the hour when Moses needed it."[10] The events of Jethro's visit to the Israelite camp clearly describe more than a simple welcome party given by the leaders of Israel. In this context instruction is given by Jethro, "the priest of God," on priesthood ritual activity and the initiation of the leaders of Israel into the (further) worship of Jehovah. (There is little agreement about how knowledgeable and faithful the Israelites had been in Egypt regarding the true worship of Jehovah. Moses, of course, had already had the visions recorded in Moses 1, but only after he fled Egypt and stayed with Jethro.)

The account in Exodus continues to highlight the theme of Jethro's instruction to Moses. On the following day, as Moses sits in judgment from morning until evening deciding the cases of the people (Exodus 18:13), Jethro, the more experienced priest, observes Moses' actions and realizes the danger in the weighty task Moses has taken upon himself. We are not explicitly told how Moses came to be judge, although as the divinely appointed priesthood leader of Israel he has that responsibility. Neither are we informed of the extent to which God revealed the method of proper judgment to him. It appears that Moses is learning as he goes along, in part. Jethro, obviously more familiar with the duties of a priesthood leader, instructs the less experienced Moses in suitable priesthood method so that Moses can judge his people effectively. The seasoned priest states, according to the New Revised Standard Version of the Bible, "Now listen to me! I will give you counsel, and God be with you! You should represent the people before God, and you should bring their cases before God; teach them the statutes and instructions. . . . You should also look for able men. . . . Let them sit as judges for the people at all times;

let them bring every important case to you, but decide every minor case themselves. So it will be easier for you" (NRSV Exodus 18:19–22). The text witnesses: "So Moses hearkened to the voice of his father in law, and did all that he had said" (Exodus 18:24). Moses acts according to the counsel of Jethro; this supports the idea that Jethro is a mentor and Moses is a pupil in this situation. Moses, like so many who lived before and after him, was learning gospel principles and practices line upon line. The Lord used Jethro to assist Moses in learning the technicalities and procedures of his calling as judge and priest of Israel.

The book of Exodus records that after Jethro's instructional visit with Moses, Aaron, and the elders of Israel, the priest of Midian "went his way into his own land" (Exodus 18:27). Although this is the end of the account of Jethro's involvement with Moses,[11] the account in Exodus 18 clearly illustrates Jethro's significant role as a mentor to Moses even after the Exodus as he coached Moses in important aspects of priestly procedure regarding judgment, and perhaps, sacrifice and sacred meals. (The extent to which Moses had already been trained by Jethro in matters of sacrifice and sacred meals before the Exodus is not clear from the text, although a significant amount of instruction had presumably already taken place.)

This view differs profoundly from the general non-Latter-day Saint view that Israelite priesthood begins with Moses. Modern revelation on ancient priesthood (D&C 84) helps us understand how Moses acquired his priesthood authority through a long line of Melchizedek Priesthood holders preceding the time of Jethro. While we believe that the Lord instructed Moses through revelation in the principles of the gospel, the Lord also called upon Jethro to play a role in the process. It was Jethro "who set in order all the officers in Israel, and gave Moses commandments how to proceed."[12] In addition, Jethro's experience as a seasoned priest of Jehovah prepared him to help train Moses in the service of God.

Conclusion

Jethro, the priest of Midian, is often overshadowed by other prophets in the Old Testament. He becomes more noteworthy when we see him in his roles as father, priest, and mentor. He stands as a patriarch to his Midianite clan and becomes the father-in-law of Moses. The father-son relationship between Jethro and Moses is emphasized by Jethro's treatment of Moses in Midian and in Moses' reunion with Jethro after the exodus from Egypt. As a priest, Jethro descends from a long line of righteous priests (possibly Midianites) and presides over the land of Midian and the mountain of God. Finally, as a mentor, he instructs and trains Moses in priesthood government and service to God. Jethro provides an important link between the ancient patriarchs and the Israelite prophets. As a descendant of a non-Israelite branch of Abraham, he provides further evidence that the gospel and priesthood were among at least one other nation and people. This study of Jethro's role as the priestly mentor of Moses does not detract from the position or achievements of Moses but rather it emphasizes the magnitude of Jethro's contribution to Moses' development.

Notes

1. For works in which *Reuel* is taken as a clan name, see William F. Albright, "Jethro, Hobab, and Reuel in Early Hebrew Tradition," *Catholic Bible Quarterly* 25 (1963): 5–6; see also *The Anchor Bible Dictionary,* ed. David Noel Freedman, 6 vols. (New York: Doubleday, 1992), s. v. "Reuel," 5:693–94.

2. Jethro probably referred to the God of the mountain by the name *Yahweh* (Hebrew)/*Jehovah,* or a similar name, as his ancestors had. Though this was the name familiar to the Midianites, it is not clear that it was still known by the Israelites in Egypt. JST Exodus 6:3 states that Moses was to tell the children of Israel that Jehovah—the God of Abraham, Isaac, and Jacob—sent him (which may indicate that Israelites still knew the name).

3. See, for example, Moshe Greenberg, *Understanding Exodus* (New York: Behrman House, 1969), 48.

4. Joseph Fielding Smith, *The Way to Perfection* (Salt Lake City: Deseret Book, 1970), 74–75. In addition, Wilford Woodruff, in *Journal*

of Discourses, 26 vols. (Liverpool: Latter-day Saints' Book Depot, 1854–86), 11:244–45, taught that Moses received his priesthood from "Jethro, his father-in-law, who received it through Abraham."

5. Erastus Snow, "On Priesthood," *Times and Seasons* 2 (2 August 1841): 489.

6. Sidney B. Sperry, *Doctrine and Covenants Compendium* (Salt Lake City: Bookcraft, 1960), 389.

7. Caleb the son of Jephunneh is associated with the tribe of Judah but is in fact a Kenezite, a group who were relatives of the Midianites (see Numbers 13:6; 14:6; 26:65; 32:12; 34:19; Deuteronomy 1:36; Joshua 14:6–14; 15:13–20; Judges 1:12, 13, 16; 1 Chronicles 4:15); Elihu from the tribe of Ram (Job 32:2) lived in the land of Uz, which was in Midianite territory (see Lamentations 4:21; Jeremiah 25:20; Genesis 36:28; see also Ernst Axel Knauf, "Uz," in *Anchor Bible Dictionary,* 6:770–71); a Jeremiah is listed with other clans with Midianite connections (1 Chronicles 1:3; 2:9, 25); in Numbers 2:14 a descendant of Gad is called the son of Reuel, a Midianite clan name.

8. See also Genesis 22:1; 37:3; 46:2; 1 Samuel 3:4–10; Isaiah 6:8.

9. See Hugh Nibley's detailed discussion on the centrality of the tribal tent in "Tenting, Toll, and Taxing," in *The Collected Works of Hugh Nibley,* vol. 10, *The Ancient State* (Salt Lake City: Deseret Book, 1991), 33–98.

10. J. Reuben Clark Jr., *On the Way to Immortality and Eternal Life* (Salt Lake City: Deseret Book, 1961), 124.

11. This is not, however, the end of Midianite contact with the children of Israel. For example, some of the Midianites become guides for the Israelites through the territories north of the land of Midian (Numbers 10:29–32), and later we read that Midianite tribes settle in the southern territory of the tribe of Judah after Israel has entered the promised land (Judges 1:16; 4:11).

12. Snow, "On Priesthood," 489. See also B. H. Roberts, *New Witness for God* (Salt Lake City: Pulsipher, 1986), 3:261: "Jethro, the priest of Midian, though not of Israel, as well as Moses, possessed divine wisdom; and even counseled the Hebrew prophet-prince, to the latter's advantage." Robert L. Simpson said: "He did not know exactly how to get organized, I guess, because the Lord finally had to have Jethro, his father-in-law, come to the rescue. The Lord inspired Jethro to counsel with Moses." *Organizing for Eternity,* Brigham Young University Speeches of the Year (Provo, 20 April 1965), 6.

CHAPTER THREE

THE PROPHET'S VOICE OF AUTHORITY

DENNIS A. WRIGHT

The book of Numbers provides evidence of a prophet's unique role as the spokesman of the Lord. Through revelation, Moses received understanding that enabled him to maintain order in the government of God as he faced his challengers. Numbers provides a response to contemporary questions regarding the authority of the living prophet.

The priest Korah[1] stood defiantly before his tent, the smoke from his censer[2] filling the air with petitions against the prophet Moses. His rebellious followers, also bearers of the holy priesthood, listened to Korah challenge Moses: "Ye take too much upon you, seeing all the congregation are holy" (Numbers 16:3). To this Moses responded, "Ye take too much upon you, ye sons of Levi" (Numbers 16:7). Warning all to stand away from the rebellious priests, Moses declared, "Hereby ye shall know that the Lord hath sent me to do all these works" (Numbers 16:28). The ground began to shake, and the rebels cried in terror as a chasm opened beneath their feet. Hoping to escape the widening abyss they turned, only to meet death in a consuming fire. Only their censers remained, dropped to the ground as the rebellious priests died.

Dennis A. Wright is associate professor of Church history and doctrine at Brigham Young University.

CHALLENGES TO A PROPHET'S AUTHORITY

While the rebellion ended with a decisive display of earthquake and fire, its implications are more subtle and complex. Events recorded in Numbers 11–17 provide insight to why members of the congregation of Israel challenged their prophet. The people initially accepted Moses' unique role with great faith, but when difficulties developed they did not hesitate to question his authority to speak for the Lord. The events at Taberah[3] (Numbers 11–17) illustrate three types of challenges. In examining each of these challenges, the relationship between the congregation and the prophet becomes clearer.

Joshua issued the first challenge by questioning the prophet's decision to delegate authority to others, which he feared would decrease the prophet's credibility. Miriam initiated the second challenge, demanding that those with spiritual gifts be given special recognition and authority. The third challenge resulted in a public rebellion because Korah, the Levite priest, coveted the position of high priest. For Joshua, the prophet delegated too much power; for Miriam he failed to grant it to those with special gifts; and for Korah, he unnecessarily restricted it to a select few. In each instance the challenger felt justified in questioning the prophet's authority to act for the Lord.

Such action is surprising since the congregation of Israel had claimed to accept their prophet as the spokesman for God. Upon leaving Egypt they acknowledged that the Lord said to Moses, "I will be with thy mouth, and teach thee what thou shalt say" (Exodus 4:12). For this reason the congregation followed the prophet and did "as the Lord had commanded Moses and Aaron" (Exodus 12:28). Like Israel of old, the Church today also accepts a living prophet. Members receive his words "as if from mine own mouth, in all patience and faith" (D&C 21:5) and recognize that "no one shall be appointed to receive commandments and revelations in this church excepting my servant" (D&C 28:2). Like their ancient counterparts, members of the contemporary Church also find reason to challenge their prophet.

For this reason, the examples from Numbers provide models with which to examine not only the relationship between the children of Israel and Moses but also the relationship between the contemporary Church and its prophet today.

Joshua Challenges the Prophet

While camped at Taberah, Moses pleaded with the Lord to lift the burden he carried as prophet. "I am not able to bear all this people alone, because it is too heavy for me" (Numbers 11:14). Earlier he faced a similar challenge and solved it with advice from his father-in-law, Jethro (Exodus 18:25). In that instance, Moses created a system of civil judges to assist in leadership matters. Building on this experience, the Lord directed Moses to select seventy elders[4] of Israel and delegate to them ecclesiastical power.[5] These faithful elders had authority to assist in ministering to the people's spiritual needs. This delegation of ecclesiastical authority complemented the earlier delegation of civil authority and greatly reduced the leadership burden on Moses.

Before discussing the response of Joshua to the calling of the seventy, it is helpful to examine the principles that guide the delegation of ecclesiastical authority. President Joseph F. Smith explained how the prophet governs every act performed under his authority.[6] This begins with God granting power to the prophet for directing His kingdom on earth. The prophet may authorize others to perform particular labors, but he alone retains the presiding authority. President Smith used the term *keys* to represent this authority. The prophet holds all keys but may delegate selected keys to others who are assigned specific responsibilities. Those who receive keys act under the prophet's direction and are subject to his authority. Moses presided over Israel and delegated keys to the seventy that enabled them to minister to the spiritual needs of the people. In this way the seventy lifted the burden of leadership from the prophet's shoulders. While delegating authority to the seventy resolved one problem, another developed—Joshua did not fully understand the principles involved, and he challenged the prophet's action.

Two of the seventy, Eldad and Medad, "went not out unto the tabernacle: and they prophesied in the camp" (Numbers 11: 26).[7] Joshua demanded that Moses restrain Eldad and Medad as he felt their service distracted from Moses' authority. With prophetic vision Moses replied, "Enviest thou for my sake? would God that all the Lord's people were prophets, and that the Lord would put his spirit upon them" (Numbers 11:29).

Joshua questioned the benefits associated with delegated authority. Rather than viewing the seventy as a strength, he feared they distracted from the authority of Moses. Moses explained that their faithful service added strength, and he desired all Israel to have sufficient faith to act in spiritual matters. As a type, Joshua represented a perspective that prefers an extreme centralization of ecclesiastical authority. This perspective frequently expects those in authority to control rather than invite counsel. It assumes that those who speak for the Lord do so without the interaction and service of others. It is surprising that Joshua resisted the service of the seventy, because the benefits of involving more servants in the Lord's work seem apparent.

Miriam Demands Recognition

As Moses delegated authority to some, it was natural that others would covet recognition for themselves. It is surprising, however, that Miriam and Aaron, members of Moses' own family, questioned his leadership. Their actions presented a second type of challenge: Unlike Joshua, they did not seek to reinforce the authority of the prophet but rather to share in that power. They sought special recognition and authority because of their spiritual gifts.

Miriam acted as spokesman, which causes most biblical scholars to consider the challenge representative of her perspective more than Aaron's.[8] She presented her credentials to the prophet. "Hath the Lord indeed spoken only by

Moses? hath he not spoken also by us?" (Numbers 12:2). She reasoned that the spiritual gifts she exhibited in her role as prophetess (Exodus 15:20) qualified her for special recognition.[9]

The manner in which Miriam presented her challenge provides important insight. From the outset, Miriam chose to make the matter personal. She first insulted Moses' wife by referring to her as a Cushite, which displays the deep emotions of the moment.[10] Aware of the special spiritual gifts granted to the seventy, Miriam then sought from her younger brother recognition of her own spiritual gifts.[11]

Miriam confused spiritual gifts with delegated power and authority. Miriam's gift of prophecy had not required a priesthood ordination.[12] As a gift of the Spirit it was available to all the faithful and had the power to make "every man a prophet and every woman a prophetess, that they may understand the plans and purposes of God."[13] Those who possess this gift receive a testimony of Christ and become prophets and prophetesses prepared to declare the principles of the gospel and provide instruction in the things of the kingdom.[14] This was not enough for Miriam; she desired additional recognition from Moses.

Moses understood the difference between the general gifts of the Spirit and the specific authority granted by the Lord. He alone presided over Israel and spoke for the Lord. Miriam's challenge recognized his unique authority but assumed that her spiritual gifts entitled her to a special position. Moses did not question the value of Miriam's spiritual gifts, but he recognized that she had lost sight of important principles. In meekness, he sought help from the Lord in what for him was a personal as well as an ecclesiastical problem.

At this point Miriam experienced the consequences of her challenge. The Lord appeared at the tabernacle door and called for Miriam and Aaron. The Lord declared, "If there be a prophet among you, I the Lord will make myself known unto him. . . . With him will I speak mouth to mouth . . . ; and the similitude of the Lord shall he behold"

(Numbers 12:6–8). Continuing, the Lord explained the difference between indirect spiritual gifts, such as dreams or visions, and the direct encounters experienced by Moses. The prophet communicated "face to face" with the Lord, which gave him the advantage of a sure knowledge of God's will. The Lord then asked Miriam why she was not afraid to challenge Moses, knowing of his special relationship with the Lord. As the cloud departed, Miriam became leprous, requiring the intervention of Moses to spare her life. The Lord granted Moses' plea but required that Miriam complete a ritual cleansing so that all Israel might know of her sin.[15] Miriam learned personally of the consequences associated with demanding of the prophet special recognition and authority.

Miriam and Joshua responded differently to situations involving the prophet's unique authority. For Joshua, the challenge related to the risk of delegated power distracting from the prophet's authority. From a different perspective, Miriam demanded that her own unique spiritual gift receive greater recognition. From Joshua's perspective, Moses delegated too much power; from Miriam's, he granted too little.

The Rebellion of Korah

The next leadership challenge to Moses developed as Korah led the Korathite branch of the Levitical Priesthood in revolt. Joined by Dathan, Abiram, and 250 other leaders, they accused Moses and Aaron, "Ye take too much upon you, seeing all the congregation are holy, every one of them, and the Lord is among them" (Numbers 16:3).[16] They recognized that Moses had previously delegated civil authority to the tribal elders and ecclesiastical authority to the seventy. These Levites now desired the right to officiate in the tabernacle. As Korathite priests they resented their assignment to the lesser tasks and sought the position of high priest.[17]

The Reubenites Dathan and Abiram supported Korah even though they presented a different complaint. These

Reubenites questioned Moses' leadership as they considered life in the wilderness inferior to the land of "milk and honey" left behind in Egypt. As leaders of the tribe of Reuben, they demanded authority suited to the descendants of the firstborn of Jacob.[18] This challenge angered Moses, as he felt he had treated them fairly (Numbers 16:15). They responded by refusing to meet with Moses. They claimed that he would only "throw dirt in their eyes"[19] and confuse the issue. Their complaint against the civil authority of Moses found an ally in Korah as he challenged Moses at an ecclesiastical level.

Acting as spokesman for the rebellion, Korah demanded that Moses recognize the "holiness" of all Israel and allow increased participation in the government of Israel. Moses perceived that Korah coveted an ordination to the "high priesthood" (JST Numbers 16:10) held by Aaron.[20] Moses responded to the rebellion by falling on his face (Numbers 16:4) as an expression of frustration and humility. Because the rebellion posed a serious threat to Israel, Moses proposed a demonstration of who the Lord approved to lead Israel. "Even to morrow the Lord will shew who are his, and who is holy; . . . the man whom the Lord doth choose, he shall be holy" (Numbers 16:5, 7).

The congregation assembled to witness the demonstration. It began with Moses reminding the rebellious priests of their sacred responsibility to care for the tabernacle. "Why did they want more?" he asked, feeling they did not appreciate their sacred calling (Numbers 16:11). The rebellious priests lit their censers as a symbolic petition to God concerning their cause. The Lord warned Moses and Aaron, "Separate yourselves from among this congregation, that I may consume them in a moment" (Numbers 16:21). Moses prayed that the congregation be spared and that only the rebels be punished. The Lord responded by commanding the congregation to move away from the rebels. The people moved, expecting the worst, but the rebels stood defiantly by their tents.

Moses cried out, "Hereby ye shall know that the Lord

hath sent me to do all these works; for I have not done them of mine own mind" (Numbers 16:28). The "earth opened her mouth, and swallowed them up, and their houses, and all the men that appertained unto Korah, and all their goods . . . and the earth closed upon them: and they perished from among the congregation" (Numbers 16:32–33). The congregation fled in fear as a fire descended from heaven to consume the remaining rebels. These events provided ample proof that the Lord accepted Moses and Aaron and rejected the rebel cause.

The experience had a surprising effect on the congregation. They murmured, saying that Moses had "killed the people of the Lord" (Numbers 16:41). The glory of the Lord appeared, and the Lord commanded Moses to move aside "that I may consume them as in a moment" (Numbers 16:45). A deadly plague swept through the people as the Lord punished the congregation for supporting the rebels. Moses cried out for Aaron to carry his censer among the people and stand between the living and dead to "make an atonement for them" (Numbers 16:46). As Aaron stood between the people, the plague stopped and the congregation survived. Fourteen thousand died that day with Korah and the rebels.

Conclusion

These examples from the book of Numbers illustrate the seriousness of challenging the Lord's prophet. The causes that motivated Joshua, Miriam, and the rebels of Korah may seem justified. The seventy may not always represent the prophet as they should. Miriam did have special spiritual gifts that had enabled her to serve the people. Korah and the Reubenites did hold positions of responsibility in the community and felt prepared to participate more fully in the government of Israel. It would be difficult for any of these people to confront Moses if they had not felt the justice of their cause; yet, the account did not focus on the rationale of the challenges but on the responsibility of those who claimed membership in the congregation.

Regarding the relevance of this discussion in a contemporary setting, President James E. Faust said, "From the beginning some from both inside and outside of the Church have sought to persuade members of the Church against following the inspired declarations of those who hold the keys of the kingdom of God on earth."[21] He continued by noting that those who challenge the prophet usually claim special knowledge and understanding or even inspiration that the prophet does not have. In the case of Joshua, Miriam, and Korah, they justified their challenge by assuming that they possessed insight which Moses did not.

The unique role of a prophet as a spokesman for the Lord does not imply he leads a perfect life. President Gordon B. Hinckley commented on this from his association with several modern prophets: "I have recognized that all have been human. But I have never been concerned over this. They may have had some weaknesses. But this has never troubled me. I know that the God of heaven has used mortal men throughout history to accomplish His divine purposes. They were the very best available to Him, and they were wonderful."[22] Miriam recognized that Moses' marriage to a non-Israelite cast doubt on his character. The Reubenites challenged his leadership decisions, and Korah felt he employed an authoritarian leadership style. These questions indicated disapproval of Moses. Given the possibility of dissatisfaction with a prophet's decisions, the Lord has asked that those who sustain prophets in modern times receive his word through the prophet "as if from mine own mouth, in all patience and faith" (D&C 21:5). Further revelation directed followers of a prophet to "not command him who is at thy head, and at the head of the church. For I have given him the keys of the mysteries, and the revelations" (D&C 28:6–7). Patience and faith enable the prophet's followers to accept that "all the words of counsel from the prophets of all generations have been given so that we may be strengthened and then be able to lift and strengthen others."[23]

Examples taken from the book of Numbers are useful in a contemporary setting. As in the time of Moses, men today "are stumbling and groping for answers to their own and world problems, and finding *their* attempts at solution to be totally inadequate."[24] In the face of such problems, President Gordon B. Hinckley pleaded "for loyalty to him whom the Lord has called and anointed . . . for steadfastness in upholding him and giving attention to his teachings. . . . [I]f we have a prophet, we have everything. If we do not have a prophet, we have nothing."[25]

As the fires died and the ground grew still, a hush fell over the camp of Israel. The censers dropped by the dying priests lay scattered where the rebellious had stood against their prophet. Following his prophet's instructions, Eleazar, the priest, walked slowly over the smoldering ground collecting the censers of those who had lost their lives. Treating them as sacred artifacts, Eleazar hammered the censers into sheets of brass to overlay the altar. "They shall be a sign unto the children of Israel" (Numbers 16:38) that all may know of the prophet in Israel.

Notes

1. Korah was a Kohathite Levite leader responsible for the "most Holy things" of the temple. The sons of Aaron strictly supervised the Kohathites as they could not touch the tabernacle furnishings on penalty of death. See *The NIV Study Bible,* ed. Kenneth Barker (Grand Rapids, Mich.: Zondervan, 1985), 195.

2. The censer was a small bronze pan that contained hot coals from the altar. The priests sprinkled incense on the coals to symbolize prayer and supplication. See Merrill F. Unger, *Unger's Bible Dictionary* (Chicago: Moody Press, 1985), 185.

3. An unknown site where Israel faced a wildfire in the uttermost parts of the camp. After the fire, the people complained about the lack of meat and the necessity of eating only manna. These complaints drove Moses to plead with the Lord for death rather than continue as leader (Numbers 11:1–11).

4. The term *elder* does not refer to an office in the Melchizedek Priesthood. Rather, it was a level of organization in Israel. In the Old Testament the elders appear to form a distinct group with tribal or family leadership responsibilities. In some circumstances they appear as religious leaders; at other times they function in civil matters.

Little understanding of their specific responsibilities exists as the Mosaic law does not describe their role. See John McKenzie, *Dictionary of the Bible* (New York: Macmillan, 1965), 225–27.

5. The "spirit" (Numbers 11:29), or authority to act in the name of the Lord, came through Moses, who acted as mediator between the Israelites and their God. Moses retained the unique role of communicating with the Lord for Israel. *The Interpreter's Bible,* ed. George A. Buttrick, 12 vols. (New York: Abingdon Press, 1953), 2:196.

6. Joseph F. Smith, *Gospel Doctrine* (Salt Lake City: Deseret Book, 1986), 136.

7. Numbers 11:26 uses "prophesied" to describe the actions of the seventy. Commentators typically explain this as an expression of praise for God and a declaration of his will. The word also seems to allow for inspired teaching as well as sharing a testimony of truth as part of the definition. Because of this broad definition the term "ministry" seemed to best represent the assignment of the seventy. See *Gesenius' Hebrew and Chaldee Lexicon to the Old Testament Scriptures,* trans. Samuel Prideaux Tregelles (Grand Rapids, Mich.: Baker Book House, 1979), 525–26.

8. In Numbers 12:1 the feminine singular word *spake* implies that Miriam initiated the leadership challenge and that Aaron played a secondary role. That may account for the punishment being limited to Miriam. See *Interpreter's Bible,* 2:201. See also Jacob Milgrom, *The JPS Torah Commentary: Numbers* (Philadelphia: Jewish Publication Society, 1990), 93.

9. Evidence points to Miriam as a recognized leader in Israel who played a significant part in the religious life of the people. Scholars debate the nature of her complaint and suggest that she served as spokesman for a larger community concern. See *The Anchor Bible Dictionary,* ed. David Noel Freedman, 6 vols. (New York: Doubleday, 1992), 4:869–70.

10. Some accept the term *Ethiopian,* quoting Josephus to support the notion that this wife was part of a political alliance Moses entered as a prince in Egypt. See Flavius Josephus *Antiquities of the Jews* 2.10.1 (Grand Rapids, Mich.: Kregel Publications, 1967), 57–58. A more accepted source translates the word as *Cushite* and views the accusation as a slur on Zipporah because she was not of Israelite origins. Dennis T. Olson, *Numbers: Interpretation* (Louisville: John Knox Press, 1989), 70–71. From either perspective most scholars agree that this was a secondary concern raised by Miriam as an excuse to challenge Moses on a more serious matter. *NIV Study Bible,* 208.

11. Milgrom, *JPS Torah Commentary,* 93.

12. James E. Talmage, *Articles of Faith* (Salt Lake City: Deseret Book, 1984), 207–8.

13. George Q. Cannon, in *Journal of Discourses,* 26 vols. (Liverpool: Latter-day Saints' Book Depot, 1854–86), 12:46.

14. Joseph F. Smith, in Conference Report, April 1918, 155–59.

15. Miriam became an outcast to complete the seclusion and purification required by the law. Cured of leprosy, she was required to complete a minimal punishment typically associated with a child's shameful act. While it communicated Miriam's error to the congregation, it did not imply serious transgression. See Martin Noth, *Numbers: A Commentary* (Philadelphia: Westminster Press, 1968), 96–97.

16. A frequent interpretation of Numbers 16 describes two rebellions, with Korah challenging Moses on ecclesiastical matters and the Reubenites upset with civil matters. These scholars consider the current text a result of combining two separate accounts. See *Interpreters Bible,* 2:220. Others believe that Korah, Dathan, and Abiram stood together as rebels and that though they may have had different complaints, they agreed in opposing Moses. See R. K. Harrison, *Introduction to the Old Testament* (Grand Rapids, Mich.: Eerdmans, 1969), 628–29; and Stephen L. Harris, *Understanding the Bible* (London: Mayfield, 1985), 72–73.

17. Milgrom, *JPS Torah Commentary,* 129.

18. F. Davidson, *The New Bible Commentary* (Grand Rapids, Mich.: Eerdmans, 1956), 182.

19. Eryl W. Davies, *New Century Bible Commentary: Numbers* (Grand Rapids, Mich.: Eerdmans, 1995), 172.

20. Some have interpreted the Joseph Smith Translation term "high priesthood" as referring to the Melchizedek Priesthood. Robert L. Millet suggests that this interpretation may be incorrect. See Robert L. Millet, "Lessons in the Wilderness," in *Studies in Scripture Series,* vol. 3, *Genesis to 2 Samuel,* ed. Kent P. Jackson and Robert L. Millet (Salt Lake City: Deseret Book, 1989), 3:196.

21. James E. Faust, in Conference Report, April 1996, 3–7.

22. Gordon B. Hinckley, in Conference Report, April 1992, 77.

23. Robert D. Hales, in Conference Report, April 1995, 7–21.

24. N. Eldon Tanner, "We Thank Thee, O God, for a Prophet to Guide Us in These Latter Days," *Ensign,* March 1975, 2.

25. Gordon B. Hinckley, in Conference Report, April 1992, 78.

CHAPTER FOUR

Isaiah and the Great Arraignment

TERRY B. BALL

The resurrected Christ gave special recognition to the writings of Isaiah. As he spoke to the Book of Mormon people gathered at the temple in Bountiful, the Savior proclaimed, "And now, behold, I say unto you, that ye ought to search these things. Yea, a commandment I give unto you that ye search these things diligently; for great are the words of Isaiah" (3 Nephi 23:1). Considering how difficult it is for many people to understand Isaiah's words, we may wish the Savior had picked an easier book to command us to study! We might be more comfortable if he had said, "Master the writings of Ruth," or perhaps, "Ponder the doctrine of Omni." But there is a reason Isaiah's writings are worthy of the distinction afforded them by the Lord. As he explained to the Nephites: "For surely he spake as touching all things concerning my people which are of the house of Israel; therefore it must needs be that he must speak also to the Gentiles. And all things that he spake have been and shall be, even according to the words which he spake" (3 Nephi 23:2–3). Thus we can be assured that Isaiah spoke not only to ancient covenant Israel but also to the latter-day covenant people. Moreover, we have the Savior's personal witness that everything Isaiah foretold has been or will be fulfilled.

Terry B. Ball is assistant professor of ancient scripture at Brigham Young University.

Not only are Isaiah's writings distinctive but the man himself seems to stand out as an anomaly when compared with other prophets of his dispensation. When we think of an Old Testament prophet, we may picture a humble, simple man, one living in the wilderness and being fed by ravens like Elijah the Tishbite (1 Kings 17:3–4), or perhaps a gatherer of sycamore fruit and a herdsman like Amos (Amos 7:14). Isaiah seems to have been a man of relatively high social station who could find audience with kings (see, for example, Isaiah 37:1–73; 38:1). Josephus proposes that King Hezekiah was actually Isaiah's son-in-law.[1] Moreover, the complexity and beauty of his writings, complete with all the poetic elements of metaphor, parallelism, and elevated language, reflect his station as a well-educated man.[2] Furthermore, Isaiah enjoyed exceptional longevity as an Old Testament prophet, serving half a century from about 740 B.C. to about 690 B.C. under four different kings of Judah: Uzziah, Jotham, Ahaz, and Hezekiah (Isaiah 1:1).[3]

While Isaiah may have differed from other Old Testament prophets in social station, education, and longevity, he was very much the same in how he fulfilled his calling as a prophet to a covenant people. As part of their calling, Old Testament prophets provided many "services" for those to whom they ministered. They taught of the coming of both the mortal and millennial Messiah. They provided instruction concerning the stewardship associated with being a covenant people. Some led their people to battle, and others controlled the elements to accomplish God's will. One of the most important roles of Old Testament prophets was to act as "spiritual physicians" for the people. As such they offered diagnoses of the spiritual maladies afflicting the people, suggested prescriptions whereby they might be healed, and gave them prophetic prognoses of what they could expect if they did or did not choose to follow the prescriptions.

The first five chapters of Isaiah are an excellent example of a prophet acting as a spiritual physician. These opening chapters of Isaiah can be called the Great Arraignment, for in them the prophet lays out the charges the Lord wishes to bring against his people. One approach that can help us understand Isaiah's teachings in the Great Arraignment is to classify, analyze, and consider the counsel contained therein as diagnoses, prescriptions, or prognoses given by the Lord's designated spiritual practitioner. Doing so not only makes the prophet's message to ancient Israel[4] clear and poignant but also reveals important counsel for a latter-day covenant people.

The Diagnosis

Despite some moments of righteousness and repentance during Isaiah's tenure as prophet, the house of Israel habitually chose to be afflicted with a number of spiritual maladies.[5] Isaiah identified ignorance, apathy, greed, worldliness, idolatry, and failure to thrive as some of the infirmities prevalent among the people of his day.

Ignorance and Apathy

Isaiah begins the diagnosis of the spiritual maladies that afflicted ancient Israel with a telling poetic verse found in the opening chapter of the Great Arraignment:

> The ox knoweth his owner,
> and the ass his master's crib:
> but Israel doth not know,
> my people doth not consider.
>
> (Isaiah 1:3)

Isaiah seems to be suggesting a hierarchy of intelligence and obedience among these creatures.[6] First is the ox, smart enough and obedient enough to know its master, whom it should obey and to whom it should look for guidance. Next is the ass, which may not know its master but at least knows where to look for the food its master provides. Last is Israel; these people know comparatively nothing concerning their master or where to receive sustenance. To make matters worse, not only do they not know these things but apparently they do not even care: "my people doth not consider." The message to Israel is vivid. They are so spiritually bankrupt that God considers them less responsive than even domesticated animals.

Isaiah uses a medicinal metaphor to reaffirm this diagnosis and explain the extent of spiritual ignorance and apathy afflicting the covenant people: "Why should ye be stricken any more? ye will revolt more and more: the whole head is sick, and the whole heart faint. From the sole of the foot even unto the head there is no soundness in it; but wounds, and bruises, and putrifying sores: they have not been closed, neither bound up, neither mollified with ointment" (Isaiah 1:5–6). Herein he questions why the people would choose to continue in their apathy when it causes illness to their entire beings, to their "whole head" or thoughts, and to their "whole heart," or desires. He marvels that in spite of the sickness filling their entire society from their "head" right down to the "sole of the foot," with "wounds, and bruises, and putrifying sores," the people could care so little that they refused to seek treatment for the malady. Rather, their wounds had "not been closed, neither bound up, neither mollified with ointment." Apparently oblivious to their condition, they had become "wise in their own eyes" (Isaiah 5:21) and sought counsel from peoples outside the covenant (Isaiah 2:6) rather than looking to the Lord for healing. Ignorance and apathy were destroying the covenant people.

Greed and Worldliness

Isaiah lamented over the city of Jerusalem: "How is the faithful city become an harlot! it was full of judgment; righteousness lodged in it; but now murderers. Thy silver is become dross, thy wine mixed with water: Thy princes are rebellious, and companions of thieves: every one loveth gifts, and followeth after rewards: they judge not the fatherless, neither doth the cause of the widow come unto them" (Isaiah 1:21–23). He marveled that this great city, which was once a seat of justice and righteousness, had become the abode of harlots and murderers. He placed much of the blame for the corruption upon the leaders of the people, who had allowed greed and worldliness to dictate their actions. Consequently they had become the friends of thieves and acceptors of gifts or bribes, who cared little for the plight of the poor and helpless. Isaiah makes it clear, however, that the disease of avarice was not confined to the leaders only. He suggests that greedy vendors were practicing deception by cutting their wine with water and adulterating their precious metals with worthless alloys: "thy silver is become dross" (Isaiah 1:22).[7] Misers were hoarding wealth (Isaiah 2:7), land mongers were monopolizing real estate (Isaiah 5:8),[8] and drunkenness, gluttony, and riotous living were becoming round-the-clock activities for many, especially the men of renown and strength (Isaiah 5:11, 22).[9] Moreover, some were challenging values, calling good evil and evil good (Isaiah 5:20). Indeed, so intent were the people on satisfying carnal desires that they went out of their way to bring themselves opportunities to sin. Isaiah pronounced woe upon such people "that draw iniquity with cords of vanity, and sin as it were with a cart rope" (Isaiah 5:18).

The prophet referred to the covenant people of this time as the "daughters of Zion." Like all good daughters of his day, they should have been keeping themselves pure and virtuous, awaiting the day when they would meet their bridegroom, or Christ. Instead, these worldly people were doing just the contrary:[10] "The daughters of Zion are haughty, and walk with stretched forth necks and wanton eyes, walking and mincing as they go, and making a tinkling with their feet" (Isaiah 3:16). Rather than virtuously preparing for marriage, they were prostituting themselves. Rather than seeking beauty in purity and devotion, they had decked themselves in all manner of worldly adornments to attract other lovers (Isaiah 3:16–23). Rather than maintaining the faith and fidelity requisite to finding everlasting joy through the Lord's covenant, they were wantonly seeking for pleasure in promiscuity and indulgence. Greed and worldliness were destroying the covenant people.

Idolatry

Historically, the Lord had blessed ancient Israel in spectacular fashion. He parted the Red Sea and the Jordan River for them, fed them manna for forty years, brought down the walls of Jericho, and rained down stones from heaven upon their enemies (Exodus 14:21–22; 16:35; Joshua 6:16–20; 10:8–11). Yet, all of these remarkable events failed to prevent Israel from turning to other gods during Isaiah's time. The prophet lamented that, "their land also is full of idols; they worship the work of their own hands, that which their own fingers have made" (Isaiah 2:8). Isaiah noted that the idolatry was widespread, as both "mean" or ordinary men and great men were bowing down and humbling themselves before idols (Isaiah 2:9).[11] In groves of trees and gardens they had established places of idol worship (Isaiah 1:29).[12] Idolatry was destroying the covenant people.

Failure to Thrive Syndrome

Some infants do not grow and develop normally or respond to the treatment that would help them do so. For some reason they refuse to eat, or if they do, their bodies do not assimilate the nourishment. These infants are clinically diagnosed as having failure to thrive syndrome. In the fifth chapter of Isaiah, the prophet uses a botanical metaphor to warn the house of Israel that they have chosen to afflict themselves with what could be called a spiritual version of failure to thrive syndrome. In this metaphor, known as the song of the vineyard (Isaiah 5:1–7), he likens the Lord to a "wellbeloved" husbandman who plants a vineyard in an exceptionally choice location and does everything requisite for producing a wonderful harvest of grapes. "And he fenced it, and gathered out the stones thereof, and planted it with the choicest vine" (Isaiah 5:2). He built a tower in the vineyard to protect it, and in anticipation of the abundant harvest, he hewed out a winepress within the vineyard itself. Imagine the husbandman's disappointment when, in spite of all his efforts, the vineyard refused to produce good grapes. Rather it brought forth "wild grapes," or in the Hebrew, *be'ushim,* literally meaning stinking, worthless things.[13] When the house of Israel should have thrived in righteousness, it floundered in sin. Such failure to thrive was destroying the covenant people.

The Prescription

Isaiah was anxious to see the house of Israel healed from its afflictions. Accordingly, in the Great Arraignment, he prescribed the course of action the people should follow to regain their spiritual health. He counseled them to put an end to their sins and become clean: "Wash you, make you clean; put away the evil of your doings from before mine eyes; cease to do evil" (Isaiah 1:16). He further instructed them to develop charity in their lives, to care for the poor and helpless, and to "learn to do well; seek judgment, relieve the oppressed, judge the fatherless, plead for the widow" (Isaiah 1:17). He commanded them to cease relying on the arm of flesh and things temporal, reminding them of the insignificance of such things: "Cease ye from man, whose breath is in his nostrils: for wherein is he to be accounted of?" (Isaiah 2:22). He pled with them to return to their God. "O house of Jacob, come ye, and let us walk in the light of the Lord" (Isaiah 2:5).

Although this prescription constitutes only a small portion of the Great Arraignment, adherence to it would have brought about a remarkable recovery in the spiritual well-being of the people of Isaiah's day. Such medicine is beneficial to a covenant people in any dispensation.

The Prognosis

In the Great Arraignment, Isaiah gave clear prophecies of what the members of the house of Israel could expect if they chose not to follow the Lord's prescription for health for a covenant people. He also made it clear what the prognosis would be if they repented and followed the prescription.

The Prognosis for Continued Rebellion

The prophet warned Israel that the prognosis for continued rebellion would include abandonment, captivity, desolation, and humiliation. Perhaps the greatest portion of the Great Arraignment is devoted to emphasizing this point.

Abandonment. In the song of the vineyard, once the wellbeloved husbandman realized that all his nurturing and efforts to produce grapes were in vain, he described how he would respond to the vineyard's refusal to thrive: "And now go to; I will tell you what I will do to my vineyard: I will take away the hedge thereof, and it shall be eaten up; and break down the wall thereof, and it shall be trodden down: And I will lay it waste: it shall not be pruned, nor digged; but there shall come up briers and thorns: I will also command the clouds that they rain no rain upon it" (Isaiah 5:5–6). In this response, the Lord does not personally go about tearing out and destroying the vines. Rather, he abandons the vineyard. He ceases his nurturing and withdraws his protection from the vineyard, leaving the rebellious vines on their own. Consequently, they are trampled, ravaged, and eventually displaced by other vegetation, or peoples. Such was indeed the eventual lot of ancient Israel.

Captivity. Isaiah cautioned Israel that once they were abandoned by the Lord, they would be easy prey for the empire-builders of the ancient Near East, who sought to conquer and enslave the weaker nations around them. He warned the southern kingdom of Judah that Jerusalem would be ruined and would fall (Isaiah 3:8), a prophecy fulfilled in 587 B.C. when the Babylonian Empire conquered the people of Judah and carried them away into captivity in Babylon. Likewise, he warned the northern kingdom of Israel that they too could expect to be overrun by a terrifying army. He described the army's attack as one that would be so swift that none would escape and declared that it would leave darkness and sorrow in its wake (Isaiah 5:26–30).[14] This prophecy was fulfilled in 721 B.C. when the

Assyrians conquered and deported many of the ten tribes of the kingdom of Israel.

Desolation. Isaiah prophesied that life would be desolate and difficult for the remnant of Israel who were not carried away into captivity: "Your country is desolate, your cities are burned with fire: your land, strangers devour it in your presence, and it is desolate, as overthrown by strangers" (Isaiah 1:7). The prophet likened the desolation to a cottage or harvest shack, and to a lodge or a watchman's hut, both left dilapidated and forsaken after the harvest is over (Isaiah 1:8).[15] He warned that as a result of the deportations there would be a shortage of food, leaders, teachers, and craftsmen in the land. Only the poor, ignorant, and unskilled would be left. In their desperation children would rule over them, and one who merely had clothing would be considered qualified to be king (Isaiah 3:1–8).[16] Moreover, the land would become unproductive, so that five acres[17] of a vineyard would produce only one bath (eight gallons) of wine, and a homer (six bushels) of seed, would yield only an ephah (four gallons) of grain. Isaiah's prognosis in these passages accurately describes the pitiful circumstances the remnant of Israel faced after the Babylonian and Assyrian deportations.

Humiliation. The prophet also warned that in the "day of the Lord"[18] the proud, the worldly, the uncharitable, and any others who trusted or looked for happiness in something outside the Lord's plan for joy would be humbled: "The lofty looks of man shall be humbled, and the haughtiness of men shall be bowed down, and the Lord alone shall be exalted in that day. For the day of the Lord of hosts shall be upon every one that is proud and lofty, and upon every one that is lifted up; and he shall be brought low" (Isaiah 2:11–12). Isaiah likened the proud and worldly to tall cedars and oaks, to high hills and mountains, to formidable towers and walls, and to luxurious ships and other desirable objects, all of which would be abased and banished (Isaiah 2:13–16; see also Isaiah 5:13–17).[19] He described the embarrassment of the worldly in that day of the Lord's coming, as they would frantically try to hide their hoarded wealth and useless idols in "holes of the rocks," and "caves of the earth," with the moles and the bats, in hopes that the Lord would not notice them. Isaiah assured them that all such attempts would be in vain as the Lord rises in "the glory of his majesty" to "shake terribly the earth" (Isaiah 2:17–21). Isaiah described further how all the temporal, vain, and worldly adornments with which the promiscuous "daughters of Zion" had hoped to beautify themselves in an effort to attract adulterous (idolatrous) lovers would be taken away, leaving them disgusting and repulsive rather than tempting and alluring (Isaiah 3:18–24): "And it shall come to pass, that instead of sweet smell there shall be stink; and instead of a girdle a rent; and instead of well set hair baldness; and instead of a stomacher a girding of sackcloth; and burning instead of beauty" (Isaiah 3:24). In their humbled and contemptible state, they would sit at the gates of the city and wail, but to no avail, for the lovers they sought would have fallen "by the sword," and those remaining would not take these foul and filthy daughters regardless of what they offered (Isaiah 3:25–4:1). Every evil thing in which they trusted and hoped to find pleasure would be lost or turned against them. Instead of finding happiness, they could expect to find abandonment, captivity, desolation, and humiliation.

The Prognosis for the Righteous and Repentant

While the abominable apostate daughters of Zion would be weeping, bald-headed, stinking, and repulsive, Isaiah promised that the righteous, the "branch of the Lord," would be lovely: "In that day shall the branch of the Lord be beautiful and glorious, and the fruit of the earth shall be excellent and comely for them that are escaped of Israel. And it shall come to pass, that he that is left in Zion, and he that remaineth in Jerusalem, shall be called holy, even every one that is written among the living in Jerusalem: When the Lord shall have washed away the filth of the daughters of Zion, and shall have purged the blood of Jerusalem from the midst thereof by the spirit of judgment, and by the spirit of burning" (Isaiah 4:2–4). The prophet further promised the obedient that the Lord would dwell with and protect them (Isaiah 4:5–6). Moreover, they could expect to enjoy the "good of the land" (Isaiah 1:19), to have righteous leaders rule over them, and to be known as "the city of righteousness" (Isaiah 1:25–27). Ancient Israel did not see these prophecies fulfilled.

For those who had strayed but were willing to repent, the prognosis was especially encouraging. Using beautiful imagery, Isaiah recorded the tender invitation of the Lord: "Come now, and let us reason together, saith the Lord: though your sins be as scarlet, they shall be as white as snow; though they be red like crimson, they shall be as wool" (Isaiah 1:18). The imagery of the scarlet and the wool points to the Atonement, the means whereby the penitent could find forgiveness. As they repented and returned to the Lord, they could expect their stained souls to be "washed white through the blood of the Lamb" (Alma 13:11).

Conclusion

The Great Arraignment offers a compelling message for any covenant people. As Isaiah diagnoses the spiritual maladies that afflicted the house of Israel in his day, a modern covenant people should learn to avoid similar sicknesses, particularly ignorance, apathy, rebellion, greed, worldliness, idolatry, and failure to thrive. Moreover, a covenant people in the dispensation of the fullness of times can learn from the Great Arraignment that repentance, charity, humility, faith, and obedience constitute proper prescriptions or medicine for a return to spiritual health. Finally, all who have entered the covenant should learn from the Great Arraignment that the prognosis for refusing to repent is abandonment, captivity, desolation, and humiliation, while those who repent and remain faithful can be assured forgiveness, prosperity, and eternal joy.

In the Great Arraignment Isaiah foresaw that "in the last days," there will indeed be a righteous and repentant covenant people. He promised that they will enjoy the blessings of having temples, "the Lord's house shall be established in the top of the mountains" (Isaiah 2:2).[20] People from all nations will be drawn to such temples to learn of God's ways and to covenant to "walk in his paths" (Isaiah 2:2–3). He prophesied that there will be holy cities for the righteous, one in Zion in the Western Hemisphere, and another in Jerusalem in the Eastern Hemisphere (Isaiah 2:3).[21] He promised that the faithful will flock to the gospel, the "ensign to the nations," as it beckons to them (Isaiah 5:26). He foretells that though they will come from "the end of the earth," their gathering will be swift and employ rapid means of transportation (Isaiah 5:26–30).[22] He acknowledges that in that day the Lord personally will "judge among the nations" and that peace will reign. Instruments of destruction will be converted to tools of production as men "beat their swords into plowshares, and their spears into pruninghooks" (Isaiah 2:4). Not only will men no longer practice war but they will cease even to learn about it (Isaiah 2:4). It will be a world in which no one finds a use for violence. It will be the millennial day for which Isaiah yearned, and for which we prepare.

Notes

1. Louis Ginsberg, *Legends of the Jews,* 7 vols. (Philadelphia: Jewish Publication Society, 1941), 4:279. In this text Josephus claims that Isaiah was killed by his own grandchild, Manasseh. Manasseh's father was King Hezekiah.

2. For an introduction to biblical poetry, see James L. Kugel, *The Idea of Biblical Poetry* (New Haven, Conn.: Yale University Press, 1981).

3. A pseudepigraphic work known as the Martyrdom and Ascension of Isaiah records that Isaiah's life ended when he was sawn in half by King Hezekiah's wicked son Manasseh, a claim supported by Josephus. See "Martyrdom and Ascension of Isaiah," in *The Old Testament Pseudepigrapha,* ed. James H. Charlesworth (Garden City, N.Y.: Doubleday, 1985), 163. See also Ginsberg, *Legends of the Jews,* 4:279. The circumstances surrounding the martyrdom are different in the Josephus account, but both accounts identify Manasseh as the one responsible for Isaiah's tragic death.

4. Isaiah was a prophet to both the kingdom of Israel and the kingdom of Judah. Because both kingdoms were a covenant people, I will use the term *Israel* to refer to either one or both.

5. One of the few periods of relative righteousness during Isaiah's ministry was King Hezekiah's reign (see Isaiah 37–38).

6. Kugel, *Idea of Biblical Poetry*, 9.

7. Ludlow suggests this interpretation for Isaiah 1:22. See Victor L. Ludlow, *Isaiah: Prophet, Seer, and Poet* (Salt Lake City: Deseret Book, 1982), 79.

8. For a clear interpretation of this verse, see footnote *c* to Isaiah 5:8 in the LDS edition of the King James Version of the Bible.

9. Nyman suggests that a modern parallel can be seen in the lives of current celebrities. See Monte S. Nyman, *Great Are the Words of Isaiah* (Salt Lake City: Bookcraft, 1980), 45.

10. The metaphor of Jehovah as the bridegroom and the covenant people as those espoused or married to him is found throughout the prophetic writings of the Old Testament. The imagery is powerful. The love, devotion, faith, and trust that should exist between God and his covenant people should be as great as, or greater than, that which should exist between a husband and wife.

11. The Book of Mormon account of this verse in 2 Nephi 12:9 reads, "the mean man boweth not down, and the great man humbleth himself not," suggesting that these men were not worshipping Jehovah.

12. For a discussion of the relationship between vegetation and idol worship, see Terry B. Ball, "Isaiah's Imagery of Plants and Planting," in *Thy People Shall Be My People and Thy God My God: The 22nd Annual Sperry Symposium* (Salt Lake City: Deseret Book, 1994), 24–25.

13. Francis Brown, *The New Brown-Driver-Briggs-Gesenius Hebrew and English Lexicon* (New York: Houghton Mifflin, 1906; reprint, n.p.: Christian Copyrights, 1983), 93. For a more thorough discussion of this botanical metaphor, see Ball, "Isaiah's Imagery," 18–20.

14. Isaiah 5:26–30 is a dualistic prophecy, meaning it applies to more than one time period and may have more than one interpretation. Latter-day Saints have traditionally placed the fulfillment of this prophecy in the last days and given it another interpretation, which will be discussed in the conclusion of this paper. Most commentators, however, see this as a prophecy that was fulfilled in Isaiah's day and interpret it as discussed above.

15. Ball, "Isaiah's Imagery," 27–28.

16. Ludlow offers a fascinating discussion of the chiasmus in these verses and suggests that the chiastic structure of the passage indicates

that the people's oppression of one another is the major cause of their difficulties. See Ludlow, *Isaiah,* 104–5.

17. The KJV here states ten acres, but the Hebrew reads ten yoke or the amount ten yoke of oxen could plow in a day, which is equivalent to about five acres.

18. The phrase "day of the Lord" is used frequently by Isaiah and seems to refer to any day of retribution or reward. For example, the day when Judah fell to the Babylonians was a day of the Lord, as will be the day of his second coming. It is both a great and dreadful day, great for the righteous and dreadful for the wicked (Malachi 4:5).

19. Footnote *a* to 2 Nephi 12:16 notes that the Hebrew Masoretic text of Isaiah 2:16 reads "upon all the ships of Tarshish," while the Greek Septuagint reads "upon all the ships of the sea." The Book of Mormon text reads "upon all the ships of the sea, and upon all the ships of Tarshish." One can offer several speculations about why both phrases appear in the Book of Mormon: (1) Perhaps Joseph Smith fabricated the Book of Mormon and somehow had access to the Septuagint. Discovering there was a discrepancy between the Septuagint and the Masoretic texts of this passage, he decided to include both text versions in the Book of Mormon to deceive readers into thinking he was actually translating a more complete ancient record, that is, the gold plates; or (2) Maybe while Joseph Smith was fabricating the Book of Mormon he accidentally, by chance, inserted into the Book of Mormon the very phrase left out of the Masoretic text; or (3) while the Prophet Joseph Smith was translating the Book of Mormon from the gold plates by the gift and power of God, he translated the phrase "upon all the ships of the sea, and upon all the ships of Tarshish" because that is exactly what the record said. Both phrases were on the gold plates Joseph Smith was translating because the brass plates of pre-600 B.C. origin, from which the gold plates text was taken, were a more ancient and complete text than either the Masoretic text (ca. A.D. 500–1000) or the Septuagint (ca. 250 B.C.). Apparently the Septuagint had lost the phrase "the ships of Tarshish" and the Masoretic text had lost the phrase "the ships of the sea." The Book of Mormon restores both.

From a purely logical point of view, the last option, option 3, is the only tenable one. From personal conviction, I testify that option 3 is the truth.

20. Isaiah's use of a mountain as a metaphor for the temple is appropriate, for there is much about a mountain that is similar to a temple. For example:

Both mountains and temples are high places were we can go to get nearer to God. Ancient prophets, such as Moses, Elijah, and Enos, and later the Savior frequently went to the mountains to communicate with God and seek answers to questions. Today, we can go to the temple to draw nearer to our Father in Heaven and receive direction from him.

Mountains are impressive, firm, and enduring. So are the doctrines taught and the ordinances performed in the temple.

It takes effort for us to reach the top of a mountain. To do so we must maintain good physical health and be willing to expend the energy required to make the climb. It is not a task for the feeble or lazy. Likewise, to enter the temple we must be in good spiritual health and be willing to live a life in harmony with the will of our Father in Heaven. It is not a task for the spiritually flabby or the unrepentant soul. As the psalmist put it, "Who shall ascend into the hill of the Lord? or who shall stand in his holy place? He that hath clean hands, and a pure heart; who hath not lifted up his soul unto vanity, nor sworn deceitfully" (Psalm 25:3–4).

The view from the top of a mountain is both spectacular and beautiful. We gain a new perspective of our surroundings from the high elevation. From a mountaintop we can see where we have come from and all the potential destinations to which we may travel. The view from the temple is equally spectacular and beautiful. There we gain an eternal perspective. We learn where we came from and where we may go if we are willing to be true and faithful to the covenants we make in the house of the Lord.

21. In view of the Hebrew poetic device of parallelism, some would argue that Zion and Jerusalem in this passage are not two different cities, but one and the same, the Old World Jerusalem. LDS theology traditionally interprets the passage as I have. For a further discussion of the two religious capitals interpretation, see Bruce R. McConkie, *The Mortal Messiah,* 4 vols. (Salt Lake City: Deseret Book, 1979–81), 1:95.

22. Elder LeGrand Richards interpreted Isaiah 5:28–30 as being a metaphorical reference to modern means of transportation. For example, he understood the phrase "their horses' hoofs be counted like flint, and their wheel like a whirlwind" to be referring to trains, while the phrase "Their roaring . . . be like a lion" was a reference to airplanes. He gives the entire passage a latter-day context and convincingly illustrates Isaiah's prophetic vision. See LeGrand Richards, *A Marvelous Work and a Wonder* (Salt Lake City: Deseret Book, 1976), 229.

CHAPTER FIVE

Isaiah's Voice on the Promised Millennium

CRAIG J. OSTLER

Many Latter-day Saints find the topic of the Millennium and the conditions that will exist during that time period most interesting. President Gordon B. Hinckley testified that "the time has come for us to stand a little taller, to lift our eyes and stretch our minds to a greater comprehension and understanding of the grand millennial mission of this, The Church of Jesus Christ of Latter-day Saints."[1] The prophetic voice of Isaiah concerning the promised millennium records the word of the Lord: "For in my own due time will I come upon the earth in judgment, and my people shall be redeemed and shall reign with me on earth. For the great Millennium, of which I have spoken by the mouth of my servants, shall come" (D&C 43:29–30).

What events will signal the beginning of the Millennium? What changes will take place to bring about one thousand years of righteousness? Who will be on earth during the Millennium? What physical changes will take place on the earth? Answers to these and other questions are found in the writings of the prophet Isaiah. Through Isaiah the Lord declared the end from the beginning (Isaiah 46:10). Isaiah's writings reveal conditions that will exist

Craig J. Ostler is assistant professor of Church history and doctrine at Brigham Young University.

during the thousand-year period the Lord set aside to accomplish his work.

Because of Isaiah's style of writing, millennial prophecies are not easily identified or understood. His practice of scattering prophecies throughout his writings makes specific analysis challenging. Additionally, Isaiah prophesied in such a manner that his words may be interpreted literally or symbolically. For example, Babylon literally was an ancient empire, but the term also symbolizes the world or the dominions of Lucifer in any time period (Isaiah 14). Moreover, the placing of Isaiah's millennial prophecies into a time frame is challenging, as he was often dualistic in his writing. In other words, he frequently referred to more than one time period or prophesied of more than one event using the same words. An example of this dualism is his prophecy of "new heavens and a new earth" (Isaiah 65:17). Isaiah describes changes in the heavens and the earth that will take place both at the beginning of the Millennium as the earth is prepared for its paradisiacal or terrestrial glory and after the Millennium as the earth is quickened and receives its celestial glory.[2]

To better identify and discuss Isaiah's millennial teachings, the prophecies discussed in this article are arranged according to the following topics: the Second Coming, social and political conditions during the Millennium; physical changes upon the earth; the binding of Satan; life during the Millennium; and the millennial kingdom of heaven on earth.

The Second Coming Ushers in the Millennium

The coming of Jesus Christ is the singular event that sets the Millennium apart from the present conditions of the world. Isaiah described the day of the Lord's coming as a day of destruction on the earth in which "he shall destroy the sinners thereof out of it" (Isaiah 13:9). The Savior will return wearing red apparel with "garments like him that treadeth in the winefat" (Isaiah 63:2). The red apparel is symbolic. The illustrative reference is to those who tread upon grapes in a vat used for making wine. As the grapes were crushed under the feet of the workmen, their clothing became red in color. Normally several individuals worked together to accomplish this task; however, the Lord indicated that he will be an exception to this custom. In response to Isaiah's question as to why He will come in red apparel, the Lord explained, "I have trodden the winepress alone; and of the people there was none with me: for I will tread them in mine anger, and trample them in my fury; and their blood shall be sprinkled upon my garments, and I will stain all my raiment. For the day of vengeance is in mine heart, and the year of my redeemed is come" (Isaiah 63:3–4). Thus, the red color of his garments represents the Lord's role in the destruction of the wicked at his coming. The Lord's role in destroying the wicked may be literal, as was the case when He caused natural disasters which destroyed the wicked of the Book of Mormon peoples (3 Nephi 9:1–12). Or it may be symbolic, as represented in latter-day revelation that describes the Lord withholding his Spirit that "the wicked shall slay the wicked" (D&C 63:33). In either case the destruction of the wicked before the Savior's coming in glory will usher in an era of peace.

The second coming of Jesus Christ is a time of redemption as well as judgment and destruction. The Lord's red apparel also represents the shedding of his blood in atoning for sin and redeeming the world.[3] In an inspired commentary on Isaiah's words, the Prophet Joseph Smith revealed that at the coming of Jesus Christ the righteous "shall mention the loving kindness of their Lord, and all that he has bestowed upon them according to his goodness, and according to his loving kindness, forever and ever" (D&C 133:52).[4] Isaiah prophesied that in that day Israel will cry and shout at the Lord's coming: "O Lord, I will praise thee: . . . Behold, God is my salvation; I will trust, and not be afraid: for the Lord Jehovah is my strength and my song. . . . And in that day shall ye say, Praise the Lord, call upon his name, declare his doings among the people, make mention that his name is exalted. Sing unto the Lord; for he hath done excellent things: this is known in all the earth. Cry out and shout, thou inhabitant of Zion: for great is the Holy One of Israel in the midst of thee" (Isaiah 12:1–2, 4–6). As Isaiah further testified, "every knee shall bow" (Isaiah 45:23) in reverence and acknowledgment that Jesus Christ is Savior and Redeemer.

Social and Political Conditions during the Millennium

One of the dramatic events that initiate the Millennium will be the destruction of the wicked associated with the second coming of the Savior. "For, behold, the Lord will come with fire, and with his chariots like a whirlwind, to render his anger with fury, and his rebuke with flames of fire" (Isaiah 66:15). Isaiah testified that the Lord "shall destroy the sinners" (Isaiah 13:9) and that "the slain of the Lord shall be many" (Isaiah 66:16). In addition, Isaiah identified that among those destroyed will be "the host of the high ones that are on high, and the kings of the earth upon the earth" (Isaiah 24:21). The destruction of many prominent leaders of the earth will open the way for the transition to the millennial government of the kingdom of heaven. The wicked who are destroyed at this time and the wicked of past ages will "be gathered together, as prisoners are gathered in the pit, and shall be shut up in the prison" (Isaiah 24:22). It appears that Isaiah was referring to the spirits of the wicked in spirit prison. They will remain in spirit prison until the end of the Millennium, when those who inherit the telestial kingdom and those who became sons of perdition in mortality are called forth from the grave to be judged.[5]

The destruction of the wicked appears to be associated, in part, with a time of war. Isaiah spoke of the Lord's indignation upon all nations and his "fury upon all their armies: he hath utterly destroyed them, he hath delivered them to the slaughter" (Isaiah 34:2). The prophet Ezekiel amplified Isaiah's message concerning the battles between Israel and the armies of Gog from the land of Magog.[6] Many will die as the Lord intervenes in behalf of his people.[7] Isaiah described the aftermath of this conflict in which "their slain also shall be cast out, and their stink shall come up out of their carcases, and the mountains shall be melted with their blood" (Isaiah 34:3).

The destruction of the wicked will also be related to the burning associated with the Second Coming as "the inhabitants of the earth are burned," with the result that there are relatively "few men left" (Isaiah 24:6). The outcome will be that "many houses shall be desolate, even great and fair, without inhabitant" (Isaiah 5:9).[8] As was the case in the destruction of ancient Israel, "in that day seven women shall take hold of one man, saying, We will eat our own bread, and wear our own apparel: only let us be called by thy name, to take away our reproach" (Isaiah 4:1). Regardless of whether such a ratio of men to women is literal or figurative, Isaiah described a world that will have fewer inhabitants due to the destruction of the wicked.

In addition to this destruction, those who remain upon the earth will witness other changes. Christ will return as the Eternal Judge of the inhabitants of the earth. Isaiah emphasized that Christ "shall not judge after the sight of his eyes, neither reprove after the hearing of his ears: but with righteousness shall he judge the poor, and reprove with equity for the meek of the earth: and he shall smite the earth with the rod of his mouth, and with the breath of his lips shall he slay the wicked. And righteousness shall be the girdle of his loins, and faithfulness the girdle of his reins" (Isaiah 11:3–5).

This explanation clarifies the concept that for the righteous and the meek, the judgment shall be a blessing. The coming of Jesus Christ as Judge will improve the justice system of nations and peoples. The courts will not be influenced by the wickedness of corrupt laws and judges that are now part of the fallen earth. As the Prophet Joseph Smith explained, "The world has had a fair trial for six thousand years; the Lord will try the seventh thousand Himself; 'He whose right it is, will possess the kingdom, and reign until He has put all things under His feet'; iniquity will hide its hoary head, Satan will be bound, and the works of darkness destroyed; righteousness will be put to the line, and judgment to the plummet, and 'he that fears the Lord will alone be exalted in that day.'"[9] The hopes and dreams of good people through the ages will be realized as righteousness becomes the standard of judgment and equity is bestowed upon all of the inhabitants of the earth.

The Prophet Joseph Smith taught that during the Millennium, "Christ will reign personally upon the earth" (Article of Faith 10). The spiritual and the temporal governments of the earth will no longer be separated. The governments of the earth and their thrones will be cast down, and the Almighty God will have "made a full end of all nations" (D&C 87:6).[10] All government and judgment will come under the direction of the King of kings and the Prince of Peace, for Jesus Christ will establish his throne forever and ever. His throne will be that of a kingly judge, and "in mercy shall the throne be established: and he shall sit upon it in truth in the tabernacle of David, judging, and seeking judgment, and hasting righteousness" (Isaiah 16:5).

The plan of God, to bring to pass his purposes, requires a reign of righteousness for one thousand years.[11] As Isaiah stated, righteousness will be hastened due to Jesus Christ's return as king and judge. Laws that individuals are given, and the manner in which they are enforced, influence the state and situation of nations and peoples. Christ revealed that "in time ye shall have no king nor ruler, for I will be your king and watch over you. Wherefore, hear my voice and follow me, and you shall be a free people, and ye shall have no laws but my laws when I come, for I am your lawgiver" (D&C 38:21–22). The peace that will exist during the Millennium will be due, in part, to the fact that Jesus Christ will reign in righteousness on the earth during this time period. He will give laws that are based on righteous eternal principles which lead to happiness and eternal life. These laws have the power to make the obedient free from sin and error. They will live in peace and have the opportunity to progress toward becoming like the Savior.[12]

Jesus Christ's government will include other rulers or, as the Bible refers to them, princes. Isaiah declared, "Behold, a king shall reign in righteousness, and princes shall rule in judgment" (Isaiah 32:1). Latter-day revelation broadens our understanding of Isaiah's messianic declaration: "For in my own due time will I come upon the earth in judgment, and my people shall be redeemed and shall reign with me on earth" (D&C 43:29). The Savior clarified that among these ruling princes would be the twelve apostles who were with him during his mortal ministry in Jerusalem. He explained that at the day of His coming these apostles would be "clothed with robes of righteousness, with crowns upon their heads, in glory even as I am, to judge the whole house of Israel, even as many as have loved me and kept my commandments, and none else" (D&C 29:12). Mormon identified the twelve Nephite disciples chosen by Christ during his ministry in the Americas as the judges over the remnant of his people. The Prophet Joseph Smith suggested that "Christ and the resurrected Saints will reign over the earth during the thousand years. They will not probably dwell upon the earth, but will visit it when they please, or when it is necessary to govern it."[13]

Isaiah alluded to the location of the seats of government during this blessed period of time "when the Lord of hosts shall reign in mount Zion, and in Jerusalem, and before his ancients gloriously" (Isaiah 24:23). He indicated that "out of Zion shall go forth the law, and the word of the Lord from Jerusalem" (Isaiah 2:3). Somewhat hidden within the apparent parallel uses of the terms *Zion* and *Jerusalem* is Isaiah's reference to the two world capitals of the millennial period. The Lord revealed to the Prophet Joseph Smith that "the place for the city of Zion" (D&C 57:2) and the center place where a temple should stand is Independence, Missouri.[14] This location and the Jerusalem of Palestine have been identified as the two world capitals from which the Lord will reign during the Millennium.[15] Temples will be built in both cities. It may be that these houses of the Lord will become the actual residences of Jesus Christ as he reigns on earth during the Millennium.

Who will be on the earth to enjoy the blessings of the Millennium? Associated with the coming of Jesus Christ will be a general separation of the righteous and the wicked. Included with those who are counted as the righteous are many classes. Clearly, the saints of the Most High, who are worthy, shall dwell on the earth and reign with the Savior.[16] This group will include both those upon the earth and resurrected beings who will return to the earth with the Lord. As the revelations declare, "these are they whom he shall bring with him, when he shall come in the clouds of heaven to reign on the earth over his people" (D&C 76:63). Elder Joseph Fielding Smith explained: "During all these years men dwelling in mortality will have the privilege of associating with those who have received their resurrection. Our Lord and Savior will be a familiar figure among the righteous saints. Instruction will be given by resurrected prophets. . . . Those who have passed through the resurrection will not, however, dwell with those in mortality. They will not stay in earthly, or human homes nor sleep in the beds of mortals."[17] As stated earlier, the Prophet Joseph Smith explained that Jesus Christ and the resurrected saints "will not probably dwell on the earth, but will visit it when they please, or when it is necessary to govern it."

On the other hand, Isaiah wrote that those who have not known the Lord's name will also be spared at the beginning of the Millennium (see Isaiah 66:19). Those who have not known the name of Jesus Christ, or the non-Christian peoples, are referred to as heathen nations. Concerning those who have not known his name, God revealed further clarification to the Prophet Joseph Smith saying that "the heathen nations [shall] be redeemed, and they that knew no law shall have part in the first resurrection; and it shall be tolerable for them" (D&C 45:54). It should be remembered that those who lived in wickedness in mortality or "the spirits of men who are to be judged, and are found under condemnation . . . live not again until the thousand years are ended" (D&C 88:100–101). But many among the heathen nations will be able to abide a terrestrial law and enjoy the blessings of the Millennium. They are good, honorable people who have been "blinded by the craftiness of men" (D&C 76:75). Further, they will receive a testimony of Jesus in the millennial day or will have received this testimony as spirits prior to coming forth in the resurrection from the dead.[18]

Additionally, Isaiah wrote of those who will be accursed during the Millennium because they are sinners (see Isaiah 65:20). Similarly, the Prophet Joseph Smith wrote, "While in conversation at Judge Adams' during the evening, I said, . . . [t]here will be wicked men on the earth during the thousand years."[19] Apparently, these references to the wicked are not to those "who are liars, and sorcerers, and adulterers, and whoremongers, and whosoever loves and makes a lie" (D&C 76:103). Such wicked characters abide a telestial law and will be destroyed when Jesus Christ comes. They will be thrust down to hell, or the spirit world, during the thousand years of the Millennium.[20] Evidently, these statements refer to those who are wicked or sinners in the sense that they exercise their agency in rejecting the fullness of the gospel. Yet, they are able to abide the terrestrial law that prevails during the Millennium. Joseph Fielding Smith explained, "There will be millions of people, Catholics, Protestants, agnostics, Mohammedans, people of all classes, and of all beliefs, still permitted to remain upon the face of the earth, but they will be those who have lived clean lives, those who have been free from wickedness and corruption."[21]

Many individuals will receive the Lord when he returns and reigns during the Millennium. The Lord's plan concerning these people was revealed to Isaiah: "For I know their works and their thoughts: it shall come, that I will gather all nations and tongues; and they shall come, and see my glory. And I will set a sign among them, and I will send those that escape of them unto the nations . . . that have not heard my fame, neither have seen my glory; and they shall declare my glory among the Gentiles. And they shall bring all your brethren for an offering unto the Lord out of all nations . . . to my holy mountain Jerusalem" (Isaiah 66:18–20). If they will hearken to the Lord and accept his gospel, the Lord revealed, "I will also take of them for priests and for Levites" (Isaiah 66:21). Thus, many will be given the opportunity during the Millennium to learn of God and receive the priesthood. The resultant blessing will be that: "Also the sons of the stranger, that join themselves to the Lord, to serve him, and to love the name of the Lord, to be his servants, every one that keepeth the sabbath from polluting it, and taketh hold of my covenant; even them will I bring to my holy mountain, and make them joyful in my house of prayer: . . . for mine house shall be called an house of prayer for all people" (Isaiah 56:6–7).

Isaiah stated that during the Millennium "the sinner being an hundred years old shall be accursed" (Isaiah 65:20). The Prophet Joseph Smith explained that the millennial wicked are those who will not receive the Lord but will be able to abide the millennial day as they are honorable and clean living.[22] Those who will die and be changed in the twinkling of an eye to a resurrected state without being converted and accepting the fullness of the gospel will have had ample time, at least one hundred years according to Isaiah, to make the choice of whether they are willing to abide celestial or terrestrial law. Furthermore, this opportunity to accept the fullness of the gospel will have been under millennial conditions in which Satan is bound and Jesus Christ reigns. At the time of their change to a resurrected state they will be quickened by a portion of the terrestrial glory, which they chose to enjoy.[23] Whether they will be caught up to dwell on another globe or remain on the earth during the Millennium has not yet been revealed.

The discussion thus far concerns those who are living on the earth when the Millennium begins. Elder Bruce R. McConkie wrote that as the Millennium proceeds, "Earth's main inhabitants . . . will be those who continue to come here from celestial realms to gain their bodies and to prepare themselves for immortal glory."[24] These are they who will be born during the Millennium, raised in millennial conditions, and "grow up without sin unto salvation" (D&C 45:58). These children "shall die an hundred years old" (Isaiah 65:20), at which time they "shall be changed in the twinkling of an eye, and shall be caught up" (D&C 101:31) to dwell with other resurrected beings awaiting the end of the Millennium and the change of the earth to a celestial globe.

PHYSICAL CHANGES UPON THE EARTH DURING THE MILLENNIUM

The Lord revealed to Isaiah that as the Millennium begins dramatic physical changes will occur on the earth and in the heavens: "Lift up your eyes to the heavens, and look upon the earth beneath: for the heavens shall vanish away like smoke, and the earth shall wax old like a garment (Isaiah 51:6). For, behold, I create new heavens and a new earth: and the former shall not be remembered, nor come into mind" (Isaiah 65:17). Isaiah explained the changes that will take place to create new heavens: "And all the host of heaven shall be dissolved, and the heavens shall be rolled together as a scroll: and all their host shall fall down, as the leaf falleth off from the vine, and as a falling fig from the fig tree" (Isaiah 34:4). It may be that the changes on the earth, of which Isaiah spoke, will cause the heavens to appear to move above the inhabitants of the earth as if the stars in the heavens are actually falling. Elder Bruce R. McConkie wrote that "it shall appear to man on earth as though the stars in the sidereal heavens are falling. And in addition, as here recorded, some heavenly meteors or other objects, appearing as stars, will fall 'unto the earth.' Indeed, the events of that day shall be so unprecedented and so beyond human experience, that the prophets are and have been at an almost total loss for words to describe those realities pressed in upon them by the spirit of revelation."[25]

Isaiah further explained the changes in the heavens: "For the stars of heaven and the constellations thereof shall not give their light: the sun shall be darkened in his going forth, and the moon shall not cause her light to shine. . . . Therefore I will shake the heavens, and the earth shall remove out of her place" (Isaiah 13:10, 13).[26] If we take Isaiah's words literally that "the earth shall remove out of her place" at the time of the changes in the heavens, it may be that the earth will be removed from its present position or place in the solar system. Such an interpretation was taught by the prophet Brigham Young regarding further, but similar, changes that will take place at the end of the Millennium, when once again the Lord will create new heavens and a new earth from that known even during the Millennium.[27] Regardless of the causes, it is evident from Isaiah's description that there will be great changes in the heavens as the millennial era dawns. The Lord testified to Isaiah of the results of these changes, saying, "I clothe the heavens with blackness, and I make sackcloth their covering" (Isaiah 50:3). The Lord did not state how long these conditions would last, but, according to Isaiah, in time "the light of the moon shall be as the light of the sun, and the light of the sun shall be sevenfold, as the light of seven days" (Isaiah 30:26).[28]

Among the physical changes upon the earth itself will be the restoring of Edenic conditions that existed at the time Adam and Eve were placed upon the earth. The Prophet Joseph Smith wrote "that the earth will be renewed and receive its paradisiacal glory" (Article of Faith 10). Isaiah referred to these conditions in his description of the earth during the Millennium: "The wilderness and the solitary place shall be glad for them; and the desert shall rejoice, and blossom as the rose. It shall blossom abundantly, and rejoice even with joy and singing: the glory of Lebanon shall be given unto it, the excellency of Carmel and Sharon, they shall see the glory of the Lord, and the excellency of our God" (Isaiah 35:1–2).

Carmel, Sharon, and Lebanon are near the Mediterranean

Sea.[29] Thus, all three locations enjoy a moderate climate and bountiful rainfall. Carmel, which refers to Mount Carmel, means "garden" or "orchard." The beauty and fertility of Carmel greatly impressed the Bible writers due to the substantial plant growth which did and still does cover its slopes.[30] The plains of Sharon border the Mediterranean Sea and extend north from Joppa on the coast to just south of Mount Carmel. The higher elevations were noted for oak forests and the lower elevations for their pastures.[31] Similarly, Lebanon was famous for its forests of cedar trees.[32] Therefore, Isaiah painted a picture of deserts, such as those found near the Dead Sea and in the Negev, becoming fertile lands covered with trees and pastures. The new earth of the Millennium will be a physical paradise of luxuriant verdure and beauty. Isaiah continued to explain the process by which the desert will be changed into a place as verdant and fruitful as Carmel, Sharon, or Lebanon: "for in the wilderness shall waters break out, and streams in the desert. And the parched ground shall become a pool, and the thirsty land springs of water" (Isaiah 35:6–7).

In addition to the changes that will come to the deserts are those that will come to areas that are fertile today. Isaiah wrote that in the fertile ground of the earth "instead of the thorn shall come up the fir tree, and instead of the brier shall come up the myrtle" (Isaiah 55:13). Thus, in place of noxious plants or weeds that have tormenting thorns and briers will be trees and leafy shrubs that are beautiful and pleasant.[33] Such a description illustrates a reversal of the curse which was put upon the earth following the fall of Adam. Adam was told that, unlike the conditions which he had enjoyed in the Garden of Eden, the ground would be cursed and bring forth thorns and thistles (Genesis 3:18). The millennial earth will be restored to conditions that existed before the Fall. Therefore, both desert and fertile field will enjoy changes in the new earth that will come to be during the Millennium.

Another change to the face of the earth will be that "every valley shall be exalted, and every mountain and hill shall be made low" (Isaiah 40:4)[34] "for the mountains shall depart, and the hills be removed" (Isaiah 54:10). In the Doctrine and Covenants the Lord included these words of Isaiah in connection with a time when the earth will tremble and "reel to and fro like a drunkard" or "as a drunken man" (Isaiah 24:20; D&C 49:23). He further stated that the rough places will become smooth.

From latter-day revelation we know that the Lord "shall command the great deep, and it shall be driven back into the north countries, and the islands shall become one land; and the land of Jerusalem and the land of Zion shall be turned back into their own place, and the earth shall be like as it was in the days before it was divided" (D&C 133:23–24). Isaiah's voice concerning this event is shrouded in poetic imagery. With reference to the renewal of the lands of Zion he prophesied: "Thou shalt no more be termed Forsaken; neither shall thy land any more be termed Desolate: but thou shalt be called Hephzi-bah ["my desire is in her"], and thy land Beulah ["married wife"]: for the Lord delighteth in thee, and thy land shall be married" (Isaiah 62:4). Elder Bruce R. McConkie saw in Isaiah's imagery of lands that are married the coming together of land masses. Further, he suggested that the joining of the Palestinian Zion and the American Zion might come through bringing the continents together amidst the present-day area of the Atlantic Ocean.[35]

It is clear from Isaiah's prophecies that the coming of the Lord and the ushering in of the Millennium will bring immense changes to the earth as we know it today. The results will become so familiar and natural to those who live during this time that "the former (heaven and earth) shall not be remembered, nor come into mind " (Isaiah 65:17).

The Spirit of God Will Be Poured Out and Satan Will Be Bound

Looking forward to the time of millennial conversion, Isaiah spoke of the need to wait "until the spirit be poured upon us from on high, and the wilderness be a fruitful field, and the fruitful field be counted for a forest. . . . [Then] the work of righteousness shall be peace; and the effect of righteousness quietness and assurance for ever" (Isaiah 32:15, 17). God will pour out his Spirit upon those who dwell on the earth during the Millennium. This blessing will aid the people in living righteously, and the Lord will reward them for heeding his counsels by additional outpouring of the Spirit. The dispensing of the Spirit and the righteousness of the people, combined with the destruction of the wicked, will bring peace to the earth. Isaiah indicated that because there will be no use for weapons and implements of war "they shall beat their swords into plowshares, and their spears into pruninghooks: nation shall not lift up sword against nation, neither shall they learn war any more" (Isaiah 2:4).

A result of the destruction of the wicked and an increased outpouring of the Spirit will be the binding of Satan. As people fill their hearts with the Spirit of God, there will be no room in their hearts for Satan's influence. Isaiah delighted in the future binding of Satan for one thousand years and the eventual banishment of Satan to outer darkness following the Millennium.

In teaching this concept Isaiah employed a satirical song. He portrayed the ancient king of Babylon as a type for Lucifer. Similar to the king of Babylon, Lucifer has ruled over an empire built upon tyranny and oppression. As Isaiah expressed concerning Lucifer, "For thou hast said in thine heart, I will ascend into heaven, I will exalt my throne above the stars of God: . . . I will be like the most High" (Isaiah 14:13–14). Isaiah prophesied that the day will come when Lucifer will "be brought down to hell, to the sides of the pit" (Isaiah 14:15). John the Revelator was shown an angel who had the key of a bottomless pit. "He laid hold on . . . that old serpent, which is the Devil, and Satan, and bound him a thousand years, and cast him into the bottomless pit, and shut him up, and set a seal upon him, that he should deceive the nations no more, till the thousand years should be fulfilled" (Revelation 20:2–3). Satan will be held in such low regard that people will mock him, saying, "Is this the man that made the earth to tremble, that did shake kingdoms; . . . that opened not the house of his prisoners?" (Isaiah 14:16–17). Truly, during the Millennium Lucifer will be bound and will "not have power to tempt any man" (D&C 101:28). Therefore, he will "have no place in the hearts of the children of men" (D&C 45:55).

Thus we see that at the beginning of the Millennium the wicked will have been destroyed and those who remain will be the righteous of the earth. Furthermore, Isaiah testified that the Lord would pour out his Spirit upon the inhabitants of the earth unto their divine empowerment for righteousness.[36] "And because of the righteousness of his people, Satan has no power; wherefore, he cannot be loosed for the space of many years; for he hath no power over the hearts of the people, for they dwell in righteousness" (1 Nephi 22:26). These blessings, together with the righteous reign of the Savior, will bring to pass peace and the binding of Satan during this thousand-year period.[37] In time, following the Millennium and the last great battle, Lucifer will be banished to outer darkness where he will "not have power over the saints any more at all" (D&C 88:114).

Life during the Millennium

The Millennium will bring to pass changes dealing with physical handicaps and deformities of the body. Similar to the miracles that blessed mankind during the mortal ministry of the Savior, Isaiah testified that "then the eyes of the blind shall be opened, and the ears of the deaf shall be unstopped. Then shall the lame man leap as an hart, and the tongue of the dumb sing" (Isaiah 35:5–6). Great blessings will come to those who have been prisoners in their own bodies, which blessings will prepare the way for freedom to act upon their righteous desires. Along with blindness and deafness, all other physical hindrances will be removed. Further, death itself will no longer bear sway over the earth. "There shall be no more thence an infant of days, nor an old man that hath not filled his days: for the child shall die an hundred years old" (Isaiah 65:20). The Lord clarified the nature of death among those who have kept the faith during that day. He explained "children shall grow up until they become old; old men shall die; but they shall not sleep in the dust, but they shall be changed in the twinkling of an eye" (D&C 63:51). That is to say that the righteous who live during the Millennium will change from a mortal paradisiacal state to an immortal resurrected state.[38] Isaiah extolled the Lord and his power when he said, "He will swallow up death in victory; and the Lord God will wipe away tears from off all faces" (Isaiah 25:8); "and the voice of weeping shall be no more heard in [Jerusalem], nor the voice of crying" (Isaiah 65:19).

Various aspects of everyday life as we know it in mortality will continue during the Millennium. For example, Isaiah explained that in that day "they shall build houses, and inhabit them; and they shall plant vineyards, and eat the fruit of them" (Isaiah 65:21). Unlike mortals in the precarious present life, in which natural calamities, war, corrupt governments, or death often prevent one from enjoying the fruits of one's labor, those who dwell upon the earth during the Millennium "shall long enjoy the work of their hands" (Isaiah 65:22).

Isaiah also spoke of those who were barren in mortality becoming fruitful during the Millennium: "Sing, O barren, thou that didst not bear; break forth into singing, and cry aloud, thou that didst not travail with child: for more are the children of the desolate than the children of the married wife, saith the Lord" (Isaiah 54:1).

The broad interpretation of this prophecy as it applies to the house of Israel will be dealt with in the next section. Doctrinally, however, Isaiah's joyous acclamation applies to individuals as well as nations. As Elder Dallin H. Oaks stated: "Singleness, childlessness, death, and divorce frustrate ideals and postpone the fulfillment of promised blessings. . . . The Lord has promised that in the eternities no blessing will be denied his sons and daughters who keep the commandments, are true to their covenants, and desire what is right. Many of the most important deprivations of mortality will be set right in the Millennium, which is the time for fulfilling all that is incomplete in the great plan of happiness for all of our Father's worthy children. We know that will be true of temple ordinances. I believe it will also be true of family relationships and experiences."[39]

Therefore, the Millennium will be a time of correcting those situations in mortal life that did not allow individuals to receive according to the desires of their hearts. Elder Joseph Fielding Smith taught that the Millennium will be a time to perform ordinances for those who did not have the opportunity during their mortal lives. He specifically mentioned that those who died in childhood would have the opportunity to choose mates and have sealings performed in their behalf for eternal marriage.[40] As Elder Oaks pointed out, these blessings will be offered to all of those who missed out on them because of the precarious nature of mortality and the limited freedom that many individuals have in acting on their own will and desires. Thus, all of the righteous barren or unmarried will have the full blessings of the gospel. As Isaiah expressed, they will be more fruitful than the married wife was in mortality previous to the Millennium. A type for the future millennial conditions regarding marriage and bearing children was evident among the Book of Mormon peoples during the period of time following the visit of the resurrected Christ: "And now behold, it came to pass that the people of Nephi did wax strong, and did multiply exceedingly fast, . . . and they were married, and given in marriage, and were blessed according to the multitude of the promises which the Lord had made unto them" (4 Nephi 1:10–11).

In general, during the Millennium "that same sociality which exists among us here will exist among us there" (D&C 130:2).[41] Brigham Young explained that outside of the changes that have been noted, "All things else shall be as they are now, we shall eat, drink, and wear clothing."[42] In contrast to present conditions, however, there will be no enmity in the animal kingdom nor between animals and mankind. Isaiah proclaimed: "The wolf also shall dwell with the lamb, and the leopard shall lie down with the kid; and the calf and the young lion and the fatling together; and a little child shall lead them. And the cow and the bear shall feed; their young ones shall lie down together: and the lion shall eat straw like the ox. And the sucking child shall play on the hole of the asp, and the weaned child shall put his hand on the cockatrice' den" (Isaiah 11:6–8).[43]

As previously considered, there will be no death as we now know it during the Millennium. Therefore, those animals that kill and feast upon their prey for sustenance will have a change of physiology and diet. Isaiah further reiterated the millennial conditions as those in which "the wolf and the lamb shall feed together, and the lion shall eat straw like the bullock: and dust shall be the serpent's meat. They shall not hurt nor destroy in all my holy mountain, saith the Lord" (Isaiah 65:25). A little reflection will lead one to conclude that many of humankind will likewise have a change of diet consistent with the physical changes in their bodies.

The Millennial Kingdom of Heaven on Earth

The Lord set aside the millennial day as a time when the knowledge of God and his salvation will cover the earth. As the Millennium proceeds "the earth shall be full of the knowledge of the Lord, as the waters cover the sea" (Isaiah 11:9). This will take place through the preaching of the gospel. Isaiah assured ancient Israel that during this time "all thy children shall be taught of the Lord" (Isaiah 54:13). Joseph Fielding Smith explained that missionary work and the preaching of the gospel will go forth "until all men are either converted or pass away."[44]

The work of building and receiving inspired teachings in the house of the Lord will continue. Many of those alive during the Millennium will desire to go to the house of the

Lord, "and many people shall go and say, Come ye, and let us go up to the mountain of the Lord, to the house of the God of Jacob; and he will teach us of his ways, and we will walk in his paths: for out of Zion shall go forth the law, and the word of the Lord from Jerusalem" (Isaiah 2:3). The Lord and his servants will teach the people concerning the way of salvation. Preachers of truth will search out listeners throughout the earth, and many will come to the houses of the Lord to learn more of his ways. The work of temple ordinances and blessings begun during this last dispensation will continue through the Millennium, and those who come into the fold of the Good Shepherd will receive the fullness of blessings offered in the house of the Lord. They will learn of the celestial law, and when they die and are changed in the twinkling of an eye to a resurrected state, they will be quickened by a portion of celestial glory.[45]

Among those who will come to the Lord are the remnants of scattered Israel. While much is being done and much will yet be done to preach the gospel in every nation, the great day of the return of Israel to the Lord will be in a millennial setting. During the Lord's visit among the peoples of the Americas, he clarified that the preaching of the gospel and the gathering of the dispersed of his people will take place following the time of his return in power and while he will be in their midst (3 Nephi 21:25–29). Isaiah foresaw that day in which "the remnant shall return, even the remnant of Jacob, unto the mighty God" (Isaiah 10:21). The return of Israel to the Lord has already begun under the direction of prophets in the latter days. The gathering has been orderly and under the Lord's watchful eye. As Isaiah prophesied, "for ye shall not go out with haste, nor go by flight: for the Lord will go before you; and the God of Israel will be your reward" (Isaiah 52:12).

The prophet Isaiah described the path upon which Israel will return, and those who will walk the path: "And an highway shall be there, and a way, and it shall be called The way of holiness; the unclean shall not pass over it; . . . but the redeemed shall walk there: and the ransomed of the

Lord shall return, and come to Zion with songs and everlasting joy upon their heads" (Isaiah 35:8–10). Thus, the path that Israel walks in the millennial day will be the same path that was given to their fathers before them. Once they have returned to the Lord and have been cleansed in the waters of baptism "it shall come to pass, that he that is left in Zion, and he that remaineth in Jerusalem, shall be called holy, even every one that is written among the living in Jerusalem: when the Lord shall have washed away the filth of the daughters of Zion, and shall have purged the blood of Jerusalem from the midst thereof by the spirit of judgment, and by the spirit of burning" (Isaiah 4:3–4). As intimated by Isaiah, the washing away of filthy sin in the waters of baptism will be followed by "the spirit of burning," or the baptism of fire which comes by receiving the gift of the Holy Ghost. Accordingly, Israel will be symbolically cleansed as a bride and "arrayed in fine linen, clean and white" (Revelation 19:8).

Isaiah identified the fulfillment of the covenant God made with ancient Israel. In poetic metaphor he explained, "for thy Maker is thine husband; the Lord of hosts is his name; and thy Redeemer the Holy One of Israel; The God of the whole earth shall he be called" (Isaiah 54:5). It was upon this point of the glorious millennial restoration of Israel that Isaiah rejoiced, "Sing, O barren, thou that didst not bear; break forth into singing, and cry aloud, thou that didst not travail with child: for more are the children of the desolate than the children of the married wife, saith the Lord" (Isaiah 54:1). Given Isaiah's exclamation, it appears that there will be more of the children of Israel who will join themselves to the Lord during the Millennium than there were in all previous generations.[46]

Moreover, Isaiah testified that in the millennial day the "dead men [of Israel] shall live" (Isaiah 26:19). The resurrected souls who will be raised from their graves, together with the converted of Israel and the converted of the heathen, will require that the people of the Lord "enlarge the place of thy tent, and let them stretch forth the curtains of thine habitations: spare not, lengthen thy cords, and strengthen thy stakes; for thou shalt break forth on the right hand and on the left; and thy seed shall inherit the Gentiles, and make the desolate cities to be inhabited" (Isaiah 54:2–3). Stakes of Zion will continue to be established throughout the earth. Zion will spread herself until she extends to cover the world over.

The work of preaching the gospel and establishing Zion has begun in this dispensation. Joseph Smith testified: "Our missionaries are going forth to different nations, and in Germany, Palestine, New Holland, Australia, the East Indies, and other places, the Standard of Truth has been erected; no unhallowed hand can stop the work from progressing; . . . the truth of God will go forth boldly, nobly, and independent, till it has penetrated every continent, visited every clime, swept every country, and sounded in every ear, till the purposes of God shall be accomplished, and the Great Jehovah shall say the work is done."[47] The complete fulfillment of Joseph Smith's prophecy will be in a millennial setting. Thus, the millennial day will be the time in which the kingdom of God on earth will become the kingdom of heaven, and the Lord will reign in glory with his saints upon the earth.

Conclusion

Isaiah presented the Millennium as a wondrous period of time in which God's purposes for his children will be realized. It is an essential part of the plan of salvation and the bringing "to pass the immortality and eternal life of man" (Moses 1:39). Yea, it is the time:

> When all that was promised the Saints will be given,
> And none will molest them from morn until ev'n,
> And earth will appear as the Garden of Eden,
> And Jesus will say to all Israel, "Come home."[48]

The equity and justice of God will be the millennial standard, and the obedient of God's children will receive all that God has in store for those who love Him. For the Millennium is the day in which the words of the Lord's servant Isaiah will come to pass in which he testified: "For since the beginning of the world men have not heard, nor perceived by the ear, neither hath the eye seen, O God, beside thee, what he hath prepared for him that waiteth for him" (Isaiah 64:4). May the Lord come quickly, and may we be prepared to enjoy the blessings of the great Millennium!

Notes

1. Gordon B. Hinckley, in Conference Report, April 1995, 95.

2. Article of Faith 10; D&C 29:27–23; 88:17–20, 25–26.

3. Hyrum M. Smith and Janne M. Sjodahl, *Doctrine and Covenants Commentary,* rev. ed. (Salt Lake City: Deseret Book, 1958), 846–47.

4. Isaiah 63:7; D&C 133:46–52.

5. See D&C 88:100–104.

6. The great battle between the forces of God and Lucifer that will take place following the Millennium is also referred to as the battle of Gog and Magog. See Joseph Smith, *History of The Church of Jesus Christ of Latter-day Saints,* ed. B. H. Roberts, 2d ed. rev., 7 vols. (Salt Lake City: Deseret Book, 1973), 5:298; and Bruce R. McConkie, *The Millennial Messiah* (Salt Lake City: Deseret Book, 1982), 488.

7. See Ezekiel 38–39.

8. Although this referred to the destruction of ancient Israel, it appears also to apply to the conditions at the beginning of the Millennium.

9. Smith, *History of the Church,* 5:64–65; see also Isaiah 28:17.

10. See Daniel 7:9.

11. D&C 29:11.

12. The Savior gave laws to the Nephites in ancient America in a sermon similar to the Sermon on the Mount in Matthew 5–7 which, as they observed these laws, brought the Nephites to a level of millennial conditions (see 3 Nephi 12–14; 4 Nephi 1:1–23).

13. Smith, *History of the Church,* 5:212.

14. D&C 57:2–3; 84:2–4.

15. Ether 13:5–11; Bruce R. McConkie, *A New Witness for the Articles of Faith* (Salt Lake City: Deseret Book, 1985), 539–40; McConkie, *Millennial Messiah,* 299.

16. D&C 43:29.

17. Joseph Fielding Smith, *The Way to Perfection* (Salt Lake City: Deseret Book, 1975), 312–13.

18. D&C 76:72–74.

19. Smith, *History of the Church,* 5:212.

20. D&C 76:84–85; 88:100–101.

21. Joseph Fielding Smith, *Doctrines of Salvation* (Salt Lake City: Bookcraft, 1954), 1:86.

22. Smith, *History of the Church,* 5:212; also see Joseph Smith, *Teachings of the Prophet Joseph Smith,* sel. Joseph Fielding Smith (Salt Lake City: Deseret Book, 1938), 268–69 n.

23. D&C 88:27–30, 99.

24. McConkie, *Millennial Messiah,* 640.

25. Bruce R. McConkie, *Doctrinal New Testament Commentary,* 3 vols. (Salt Lake City: Bookcraft, 1973), 3:486.

26. Also see Isaiah 24:23.

27. "This earth is our home, it was framed expressly for the habitation of those who are faithful to God, and who prove themselves worthy to inherit the earth when the Lord shall have sanctified, purified and glorified it and brought it back into his presence, from which it fell far into space. . . . When the earth was framed and brought into existence and man was placed upon it, it was near the throne of our Father in heaven. And when man fell—though that was designed in the economy, there was nothing about it mysterious or unknown to the Gods, they understood it all, it was all planned—but when man fell, the earth fell into space, and took up its abode in this planetary system, and the sun became our light. . . . This is the glory the earth came from, and when it is glorified it will return again unto the presence of the Father, and it will dwell there, and these intelligent beings that I am looking at, if they live worthy of it, will dwell upon this earth." Brigham Young, in *Journal of Discourses,* 26 vols. (London: Latter-day Saints' Book Depot, 1854–86), 17:143.

28. It is difficult to know whether Isaiah is referring to events that are millennial or postmillennial. I have taken the approach that Isaiah was writing of both time periods as similar changes will take place at each time. The changes that will take place at the beginning of the Millennium will prepare the earth as a terrestrial sphere and those that will take place after the Millennium will prepare the earth as a celestial sphere. (D&C 88:25–26.)

29. See Victor L. Ludlow, *Isaiah: Prophet, Seer, and Poet* (Salt Lake City: Deseret Book, 1982), 313.

30. *The Interpreter's Dictionary of the Bible,* ed. George A. Buttrick, 12 vols. (New York: Abingdon Press, 1962), 1:538.

31. Ibid., 4:308.

32. Ibid., 1:545.

33. Ibid., 3:479.

34. Although Matthew and Luke cite this prophecy in connection

with the ministry of John the Baptist, in the Doctrine and Covenants the Lord focused on the fulfillment being millennial as discussed in the text (Matthew 3:3; Luke 3:3–5).

35. McConkie, *Millennial Messiah,* 624–25.

36. Isaiah 32:15.

37. See 1 Nephi 22:15, 26; D&C 43:31; 45:55; 84:100.

38. Doctrine and Covenants 43:32 explains, "And he that liveth in righteousness shall be changed in the twinkling of an eye." For a discussion concerning these states, see McConkie, *Millennial Messiah,* 645–49.

39. Dallin H. Oaks, in Conference Report, October 1993, 101.

40. Smith, *Doctrines of Salvation,* 3:65–66.

41. Doctrine and Covenants 130:1 places this statement in the context of the time "when the Savior shall appear."

42. Brigham Young, in *Journal of Discourses,* 1:203.

43. The asp and the cockatrice are venomous serpents or snakes.

44. Smith, *Doctrines of Salvation,* 1:86.

45. D&C 88:28–29.

46. Ludlow, *Isaiah,* 459–60; Monte S. Nyman, *Great Are the Words of Isaiah* (Salt Lake City: Bookcraft, 1980), 211–12.

47. Smith, *History of the Church,* 4:540.

48. "Now Let Us Rejoice," *Hymns of The Church of Jesus Christ of Latter-day Saints* (Salt Lake City: The Church of Jesus Christ of Latter-day Saints, 1985), no. 3.

CHAPTER SIX

The Prophets of the Exile: Saviors of a People

RICHARD D. DRAPER

The thunder of Nebuchadnezzar's battering rams should have sounded the death knell of the Jews as a people, but it did not. To say it another way, Jerusalem's destruction, followed by the Babylonian captivity, marks a major break in the course of Jewish history but not its end. Those battering rams were instrumental in ending both Judah's institutional and corporate life but not that of the people or their religion. Some things, however, did come to an end. Never again would the old social and religious pattern be constructed in exactly the same way. The destruction of the Jewish capital with its temple successfully demolished the Jewish state and ended its priestly activities. In 580 B.C. the Jewish people, beaten and scattered, were but an agglomeration of individual refugees living under foreign rule.[1] The threat posed by the exile must not be minimized or trivialized.[2] Loss of identity threatened the Jewish people more fully than at any other time in their existence with the possible exception of the Egyptian bondage. The possibility is underscored by the fact that a number of Jewish communities that took root outside Palestine eventually lost their Jewish character and eroded into the cultures of the area.[3] That Judah's history did not end with the Babylonian captivity is nothing short of a miracle, but Judah not only

---

Richard D. Draper is associate professor of ancient scripture at Brigham Young University.

survived the calamity but also formed a new and viable society built on the ruins of the old.[4] In the process, she refined, disciplined, and strengthened her faith, giving it a vigor and direction that would carry it into and beyond New Testament times.[5]

One aspect of that miracle central to the success of all the others is prophecy. Judah's prophets kept her faith from extinction and her culture from decay. They did this, in part, by reminding her of her unique relation to her God and the mission he had assigned her. The prophets also fueled the Jews' desire to return to their own land, build God's temple, and once more become his people. Further, these inspired men facilitated the miracle by satisfactorily answering the exile's most urgent questions and, in the process, giving the Jews both hope and direction.[6]

It is noteworthy that the impetus of the miracle did not come, as one might suppose, from those Jews still living in and around Judea. The Babylonians left quite a nucleus of Jews in the land. Though the disruption of their life was extreme, it was by no means complete.[7] Many were able to eke out a living in various parts of Judea.[8] Evidence suggests that most of these Jews continued to practice an impure form of Jehovah worship.[9] Still, some, if not many, would have been loyal to their religion. These godly souls would have mourned for Zion and wished for her return. But for seventy years, all they did was wish. There was no spark, no energy, no attempt at restoration from this source.[10]

To the north, the Jewish communities experienced little disruption of life compared to their southern neighbors. Many hundreds of Jews continued to exist in Samaria and Galilee. Nebuchadnezzar destroyed few buildings and no cities in these areas. Few of these Jews, if any, were taken hostage by the king. They were the dominant population throughout the Jezreel and Galilee. Their worship, like that of the unfaithful Jews around Judea, would have contained many pagan elements.[11] But even here an orthodox strain would have yearned for the temple and prayed to their God. But pray was all they did. No restoration pressure existed here,[12] no fires of nationalistic zeal burned in the area. At best, it smoldered well beneath the surface, unable to produce the energy necessary to renew and rebuild what was lost.

The same is true of those Jews living in lands outside of Palestine. Even before the Babylonians marched, Jews had established a few communities and bolstered the population of others as they attempted to escape to more secure climes.[13] As chapters 42 through 44 of Jeremiah show, Egypt became very attractive for many of these. Quite a number of Jews settled in Daphnae, a city in the Nile delta; others moved farther south. Some were hired as mercenaries and developed a colony at Elephantine, near the first cataract of the Nile.[14] The successful Jewish communities in Egypt acted as magnets, and more Jews flowed into that country. But Egyptian favoritism did not act to stir into flame the coals of Judah's desire to return. Rather, Egyptian wiles seem to have acted more to cool what little heat there was.

Both Transjordan and Syria received an influx of Jewish refugees. Jewish villages grew up here and there on the eastern end of the Mediterranean area,[15] but no pressure for restoration came from these Jews, either. Though they were much closer to Jerusalem and had influence with local leaders and sufficient resources to reenter the land of Judea and at least lay the foundation for further growth, none are known to have stirred. Indeed, the embers of gathering lay cold in these lands.

The scattered circumstance of the Jews underscores one point: Prophecy was being fulfilled. Though Judah was not yet scattered the world over, the process was beginning in earnest. Never again would all, or even most, of her sons and daughters reside in Palestine. Never again would there be a full return before her Messiah came in glory.[16] But, considering the magnitude of the calamity that overtook her, the wonder is that she did not disappear into the vortex of history forever, as had so many nations before and after her. Many of these, like Judah's northern sister, Ephraim, and her great enemy, the Philistines, lost their identity as a people during this time.[17] That Judah did not stems in large measure from the Jews in Babylon and the work going on among them.

It was in Babylon, in a land far away from Judah, that the desire for return actually burned. It is to these Jews, those who were actually taken into captivity by Nebuchadnezzar, that one must give the largest credit for the survival of the people. Three major factors contributed. First, the policy of deportation carried out by the Babylonians meant that the Jews in Babylon were the top of Judah's intellectual, political, and ecclesiastical leadership. Jeremiah gives the total number of those deported (in 597, 587, and 582 B.C.) as forty-six hundred (Jeremiah 52:28–30). This figure most likely represents only adult males, suggesting that the actual number was closer to twenty thousand.[18] That is not very many Jews, certainly far fewer than those living in either Palestine, Syria, or Egypt.

On the surface it seems surprising that the force that would preserve the nation would come from so few people, even if they were the more elite, but here the second factor came into play. Conditions in Babylon contributed markedly to their success. Though the Jews did suffer some discomfort and instability (especially during the first few years of exile) and were not free to return to their homeland, they were not prisoners, either. Theirs was a kind of modified, somewhat benevolent, internment that allowed them to buy land, open shops, move into civil service, and attend to their many chores. Eventually many of them settled into a comfortable, if unconnected, lifestyle.[19] The historical writings of the Bible suggest that they developed communities of their own and prospered in peace.[20] The Babylonians allowed them to assemble and to carry out certain civil and religious duties among themselves.[21] Many Jews entered trade, and some became quite wealthy.[22] Facilitating that favorable internment would have been the Jewish administrators, such as Daniel, Shadrach, Meshach, and Abednego, who were moving up in the ranks of Babylonian government. By the year 531 B.C., Zerubbabel had risen to the position of cup bearer, second in command among the palace bureaucrats. Some of the Jewish leaders were in an excellent position both to assist the captives and to enhance their desire to return and restore their homeland and temple.

In all, the Jews in Babylon produced the capital and manpower necessary to do the work essential for the return. But other areas of Jewish settlement had all these things as well. What they lacked was the one thing the Babylonian Jews had uniquely: the prophets. The Jews taken captive to Babylon included not only the socially elite but the spiritually elite as well. This brings us to the third factor that helped these Jews keep alive the spirit of restoration. It was here—not in Palestine, Syria, Jordan, or Egypt—where God placed his prophets. From them came the explanation, the direction, and the impetus for the restoration of the whole community and the religion.[23]

Nevertheless, Judah's restoration, even with the prophetic push, did not transpire easily or automatically. It took a lot of soul-searching and a profound readjustment in her theological understanding to get things moving.[24] Yet, the role played by the prophets must not be underestimated. Hindsight makes it easy for the modern reader to understand why Judah fell. But to many of the Jews living at the time, it was anything but clear. They questioned Jehovah's dealings with his people, and some felt betrayed.

Because of that, Judah's danger of apostatizing in Babylon was real and immediate. It may have been more acute here than anywhere else. Though the state and the religion of Judah emphasized the worship of Jehovah alone, insisting that all other gods were "no gods," Judah was never more than a step away from polytheism. Archeological evidence seems quite convincing that the common people practiced a symbiotic religion mixing elements of Jehovah worship with worship of the gods of the land.[25] The writings of the prophets show that the people felt justified in doing this and were sure they should receive

Jehovah's blessings (see, for example, Hosea 9:9–10; Jeremiah 11:12–13).

The fall of Jerusalem did not immediately shatter those beliefs. Some felt that somehow Jehovah had failed them. When many of the Jews looked at what they considered Jehovah's broken promise, evidenced in the victory of Babylon, they might have wondered if Babylon's gods were not more real or at least more mighty than theirs.[26] To some it might have appeared that Jehovah was a petty god unable to protect even his petty state.

Others were not so willing to give credit to foreign gods. They felt Jehovah was responsible, but they questioned if he were really just. Many whined that their lot was unfounded and unfair.[27] Their attitude is perfectly reflected in the Book of Mormon, in the insistence of Laman and Lemuel that "we know that the people who were in the land of Jerusalem were a righteous people; for they kept the statutes and judgments of the Lord, and all his commandments, according to the law of Moses; wherefore, we know that they are a righteous people" (1 Nephi 17:22). Nothing could have been further from the truth, but the attitude displayed by these two ruthless brothers was popular in Judah as well. The prophet Habakkuk's willingness to question God's justness in using Babylon as his tool to chastise Judah underscores how pervasive the feeling was (Habakkuk 1:1–17).

A third group, those who believed in the words of the prophets, feared that Judah had committed a mortal sin for which she could never be forgiven. As a result of this sin she had lost her place as the covenant people as well as her homeland.[28] The Jews cried to their God for mercy, but, seemingly, without hope. They knew that Jerusalem's "gates are sunk into the ground; he [God] hath destroyed and broken her bars: her king and her princes are among the Gentiles: the law is no more; her prophets also find no vision [of hope] from the Lord" (Lamentations 2:9). Even for the faithful, the future appeared hopeless.

As a result, wholesale abandonment of Jehovah and his

word threatened the Jews; the seductive power of Babylon compounded the problem. Jerusalem, seen through the eyes of parochialism, had seemed strong, beautiful, and mighty. Now, more cosmopolitan eyes, having looked upon the strength and splendor of Babylon and all she had to offer, saw Jerusalem as small, dingy, weak, and unsophisticated. Judah could neither ignore nor forget what had happened. She was forced to clarify her position in relation to the national tragedy and Babylon and its gods. The only other alternative was to perish.[29]

On the positive side, the captivity did deal a mortal blow to the dogma propagated by such false prophets as Hananiah and others. This false doctrine was based on two misconceptions. The first was the belief that Jehovah would never allow his temple to fall. Just what precedents caused the people to believe and the false prophets to propagate this idea are unknown, but the common proverb was "The temple of the Lord, The temple of the Lord, The temple of the Lord, are these" (Jeremiah 7:4), meaning that as long as the temple stood, God would protect the people. Jeremiah castigated the Jews for believing "in lying words, that cannot profit. Will ye steal, murder, and commit adultery, and swear falsely, and burn incense unto Baal, and walk after other gods whom ye know not," asked his God, "and come and stand before me in this house, which is called by my name, and say, We are delivered to do all these abominations?" (Jeremiah 7:8–10).

It would not work, the Lord testified, and urged them to go to "Shiloh, where I set my name at the first, and see what I did to it for the wickedness of my people Israel" (Jeremiah 7:12). Judah should have understood the idiocy of the position taken by these pseudoprophets, for Shiloh, the chief sanctuary of Jehovah for centuries, now lay in ruins. Their own hymn mourned the extent of that loss, saying that God "forsook the tabernacle of Shiloh, the tent which he placed among men; and delivered his strength into captivity, and his glory into the enemy's hand. He gave his people over also unto the sword; and was wroth with his inheritance. The fire consumed their young men; and their maidens were not given to marriage. Their priests fell by the sword; and their widows made no lamentation" (Psalm 78:60–64). Still, few seem to have gotten the message, and its echoes must have haunted those in Babylon.

The second misconception lay in the false belief that God would uphold the Davidic dynasty no matter what. Here we can see how the Jews came to believe this idea. Nathan, the prophet, had told David that "thine house and thy kingdom shall be established for ever before thee: thy throne shall be established for ever" (2 Samuel 7:16). David himself exulted that Jehovah "hath made with me an everlasting covenant, ordered in all things, and sure: for this is all my salvation, and all my desire" (2 Samuel 23:5).[30] The theology quickly developed that each king, as Jehovah's anointed "son" (Psalm 2:7–11), would be protected from his foes and lead Israel to an ever-expanding kingdom (see, for example, Psalm 72:8–11).

As Jeremiah had worked to redirect Israel's thinking about the temple, Micah had earlier tried to make a course correction concerning God's covenant with her princes. He declared in no uncertain terms that he had full authority to "declare unto Jacob his transgression, and to Israel his sin. Hear this, I pray you, ye heads of the house of Jacob, and princes of the house of Israel, that abhor judgment, and pervert all equity. They build up Zion with blood, and Jerusalem with iniquity. The heads thereof judge for reward, and the priests thereof teach for hire, and the prophets thereof divine for money: yet will they lean upon the Lord, and say, Is not the Lord among us? none evil can come upon us. Therefore shall Zion for your sake be plowed as a field, and Jerusalem shall become heaps, and the mountain of the house as the high places of the forest" (Micah 3:8–12).

Micah did not stand alone in his testimony. Isaiah also assailed the nobles, judges, and priests for their unscrupulous willingness to rob from the poor and defenseless. God would not allow prince, priest, or prophet to lead Judah astray without severe consequences. Indeed, Judah, with all her seeming splendor, would fall.[31]

But Judah ignored these clear warnings. The false dogma proved too intoxicating because of the acute sense of security it offered. It further allowed Judah to reject Jehovah's laws and his true prophets and foolishly believe that the scion of David's line—the Messiah—would soon come and establish his world-embracing kingdom over which the Jews would triumphantly rule.

Babylonian battering rams destroyed that belief as surely and completely as they breached Jerusalem's walls. Those who had put trust in it now found their spiritual lives in peril, much as their ancestors' physical lives had been in danger under the Egyptian pharaohs. What Judah desperately needed was another Moses to lead her out of the way not of physical harm but of spiritual. And she had one in the form of the prophets.

Judaism in Babylon survived because of three interconnected phenomena. First, the spiritually weak apostatized, leaving the ranks of the faithful more pure and determined; second, the spiritually strong repented and became more orthodox; and, finally, those who remained in the faith began to listen with hearing ears to the voices of the prophets. They quickly found that these inspired men had answered and continued to answer Judah's most pressing questions. The prophets carefully and fully identified her problems and gave counsel on how to correct them, promising that the people could once again return to God's covenant and the land tied thereto.

Through the prophets, Judah became convinced that God's judgment had been righteous and well deserved.[32] Her job was to repent; then God would restore the covenant. Hosea's gracious act of taking to himself a wife who had turned to prostitution (see Hosea 1:1–2:23) must have given the Jews comfort and hope. The prophets' love, mirroring that of Jehovah for Judah, testified that God would gladly welcome back the penitent with full forgiveness.

The prophets did not underplay the tragedy that had

occurred. Nonetheless, they offered hope in Jehovah's redemptive purpose. Judah would not stay in captivity. She was but a stranger in a strange land, a sojourner in a foreign country from which she would eventually be released. Jeremiah even supplied the parameters of her stay, promising Judah that she would "serve the king of Babylon seventy years. And it shall come to pass, when seventy years are accomplished, that I [God] will punish the king of Babylon, and that nation, saith the Lord, for their iniquity, and the land of the Chaldeans, and will make it perpetual desolations" (Jeremiah 25:11–12). Therefore, Judah's challenge was to make sure that she did not become integrated into the culture of this foreign land, or she might forget her true home and temple.

An important task of the prophets was to assure Judah that, even in Babylon, Jehovah was with her. They did that by reinforcing the idea that Jehovah governed and controlled the destiny of all nations, including Babylon. Here the writings of Daniel were particularly poignant. The historical portion of his work contains two stories that bear directly on the point.[33] The first dealt with Nebuchadnezzar's dream of the great image. The important point of the story was not only that Daniel interpreted the king's dream but also that he had the ability to do it. The story really plays upon the latter point. The king insisted that his auditors, consisting of many of his wise men, astrologers, magicians, and soothsayers,[34] tell him the dream before they interpreted it, as insurance that their interpretation was true. His demand brought forth the excuse that "there is none other that can shew it before the king, except the gods, whose dwelling is not with flesh" (Daniel 2:11). Here the Babylonian priests admit that they could not get in contact with their own local gods on such matters. Daniel, however, was able to tell the king the dream because his God, who possessed both wisdom and might, also "giveth wisdom unto the wise, and knowledge to them that know understanding: he revealeth the deep and secret things: he knoweth what is in the darkness, and the light dwelleth with him" (Daniel 2:21–22). The irony is important; the response of the Babylonian wise men underscores their belief that their own gods were distant and impersonal, while Daniel's shows that Jehovah, even in Babylon, was immediate and personal.

So that his readers would not miss the point, Daniel further testified that Jehovah was also the one who "changeth the times and the seasons: he removeth kings, and setteth up kings" (Daniel 2:21). Nebuchadnezzar's dream emphasized the last point. It was Jehovah who chose Nebuchadnezzar to be king and who would set up all the kingdoms to follow until God's own eternal kingdom overmastered and ruled the rest (see Daniel 2:36–45).

Daniel's second point, showing that the Lord governed Babylon, centered on Jehovah's work in convincing its kings that he was the living God. We see the progression in four events. The first, already noted, was Daniel's ability to tell Nebuchadnezzar both his dream and its meaning. Daniel ascribes the power to "the God of heaven" (Daniel 2:19, 44). The Jews used this term to designate the almighty and true God.[35] The point Daniel may have been making with the king is that the prophet's God overmastered the whole heaven, including the stars that the Babylonians worshipped as symbols of their gods. As a result, the king concluded that "your God is a God of gods, and a Lord of kings, and a revealer of secrets, seeing thou couldest reveal this secret" (Daniel 2:47). We see in this admission the king allowing Jehovah a place among the pantheon of Babylonian gods and even according him the special place as revealer. But to have the Lord as one among the many gods would not do, so Jehovah instituted the next step.

The king set up an idol and wanted all to worship it. When Shadrach, Meshach, and Abednego refused, he ordered them burned (see Daniel 3:13–22). When they emerged from the fire, not only unharmed but not even smelling of smoke, the king exclaimed, "There is no other God that can deliver after this sort" (Daniel 3:29). Jehovah had definitely climbed a few more rungs up the ladder of the pantheon. Still, that was not far enough. The next event would push his position all the way to the top.

The king again had a dream that Daniel interpreted. The king, according to the revelation, would go mad for seven years, "till thou know that the most High ruleth in the kingdom of men, and giveth it to whomsoever he will" (Daniel 4:25). Nebuchadnezzar may rule over Babylon and its temples, but Jehovah ruled over him. The malady struck that very hour.[36] Then, as the record reports, "at the end of the days I Nebuchadnezzar lifted up mine eyes unto heaven, and mine understanding returned unto me, and I blessed the most High, and I praised and honoured him that liveth for ever, whose dominion is an everlasting dominion, and his kingdom is from generation to generation" (Daniel 4:34). It is hard to know from the text if Nebuchadnezzar moved from polytheism to henotheism or monotheism. One thing is sure: He reckoned Jehovah as "the King of heaven, all whose works are truth, and his ways judgment: and those that walk in pride he is able to abase" (Daniel 4:37).

Darius took the last step, which occurred when Daniel's enemies tricked the king into throwing Daniel into the lion's den. The king confessed his belief that Daniel's God could save him (see Daniel 6:16). When he did, Darius made a decree commanding, "That in every dominion of my kingdom men tremble and fear before the God of Daniel: for he is the living God, and stedfast for ever, and his kingdom that which shall not be destroyed, and his dominion shall be even unto the end" (Daniel 6:26). Jehovah no longer stood as one of the many gods nor as the head of the gods: he was *the* living God whose kingdom and dominion were everlasting.

It would be helpful to know when Daniel, or an editor, composed and circulated his works. Because his record does not conclude until the reign of Cyrus the Persian, the book as we know it probably did not come into being until the Jews either had departed or were preparing to depart for the land of Judea. But because Daniel was a high official—

second only to the king some of the time, according to the record (see Daniel 6:1–3)—his teachings and experiences should have been well known to his fellow Jews. If that is the case, his testimony would have reinforced the idea that God was with them and directing the affairs not only of Babylon but also of all nations through time. Further, it promised the Jews that even in Babylon, Jehovah could and did sustain and protect those who remained true to the faith.

We are on firmer ground dating the work of Jeremiah. His prophecies were written down throughout his long ministry, beginning under the reign of Josiah (626–608 B.C.) and concluding after Zedekiah's fall in 586 B.C. Though his messages made him unpopular with some of the most influential and powerful people in Jerusalem, to the point where he was incarcerated and persecuted, others, in addition to his scribe Baruch, were carefully recording and preserving them.[37]

Jeremiah was of the priestly house. He lived in the village of Anathoth, about three miles north of the Jerusalem temple. Shortly before 608 B.C., his fearless voice rang out in clear warning. To the Jews who gathered for worship, he warned:

"The Lord said unto me, Proclaim all these words in the cities of Judah, and in the streets of Jerusalem, saying, Hear ye the words of this covenant, and do them.

"For I earnestly protested unto your fathers in the day that I brought them up out of the land of Egypt, even unto this day, rising early and protesting, saying, Obey my voice.

"Yet they obeyed not, nor inclined their ear, but walked every one in the imagination of their evil heart: therefore I will bring upon them all the words of this covenant, which I commanded them to do; but they did them not.

"And the Lord said unto me, A conspiracy is found among the men of Judah, and among the inhabitants of Jerusalem.

"They are turned back to the iniquities of their forefathers, which refused to hear my words; and they went after other gods to serve them: the house of Israel and the house of Judah have broken my covenant which I made with their fathers.

"Therefore thus saith the Lord, Behold, I will bring evil upon them, which they shall not be able to escape; and though they shall cry unto me, I will not hearken unto them" (Jeremiah 11:6–11).

The warning was clear: Judah must repent and follow her God or the coming evil would bring her great suffering. But she would come to repentance, he warned, one way or another. If she would not do it on her own, then "thine own wickedness shall correct thee, and thy backslidings shall reprove thee" (Jeremiah 2:19). The evil agent, he warned, already gathering to the north, was ready to move against this vile and sinful nation. The agent of destruction, the Lord warned, "is a mighty nation, it is an ancient nation, a nation whose language thou knowest not, neither understandest what they say. . . . And they shall eat up thine harvest, and thy bread, which thy sons and thy daughters should eat: they shall eat up thy flocks and thine herds: they shall eat up thy vines and thy fig trees: they shall impoverish thy fenced cities, wherein thou trustedst, with the sword" (Jeremiah 5:15–17; see also 2:16; 4:5–8, 11–17; 6:22–26). When the destruction came, the Jews would lament, "The Lord our God has put us to silence, and given us water of gall to drink, because we have sinned against the Lord" (Jeremiah 8:14).

Jeremiah did not deny the validity of the Davidic covenant in which so many trusted; however, he pushed it into the future and made its realization contingent on the righteousness of the people (see Jeremiah 23:5–8). For now, he warned David's heir, "Execute ye judgment and righteousness, and deliver the spoiled out of the hand of the oppressor: and do not wrong, do no violence to the stranger, the fatherless, nor the widow, neither shed innocent blood in this place. . . . But if ye will not hear these words, I swear by myself, saith the Lord, that this house shall become a desolation" (Jeremiah 22:3–5).

Jeremiah's message must have haunted those captives on the way to Babylon who had heard and spurned it. Yet it still took them some time before they accepted it and were finally healed by it. This spiritual balm of Gilead, once applied, worked upon the captives and those living in Judah and elsewhere. The message made sense and found reinforcement in other scriptures. But the powerful voice of another prophet backed up Jeremiah and acted to fulfill the divine law of witnesses[38]: Ezekiel.

Like Jeremiah, Ezekiel was a priest (Ezekiel 1:3). That explains in part why he became one of Nebuchadnezzar's many hostages, the Babylonians concentrating on children of the gentry, clergy, and aristocracy. His captors would have taken him into Babylon about 597 B.C., with a group of Jewish exiles deported about a decade before Jerusalem was destroyed.[39] Because Jeremiah had been prophesying for more than ten years by that time, it is very likely that Ezekiel would have heard his testimony and caught the same fire. God called him to carry the message into the streets of the Babylonian captives as Jeremiah did in the streets of Jerusalem.

He used the prophetic *'ot,* rather exaggerated symbolic acts, as the means of drawing attention to his message. Among other things, he symbolized the coming fate of Jerusalem by drawing a picture of the city on a brick and then, while eating rationed foods, simulating a siege against it (see Ezekiel 4:1–15).

A little later, he shaved off his hair and beard. That act alone, especially shaving his beard, would have brought him a great deal of attention. Men in both the Babylonian and the Jewish cultures wore beards, and the Jews viewed them as a sign of adult male vitality and glory.[40] The prophet's clean-shaven face would have startled those who viewed it. But they would have sensed his message, for the shaved beard symbolized a radical change in the state of affairs.[41] He did not leave his audience guessing as to which way affairs were going to change. One-third of his hair he burned with fire, another he hacked with the sword, and the last he scattered to the wind. He did retain a few strands, which he tied to the hem of his robe (see Ezekiel 5:1–5).

This ritual act he followed with a stern warning. "This is Jerusalem," he explained, and because "she hath changed my [that is, God's] judgments into wickedness more than the nations," God "will execute judgments in the midst of thee in the sight of the nations." The judgment would be horrible, for "fathers shall eat the sons in the midst of thee and the sons shall eat their fathers; and I [God] will execute judgments in thee, and the whole remnant of thee will I scatter into all the winds." Underscoring the reason for such severe judgment, the Lord chastised, "Surely, because thou hast defiled my sanctuary with all thy detestable things, and with all thine abominations, therefore will I also diminish thee; neither shall mine eye spare, neither will I have any pity" (Ezekiel 5:5–7, 9–11).

Ezekiel clearly preached against the idea that the temple alone would save the people. He recounted a vision in which he saw the Lord's Spirit lift from the sanctuary, hover over the temple for a moment, and then depart to the east (see Ezekiel 9:8; 10:18; 11:23). His message was both clear and simple: It was not the temple but righteousness that would be Judah's only shield. Where there was no righteousness, there was no hope.

Ezekiel's words stung the Jews of the captivity, but they refused, at least initially, to respond. Jehovah castigated them because "they hear thy words, but they do them not." But they would soon learn a stern lesson, for "when this [the fall of Jerusalem] cometh to pass (lo, it will come,) then shall they know that a prophet hath been among them" (Ezekiel 33:32–33).

Not many months later the captive Jews received a startling witness that they, indeed, had a prophet among them. An escapee from the siege of Jerusalem was able to make his way to the captives and testify, "The city is smitten" (Ezekiel 33:21). The shock of that testimony and, a short time later, the confirmation by several thousand refugees moving into the area, stirred the Jews to listen to Ezekiel. He assured them that God took no pleasure in his people's pain, but it was the only way he could get Judah to turn from her wicked ways (see Ezekiel 33:11). He moved to allay their fears with as much energy as he had used to provoke their righteousness.

Again his voice was not alone. Former and present prophets continually assured the people that there would be a homecoming. Even the most dire prophecies were tempered by the assurance that Zion would be delivered, God's temple would stand again, and Israel would be restored (note particularly Jeremiah 32:6–15). Ezekiel's famous vision of the dry bones testified not only to the eventual resurrection of Israel but the more immediate restoration of Judah:

"Then he said unto me, Son of man, these bones are the whole house of Israel: behold, they say, Our bones are dried, and our hope is lost: we are cut off for our parts.

"Therefore prophesy and say unto them, Thus saith the Lord God; Behold, O my people, I will open your graves, and cause you to come up out of your graves, and bring you into the land of Israel.

"And ye shall know that I am the Lord, when I have opened your graves, O my people, and brought you up out of your graves, and shall put my spirit in you, and ye shall live, *and I shall place you in your own land:* then shall ye know that I the Lord have spoken it, and performed it, saith the Lord" (Ezekiel 37:11–14; emphasis added).

God commanded Ezekiel to "take thee one stick, and write upon it, For Judah, and for the children of Israel his companions: then take another stick, and write upon it, For Joseph, the stick of Ephraim, and for all the house of Israel his companions" to show that the whole house of Israel, not just Judah, would be restored (Ezekiel 37:16). Therefore, the Lord said, "Join them one to another into one stick; and they shall become one in thine hand.

"And when the children of thy people shall speak unto

thee, saying, Wilt thou not shew us what thou meanest by these?

"Say unto them, Thus saith the Lord God; Behold, I will take the stick of Joseph, which is in the hand of Ephraim, and the tribes of Israel his fellows, and will put them with him, even with the stick of Judah, and make them one stick, and they shall be one in mine hand.

"And the sticks whereon thou writest shall be in thine hand before their eyes.

"And say unto them, Thus saith the Lord God; Behold, *I will take the children of Israel from among the heathen,* whither they be gone, and will gather them on every side, *and bring them into their own land"* (Ezekiel 37:17–21; emphasis added). Though this scripture looks to the last days, it had immediate application to Judah's return from captivity. Ezekiel's commission to join together the sticks—or better, writing tablets—becomes a harbinger of the restoration of all Israel. As Latter-day Saints we understand that the passage referred to the Book of Mormon and the Bible. The captive Jews, however, would have seen it as a plea to accept the message of the prophets of the north (for example, Amos, Hosea, and Isaiah) combined with those of the south (for example, Micah, Jeremiah, and Habakkuk) that Jehovah reigned and would see that his people returned.

Once Judah began to look, the scriptural evidence of her restoration must have been very reassuring. Further, the scriptures even outlined the events that would lead to her return. Isaiah foresaw the fall of her captor Babylon and the coming of her Median liberator, Cyrus.[42] Jehovah's doleful words promised Babylon a tragic end: "I will stir up the Medes against them, which shall not regard silver; and as for gold, they shall not delight in it. Their bows also shall dash the young men to pieces; and they shall have no pity on the fruit of the womb; their eye shall not spare children. And Babylon, the glory of kingdoms, the beauty of the Chaldees' excellency, shall be as when God overthrew Sodom and Gomorrah" (Isaiah 13:17–19).

The reaction of the exiles after the fall of Jerusalem to the promises of deliverance and restoration brought to the prophets all they could have hoped for. The people confessed their sins and turned to their Lord. Solomon's inspired prayer had seen them "repent, and make supplication unto thee [Jehovah] in the land of them that carried them captives, saying, We have sinned, and have done perversely, we have committed wickedness" (1 Kings 8:47). Then would they "return unto thee with all their heart, and with all their soul, in the land of their enemies, which led them away captive, and pray unto thee toward their land, which thou gavest their fathers" (1 Kings 8:48). Isaiah quoted their prayer for restoration. They would ask the Lord to "return for thy servants' sake, the tribes of thine inheritance. The people of thy holiness have possessed it but a little while: our adversaries have trodden down thy sanctuary. We are thine: thou never barest rule over them; they were not called by thy name" (Isaiah 63:17–19). To their prayer the Lord would respond, "I will bring forth a seed out of Jacob, and out of Judah an inheritor of my mountains: and mine elect shall inherit it, and my servants shall dwell there" (Isaiah 65:9).

The promise seemed sure. Judah's job was to turn to her God with full purpose of heart and the reward would come. Yet there was tension between those who desired to establish the new nation on the basis of its old Davidic theology (see Ezekiel 34:23–27; 37:24–28) and those with the grander vision of an idealized confederation based on the old pattern of the tribal league. These saw the nation presided over by the Zadokite priesthood with the restored Davidic monarchy playing the reduced role of protector of the state and the religion[43] (see Ezekiel 43–45; especially 43:1–7; 44:4–31). The difference of opinion, however, could not be resolved while the Jews were in Babylon, but it does illustrate their growing faith in the prophecies. They hoped that they would have the opportunity to create a distinctly Jewish society in the land of Palestine.

The promises of the scriptures and the hope that they

generated moved Judah to place high value upon them. She began to prize God's law as the means of salvation in both a temporal and a spiritual sense. As a result, she embarked upon a kind of "operation salvage," collecting, editing, compiling, and copying the Law and the Prophets. Details are unknown of how the Jews proceeded, but the movement was unstoppable once it began.[44] How the Jews in Babylon happened to have quite a collection of scriptures remains somewhat of a mystery. The Book of Mormon indicates that an extensive collection was kept by one of Jerusalem's generals (see 1 Nephi 3:3; 5:10–13). We don't know if other copies existed, but it seems reasonable that there were other collections as well as individual pieces treasured by their owners. The wealth of source material in the Bible, especially the historical records and writings of the early prophets, suggests that the records were composed in Jerusalem well before 587.[45] Many of these records may have been taken to Babylon by various hostages, especially those of priestly and royal rank, and finally, by the last deportees. At any rate, the Jews in Babylon were able to collect and begin to duplicate a large number of scriptures, further evidence of their growing trust in God's word through his prophets.

Thus, while the Jews were still in captivity, the voice of their former and present prophets provided the answers to Judah's questions and gave her hope and direction for the future. Under their auspices, she was able to keep her integrity in Babylon and prepare for the realization of the blessings of her restoration. In the meantime, the prophets gave her a role to play even in Babylon. They allowed her to see herself as the servant of Jehovah responsible for carrying his law to later generations. By encouraging Judah to see herself in this role, the prophets gave a most profound interpretation to both her present distress and her eventual destiny.[46] By doing so, they gave meaning to the whole and reinforced the need for total loyalty to her God. This bound the people to a common ideal and kept many of them from becoming lost in Babylon. When proper circumstances arose, she had the will and determination to appeal to her captors for her freedom. Under the guidance of her leaders, she returned home and began to rebuild her national identity.

Notes

1. John Bright, *A History of Israel,* 3d ed. (Philadelphia: Westminster Press, 1981), 343.

2. Such has been done by Charles C. Torrey, *The Chronicler's History of Israel* (New Haven, Conn.: Yale University Press, 1954).

3. H. H. Ben-Sasson, *A History of the Jewish People* (Cambridge: Harvard University Press, 1976), 160.

4. Cecil Roth, *A History of the Jews* (New York: Shocken Books, 1970), 57–60.

5. Bright, *History of Israel,* 343.

6. Epigraphic sources for the sixth and fifth centuries are meager. Even so, a fairly clear picture can be drawn from Jeremiah, Daniel, Ezekiel, 2 Kings, 2 Chronicles, Ezra, Nehemiah, Esther, 1 Esdras, the postexilic prophetic books, and the few extrabiblical sources that exist.

7. On the extensive damage done to Jerusalem, see Kathleen M. Kenyon, *Jerusalem* (London: Thames and Hudson, 1967), 78–104. Jerusalem was completely pillaged and much was destroyed, but little of it, including the temple mount, was actually leveled. Until 1925, scholars did not realize the extent of the catastrophe. Archaeology has shown that the Babylonians razed virtually every fortified town in Judea. See Hugh Nibley, *The Collected Works of Hugh Nibley,* vol. 5, *Lehi in the Desert/The World of the Jaredites/There Were Jaredites,* ed. John W. Welch (Salt Lake City: Deseret Book, 1988), 9–10.

8. Amihai Mazar, *Archaeology of the Land of the Bible 10,000–586 B.C.* (New York: Doubleday, 1990), 548–50.

9. See Ezekiel 33:24–29 in light of Isaiah 57:3–13; 65:1–5, 11 for example.

10. Peter R. Ackroyd, *Exile and Restoration: A Study of Hebrew Thought of the Sixth Century B.C.* (Philadelphia: Westminster Press, 1968), 18–25; Bright, *History of Israel,* 345.

11. See Hosea 4:6, 12–13; 8:11–14 for examples. Less devout and more ignorant Jews moving into the area would likely have been influenced by them. These areas also contained non-Israelites, many of whom had been moved here by the Assyrians in the late 700s (2 Kings 17).

12. Bright, *History of Israel,* 345.

13. Ben-Sasson, *History of the Jewish People,* 160–61.

14. James B. Pritchard, *Ancient Near Eastern Texts Relating to the Old Testament,* 3d ed. (Princeton, N.J.: Princeton University Press, 1969), 491–92.

15. Ben-Sasson, *History of the Jewish People,* 161–62; Ackroyd, *Exile and Restoration,* 20–23.

16. Bright, *History of Israel,* 346–47.

17. Ibid., 347. On the demise of the Philistines, see *The Anchor Bible Dictionary,* ed. David Noel Freedman, 6 vols. (New York: Doubleday, 1992), s.v. "Philistines."

18. See Ackroyd, *Exile,* 20–23; Ezra Janssen, "Judah in der Exilszeit," *Forschungen zur Religion und Literatur des Alten und Neuen Testaments* (Göttengen: Vandenhoeck and Ruprecht, 1956), 25–39, for further discussion and source material.

19. Adolf Alt, *Kleine Schriften zur Geschichte des Volkes Israel,* 3 vols. (Munich: C. H. Beck'she Verlagsbuchhantlung, 1953–59), 2:326, argues persuasively that the Babylonians placed the Jews under a very different internment than that used by the Assyrians.

20. See Ezra 3:15; 2:59; 8:17; Jeremiah 29:5–7, for example.

21. See Ezekiel 8:1; 14:1; 33:30–35 for examples.

22. Bright, *History of Israel,* 346.

23. Ibid., 345.

24. Ben-Sasson, *History of the Jewish People,* 163–64; Bright, *History of Israel,* 347. For a discussion of the whole issue see David Noel Freedman, "Son of Man, Can These Bones Live?" *Interpretation* 29 (1975): 171–86.

25. Mazar, *Archaeology,* 348–52.

26. Jeremiah 44:15–19 and Ezekiel 20:32 show how acutely some Jews were tempted to leave the old faith. See also Bright, *History of Israel,* 347.

27. See, for example, Ezekiel 18:2, 25; Lamentations 5:7.

28. Isaiah 63:19 reflects the idea that the covenant could be lost, and Ezekiel 33:10; 37:11 shows that some of the Jews were really concerned about it.

29. Bright, *History of Israel,* 348.

30. The same idea is expressed in a number of the hymns. See, for example, Psalms 2, 18, 20, 21, 45, 72, 89, 101, 110, and 132. For discussion on the development of the kingship theology within Israel, see Hans J. Kraus, *Worship in Israel: A Cultic History of the Old Testament* (Richmond: John Knox Press, 1966); R. E. Clements, *Abraham and David: Genesis XV and Its Meaning for Israelite Tradition*

(London: SCM Press, 1967), 4–96; and Bright, *History,* 224–25, 289–98.

31. See, for example, Isaiah 1:21–23; 3:13–15; 5:8, 23; 10:1–4.

32. Bright, *History of Israel,* 349.

33. Because the apocalyptic portion has been sealed (see Daniel 12:4, 9) and no prophet of the Restoration has opened it, much that is there remains a mystery. As a result, it requires too much speculation to be of worth for the purposes of this paper.

34. The Aramaic word designated magicians but would have included all those claiming ability to understand mysteries. Though Daniel would not have been viewed as a magician, he would have been viewed as one with powers of God, and, therefore, would have been caught in the king's net.

35. The title designated the high place of Jehovah and stressed his rank above all things. See Genesis 24:7; Ezra 1:2; 6:10; Nehemiah 1:5; 2:4; Psalm 136:26.

36. Nabonidus may have suffered also from a period of madness. A fragment from Qumran shows that a Jewish tradition existed ascribing his long absence from Babylon to mental illness as a vengeance which came upon him from God. See Joan Oates, *Babylon* (London: Thames and Hudson, 1979), 133.

37. The Book of Mormon suggests that there were record keepers in charge of preserving prophecies among the people. The brass plates, taken by Nephi from Laban, contained "prophecies of the holy prophets, from the beginning even down to the commencement of the reign of Zedekiah; and also many of the prophecies which have been spoken by the mouth of Jeremiah" (1 Nephi 5:12). Because Jeremiah continued to prophesy for some time after 600 B.C., someone was collecting and recording his prophecies while they were being given.

38. See the biblical instruction in Deuteronomy 17:6 and in Matthew 18:16.

39. Because of Ezekiel's call while in Babylon about 593, some date his captivity to that point; however, the Babylonians took quite a few of the priestly families captive five years earlier. That seems the better date. See Harold H. Rowley, "The Book of Ezekiel in Modern Study," *Men of God* (London: T. Nelson, 1963), 169–210.

40. In most ancient Near Eastern languages, the word describing an adult male was a cognate of the word for beard. See *The New Bible Dictionary,* ed. J. D. Douglas (Grand Rapids, Mich.: Eerdmans, 1962), s.v. "Beard."

41. Merrill C. Tenney, *The Zondervan Pictorial Encyclopedia of the Bible* (Grand Rapids, Mich.: Zondervan, 1976), s.v. "Beard."

42. Isaiah 44:28; 45:1 mentions Cyrus by name.

43. See Martin Noth, *The Law in the Pentateuch and Other Studies* (Philadelphia: Fortress Press, 1967), 67–70.

44. Bright, *History of Israel,* 350. Note 2 Kings 25:27–30, which had to be added to the text by the Babylonian Jews. The addition shows that the Jews were actively working on their records during the captivity.

45. Martin Noth, *Überlieferungsgeschichtliche Studien I* (Halle, Germany: M. Niemeyer, 1943), argues that material had been written down from at least the tenth century and that more than one collection existed between 622 and 587. See that study for sources and background material.

46. H. H. Rowley, *The Servant of the Lord and Other Essays,* rev. ed. (Oxford: Blackwells, 1965), 1–60, has completed an excellent study on this motif and its effects on the Jews of the captivity and afterwards.

CHAPTER SEVEN

EZEKIEL'S "MISSING PROPHECY"

JOHN A. TVEDTNES

In Doctrine and Covenants 29:21, we read that "the great and abominable church, which is the whore of all the earth, shall be cast down by devouring fire, according as it is spoken by the mouth of Ezekiel the prophet." While the "great and abominable church" is described by Nephi (1 Nephi 13:5–9, 26–28; 14:3, 9–11, 15–17; 22:13–14; 2 Nephi 6:12; 28:18), this term is not used in Ezekiel nor elsewhere in the Bible. In 1 Nephi 14:11 and 2 Nephi 28:18, this church is also called "the whore of all the earth" (compare 1 Nephi 22:14), while in 1 Nephi 14:17 it is termed the "mother of harlots." These terms are also used by the apostle John (Revelation 17:1, 5, 15–16; 19:2), who experienced the same vision as Nephi (1 Nephi 14:18–27). In Ezekiel, however, the words *whore* and *harlot* are reserved for sinful Israel. Yet none of the key terms used in Doctrine and Covenants 29:21 is found in the book of Ezekiel (including the Joseph Smith Translation[1]). How, then, can the Doctrine and Covenants attribute such a prophecy to Ezekiel?[2] I believe there are three possibilities:

1. The text of the book of Ezekiel may have been modified, resulting in the loss of this prophecy from the Bible.
2. Ezekiel may have written another book containing the prophecy, which is not found in our current Bibles.

John A. Tvedtnes is senior project manager at the Foundation for Ancient Research and Mormon Studies (FARMS) in Provo, Utah.

3. The prophecy, though distorted, is found in the biblical Ezekiel.

Was the Text of Ezekiel Modified?

Nephi noted that the "great and abominable church" would remove "from the gospel of the Lamb many parts which are plain and most precious; and also many covenants of the Lord have they taken away" (1 Nephi 13:26). It is therefore possible that the prophecy in question was lost from the biblical book of Ezekiel. Critics dismiss this as too simplistic an explanation. After all, were one to admit such an idea, where would it end? Whenever the revelations of Joseph Smith contradicted the Bible, one might simply declare that the Bible lacks the information because it was removed. In this case, however, there is clear evidence from early Christian and Jewish sources that the text of Ezekiel was, in fact, modified.

Several of the Church Fathers of the first centuries of the Christian era quoted items from Ezekiel that are not found in the biblical book of that name. Epiphanius (ca. A.D. 315–403) attributes to Ezekiel the story of the blind and lame men,[3] which is also found, without attribution, in TB *Sanhedrin* 91a–b[4] but which is unknown from the biblical Ezekiel. Clement of Alexandria (ca. A.D. 153–217) cites a passage he attributes to Ezekiel which, while clearly like Ezekiel 34:14–16, is a variant reading.[5] Tertullian (ca. A.D. 145–220) noted that Ezekiel wrote about a cow that gave birth and did not give birth[6]—a story repeated by Epiphanius,[7] Gregory of Nyassa (ca. A.D. 335–96),[8] Clement of Alexandria,[9] and in an early pseudepigraphic text, *Acts of Peter* 24.[10] Again, this information is not extant in the book of Ezekiel. Clearly, these early writers had access to material attributed to Ezekiel that is no longer found in the book of that name.[11] Whether the differences were due to Christian emendation of the text or the expunging of passages by Jewish scribes cannot be ascertained.

First Clement 8:3,[12] citing Ezekiel 18:30–31, has a reading different from that found in our current Old Testament but which is included in the version in one of the Nag Hammadi texts, *The Exegesis on the Soul* (II, 6) 135–36.[13] The latter attributes the words to "the spirit to the prophet," without naming Ezekiel. *First Clement* has no attribution, but it is clear from the passage that the writer understood it to be from Ezekiel, for he quotes Ezekiel 33:11 and then immediately introduces the quotation from Ezekiel 18 with the words "adding moreover, this gracious declaration." Here is a comparison of the three versions of the passage:

Ezekiel 18:30–31 (King James Version)	*First Clement* 8:3[14]	*The Exegesis on the Soul* II, 6:135–36[15]
Therefore I will judge you, O house of Israel, every one according to his ways, saith the Lord God. Repent, and turn yourselves from all your transgressions; so iniquity shall not be your ruin. Cast away from you all your transgressions, whereby ye have transgressed; and make you a new heart and a new spirit: for why will ye die, O house of Israel?	Repent, O house of Israel, of your iniquity. Say to the children of my people, Though your sins reach from earth to heaven, and though they be redder than scarlet, and blacker than sack-cloth, yet if ye turn to me with your whole heart, and say, Father! I will listen to you, as to a holy people.	Say to the children of my people, "[If your] sins extend [from earth to] heaven, and if they become [red] like scarlet and blacker than [sack-cloth and if] you return to me with all your soul and say to me, "My father," I will heed you as a holy people."

Similarly, Clement of Alexandria attributes to Ezekiel words that partially parallel the thoughts in Ezekiel 34:11–16 but which are quite different.[16] From these examples, it is clear that the Ezekiel text possessed by the early Church differed from the one in today's Bible. But we have more than vague suggestions that the text of Ezekiel was modified; we have the testimony of the rabbis.

During the rabbinic council held in Yabneh (Yamnia) in A.D. 90 to determine which books would be accepted as authentic scripture, there were many disagreements over the canonicity of Ezekiel, whose description of the temple service in the last days (chapters 40–48) contradicted the rules laid down in the Torah. Of this, one of the rabbis said, "When Elijah comes, he will explain the difficulty." Others were not content to wait so long. Rabbi Hananiah literally burned the midnight oil for many nights *revising* the text of Ezekiel. The Talmud said of him: "Blessed be the memory of Hananiah, son of Hezekiah: if it had not been for him, the book of Ezekiel would have been 'hidden' (i.e., withdrawn from public reading), . . . What did he do? They brought him three hundred measures of oil, and he sat down and explained it."[17] By this, it was understood that the rabbi had modified the text to make it acceptable to the council.[18]

This story suggests the possibility that the passage relating to the latter-day destruction of "the great and abominable church" may have been omitted from the book of Ezekiel, either inadvertently or during a deliberate modification of the text.

At this point, it is fair to ask whether there is documentary support for such changes to the book of Ezekiel. For example, do the Dead Sea Scrolls, some of which were written before the council of Yabneh, differ from the Ezekiel known to us in later Hebrew Bibles? Alas, the copies of Ezekiel found near Qumran are so fragmentary that they do not shed light on this subject. The single scroll from Cave 3 (3Q1, also called 3QEz) has only fragmentary remains of Ezekiel 16. Three Ezekiel scrolls were found in Cave 4, but they, too, are much too fragmentary: 4Q73 (also called 4QEz[a]) contains Ezekiel 10:17–11:1, 4Q74 (4QEz[b]) has a few remains of Ezekiel 1, and 4Q75 (also called 4QEz[c]) is a minute fragment with remains of Ezekiel 24:2–3. From other biblical texts found among the Dead Sea Scrolls, it is clear that by the time of Christ, there were variant versions of different books of the Bible. This makes it impossible to determine which version, if any, is closer to the original.

Another potentially useful check is the Septuagint, the Greek translation of the Old Testament made in the third century B.C. Does it differ from the Hebrew text supposedly modified by Rabbi Hananiah? Here, again, we are disappointed because no copies of the Greek version of Ezekiel can be dated prior to the council of Yabneh. One very early document (third century A.D.), known as 967, whose leaves are scattered in several separate collections, is often considered to be the closest to the original Septuagint. But even 967, like other Septuagint manuscripts, bears evidence of a Greek text that has been revised to correspond with the Hebrew version. This type of "back correction" is a common phenomenon in biblical manuscripts. It is, nevertheless, interesting that 967 omits Ezekiel 36:23c–38 and places chapter 37 after chapter 39 (a transposition also attested in an Old Latin manuscript, Codex Wirceburgensis).[19] Evidence from the Septuagint, while inconclusive, does not contradict the rabbinic story about the revision of Ezekiel.

Did Ezekiel Write Two Books?

Another possible explanation for the absence of the passage from the book of Ezekiel is that it was included in another of Ezekiel's books that is no longer extant. Flavius Josephus, a Jewish historian of the first century A.D., declared that Ezekiel had "left behind him in writing two books" containing prophecies about the calamities that would befall the Jews.[20]

Among the Dead Sea Scrolls are five fragmentary copies (4Q385, 4Q386, 4Q387, 4Q388, 4Q391) of a text that has been termed "Pseudo-Ezekiel" because it contains passages from the biblical Ezekiel that vary from what is found in the standard Masoretic Hebrew text and some material not found in Ezekiel at all. It is unclear whether these represent a variant form of the book of Ezekiel or a separate book, though Strugnell and Dimant have referred to the text as

"Second Ezekiel."[21] In one of the documents (4Q385, frag. 3, line 4), the Lord addresses Ezekiel by name.

Another Possible Explanation

While it is true that the words of Doctrine and Covenants 29:21 are not found in the book of Ezekiel, it is important to note that the Doctrine and Covenants passage does not claim that Ezekiel spoke those very words, only that the prophecy about the great and abominable church being destroyed by fire was "spoken by the mouth of Ezekiel the prophet." It does not say that he wrote the prophecy. But if Ezekiel did record that prophecy without using the expression "great and abominable church," it may be possible to identify one of his prophecies as a parallel to the one in Doctrine and Covenants 29:21.[22]

The Gog and Magog prophecy of Ezekiel 38–39 is paralleled by John's vision in Revelation 17–20, part of which speaks about the great "whore," the "mother of harlots" (Revelation 17:1–6, 15–18) which falls (Revelation 18:1–3) and whose "smoke rose up for ever and ever" (Revelation 19:1–3). John wrote of the war of Gog and Magog, wherein the forces of evil are devoured by fire from heaven and the devil who deceived them is "cast into the lake of fire and brimstone" with his followers (Revelation 19:20; 20:7–10, 14; 21:8). The fire from heaven that destroys the army of Gog and Magog is also mentioned in Ezekiel 39:6, while fire and brimstone are in Ezekiel 38:22.

John saw that, in preparation for the battle, an angel calls to the fowls to "gather yourselves together unto the supper of the great God; that ye may eat the flesh of kings, and the flesh of captains, and the flesh of mighty men, and the flesh of horses, and of them that sit on them, and the flesh of all men, both free and bond, both small and great" (Revelation 19:17–18). John borrowed these words from Ezekiel 39:17–20, where the prophet himself is told to call the birds to eat the flesh of those who would be slain in the great battle.

It is clear, from these parallels, that Ezekiel and John

both saw the results of this great battle that takes place after the Millennium, when Satan is released for a brief period and fights against God. Another prophet who experienced the same vision was the Book of Mormon prophet Nephi, who, having been informed that John would record the vision, was told to write only part of what he saw (1 Nephi 14:25–28). It is Nephi who employed the term "great and abominable church" in reference to the great whore of the vision (1 Nephi 13:6–8, 26–28; 14:3, 9, 15–17; 22:13–14; 2 Nephi 6:12; 28:18–19).

When mentioning that John would record the rest of the vision, Nephi noted that there were "also others who have been" who had seen and written about these things, "and they are sealed up to come forth in their purity . . . in the own due time of the Lord" (1 Nephi 14:26). This may imply that others, such as Ezekiel, wrote things seen in the vision that would not be available to us until the last days. As we saw earlier, there are indications that some of Ezekiel's writings are no longer extant. It is possible that such missing writings provide more details than the current book of Ezekiel about the destruction of the great and abominable church.

Nephi's brother Jacob, speaking about "they that fight against Zion" and specifically mentioning the "great and abominable church" (2 Nephi 6:12–13), adds that the unbelievers "shall be destroyed, both by fire, and by tempest, and by earthquakes, and by bloodsheds, and by pestilence, and by famine. And they shall know that the Lord is God, the Holy One of Israel" (2 Nephi 6:15). A similar passage is found in Ezekiel's description of the fate of Gog's army, which will be destroyed by the same forces, adding, "and I will be known in the eyes of many nations, and they shall know that I am the Lord" (Ezekiel 38:18–23).[23] It is unlikely that Nephi and Jacob had access to the writings of their contemporary, Ezekiel, for he lived in Babylon at the time that Lehi's family left Jerusalem. But the similarity between the prophecies suggests that Ezekiel, like John and Nephi, shared the same vision of the future destruction of the wicked.

Matthew Roper noted another tie between the prophecies of Nephi and Ezekiel.[24] Nephi writes of the "great and abominable church," while Ezekiel 38:7 speaks of Gog's assembly ("they that are assembled unto thee"), which is the meaning of the word *church.* The tie is somewhat lost in the King James translation, which speaks of "thy company that are assembled unto thee." In the Hebrew text, both the verb and the noun derive from the root *qhl,* which means "to assemble." Significantly, Nephi notes that the "great church" would be formed "among the nations of the Gentiles" (1 Nephi 13:4).

One problem with this scenario is the timing of the events. Joseph Smith declared that "the battle of Gog and Magog will be after the millennium. The remnant of all the nations that fight against Jerusalem were commanded to go up to Jerusalem to worship in the millennium."[25] Clearly, the final battle described in Revelation 20 will take place after the Millennium, for the binding of Satan is noted in verses 1 through 3, while it is only after Satan is released (v. 7) that Gog and Magog assemble their forces (v. 8). But some LDS authorities have identified the battle of Gog and Magog described in Ezekiel with the battle of Armageddon, which takes place before the Millennium (Revelation 16:16–18; compare Zechariah 11–13), while continuing to apply the names Gog and Magog to the final battle that will take place after the Millennium.[26] This suggestion has merit, for the "mother of harlots and abominations of the earth" is also called "Babylon" in Revelation 17:5, and the destruction of this latter-day Babylon is described in connection with events surrounding the battle of Armageddon. In Revelation 14:8–11, John wrote of an angel announcing the forthcoming destruction of "Babylon." Following the battle of Armageddon (Revelation 16:16), he notes the fate of "Babylon" (Revelation 16:19) and is shown "the judgment of the great whore that sitteth upon many waters" (Revelation 17:1–2). Immediately following this, another angel declares, "Babylon the great is fallen, is fallen" (Revelation 18:2–3). From this, it appears that the fall of the great and abominable church precedes the Millennium.

In this light, it is important to determine whether the prophecy mentioned in Doctrine and Covenants 29:21 best fits the premillennial battle of Armageddon or the postmillennial war against the forces of evil. In Doctrine and Covenants 29:11, Christ speaks of his coming in glory to reign for a thousand years on earth. "But," he declares three verses later (D&C 29:14), other events must occur "before this great day shall come." The reference to the Ezekiel prophecy is one of the events in the list that follows. Indeed, immediately after that passage, the Lord begins to speak of events that will take place "when the thousand years are ended, and men again begin to deny their God" (D&C 29:22).

Other modern revelations also indicate that the great and abominable church will fall before Christ's millennial reign. Thus, for example, in Doctrine and Covenants 88:94–95, we read of the burning of "that great church, the mother of abominations," followed by "silence in heaven for the space of half an hour; and immediately after shall the curtain of heaven be unfolded, as a scroll is unfolded after it is rolled up, and the face of the Lord shall be unveiled" (compare D&C 88:105).[27] Similarly, the burning of Babylon is placed at the time of "the coming of the Son of Man" in Doctrine and Covenants 64:23–24.

Conclusion

In this paper, I have presented three possible scenarios for explaining the reference in Doctrine and Covenants 29:21 to a seemingly unattested prophecy by the prophet Ezekiel. The first two assume that the prophecy was lost, either because it was removed from the biblical book of Ezekiel when revised by Rabbi Hananiah or because it was included in a second book of Ezekiel that is no longer extant. I have elicited evidence from early Jewish and Christian sources to show that both scenarios are possible.

The third suggestion is that the reference to the "great and abominable church" in Doctrine and Covenants 29:21 does not reflect Ezekiel's original wording, making it possible that the prophecy in Ezekiel 38–39 refers to the same event mentioned in the modern revelation. Again, we have seen that this scenario is entirely plausible. While I lean toward this latter explanation as the most likely, I cannot state with certainty which, if any, of the three suggested scenarios is correct. I can, however, state unequivocally that the attribution of the prophecy to Ezekiel in Doctrine and Covenants 29:21 is perfectly reasonable.

Notes

1. *Joseph Smith's "New Translation" of the Bible* (Independence, Mo.: Herald Publishing House, 1970), 221–24.

2. The passage is found in all manuscripts and early publications of this revelation with only minor variations, none of which affect the wording that is the subject of this paper.

3. *Against Heresies* 64.70.5–17.

4. The parable is also found in other rabbinic works: *Midrash Vayiqra Rabbah* 4:5; *Mekilta de Rabbi Shimon ben Yohai* to Exodus 15:1; *Midrash Tanhuma* (Buber 8).

5. *Paedagogus* 1:9, in Alexander Roberts, James Donaldson, and A. Cleveland Coxe, *Ante-Nicene Fathers* (reprint, Peabody, Mass.: Hendrickson, 1994), 2.231.

6. *De Carne Christi* 23.

7. *Panarion Haeresies* 30.30.3.

8. *Against the Jews* 3.

9. *Stromata* 7:16.

10. The *Apocalypse of Peter* was widely circulated as early as the second century after Christ.

11. Tertullian is the only one to credit the story to the writings of Ezekiel, while Clement merely says that it is found in "the scriptures."

12. *1 Clement* was cited by Church Fathers as early as the second century after Christ and was included in some fourth century Bible codices.

13. The Nag Hammadi texts were buried in a jar in Egypt not long before A.D. 400 and were discovered in 1945.

14. John Keith, "The Epistles of Clement," in *Ante-Nicene Fathers,*

ed. Allan Menzies, 4th ed. (Peabody, Mass.: Hendrickson, 1994), 9.231.

15. William C. Robinson Jr., "The Exegesis on the Soul," in *The Nag Hammadi Library in English,* ed. James M. Robinson, rev. ed. (San Francisco: Harper, 1990), 197.

16. *Paedagogus* 1:9, in Roberts, Donaldson, and Coxe, *Ante-Nicene Fathers,* 2.231.

17. Babylonian Talmud *Hagigah* 13a–b. The translation given here is by F. F. Bruce, *The Books and the Parchments* (Old Tappan, N.J.: Fleming H. Revell, 1984), 89.

18. According to *Abot de Rabbi Nathan* 1, the books of Proverbs, Song of Songs, and Ecclesiastes were originally considered parables only and became accepted as scripture only after being "interpreted."

19. For a discussion, see Leslie John McGregor, *The Greek Text of Ezekiel: An Examination of Its Homogeneity,* Septuagint and Cognate Studies 18 (Atlanta: Scholars Press, 1985), 10–19.

20. *Antiquities of the Jews* 10.5.1, in William Whiston, trans., *The Complete Works of Flavius Josephus* (reprint, New York: Holt, Rinehart and Winston, 1980), 305.

21. John Strugnell and Devorah Dimant, "4QSecond Ezekiel," *Revue de Qumran* 13 (1988): 54–58; Devorah Dimant and John Strugnell, "The Merkaba Vision in Second Ezekiel (4Q385 4)," *Revue de Qumran* 14 (1989): 331–48.

22. I found that virtually none of the commentaries on the Doctrine and Covenants address this issue. The exception was Sperry, who wrote, "The special words of the Prophet Ezekiel are not indicated, but the general effect could be as shown in Ezekiel 8:14–23." Sidney B. Sperry, *Doctrine and Covenants Compendium* (Salt Lake City: Bookcraft, 1960), 136. Sperry then cited Ezekiel 8:21–22, which speaks of pestilence and blood, internecine warfare, and a rain of fire and brimstone. He compares this with 1 Nephi 22:13–14, where we read of blood and warfare within the great and abominable church. While the Book of Mormon passage is relevant to our study, the clear context of Ezekiel 8 is the wickedness in the kingdom of Judah in Ezekiel's time, not latter-day wickedness.

23. I am indebted to Matthew Roper for pointing out the parallel between these two passages.

24. Private communication to the author.

25. Joseph Smith, *History of The Church of Jesus Christ of Latter-day Saints,* ed. B. H. Roberts, 2d ed. rev., 7 vols. (Salt Lake City: Deseret Book, 1951), 5:298. That this was the view held in the early restored Church is supported by an article by Sidney Rigdon, "Millennium," *Evening and Morning Star* 2, no. 19 (April 1834): 147.

26. Joseph Fielding Smith, *Doctrines of Salvation,* 3 vols. (Salt Lake City: Bookcraft, 1954), 3:45; *Answers to Gospel Questions,* 5 vols. (Salt Lake City: Deseret Book, 1958), 2:109; *The Restoration of All Things* (Salt Lake City: Deseret Book, 1973), 295; *The Signs of the Times* (Salt Lake City: Deseret News Press, 1942), 155; Bruce R. McConkie, *Mormon Doctrine,* 2d ed. (Salt Lake City: Bookcraft, 1966), 74, 324–25, 695, 827; *The Millennial Messiah* (Salt Lake City: Deseret Book, 1982), 22, 63–64, 66–67, 449–50, 455–56, 476–94, 696; *A New Witness for the Articles of Faith* (Salt Lake City: Deseret Book, 1985), 638–39, 651; *Doctrinal New Testament Commentary,* 3 vols. (Salt Lake City: Bookcraft, 1965), 3:543, 575–76.

27. The fall of Babylon is also discussed in D&C 1:16; 35:11; compare D&C 86:2–3; 133:5–7, 12–14.

CHAPTER EIGHT

Obadiah's Vision of Saviors on Mount Zion

GARY P. GILLUM

The prophet Obadiah's claim to fame among Latter-day Saints is the final verse of his twenty-one-verse prophecy against Edom: "And saviours shall come up on mount Zion to judge the mount of Esau; and the kingdom shall be the Lord's." Joseph Smith and succeeding latter-day prophets and other Church leaders are nearly unanimous in their interpretation of this scripture: Obadiah was referring to temple work for our kindred dead.[1] The purpose of this discussion is to explore a broader interpretation of Obadiah's prophecy and enlarge upon the definition of *saviors* to include work for the living as well as for the dead. I believe that the great truths contained in Obadiah's vision relate not only to the ongoing restoration of the Church but to individual restoration and progression as well.[2]

The book of Obadiah was probably written sometime after 587 B.C., when Jerusalem was destroyed by the Babylonians with the help of the Edomites. (While Edomite participation in the destruction of Jerusalem is not specifically described in the Old Testament, it is mentioned in the apocryphal 1 Esdras 4:45 and alluded to in Lamentations 4:21–22.) Nothing is known of the prophet for whom the book is named, although Obadiah most likely lived in Judah about the time of Jeremiah, Lehi, and their

Gary P. Gillum is religion and ancient studies librarian at Brigham Young University.

contemporaries. The Edom against which he prophesied is now known as Petra, the mountainous region southeast of the Dead Sea.

Christian scholars recognize that the name *Obadiah* is attributed to at least twelve different men in the Old Testament, none of whom fit the time and place of the author of the book. *Obadiah,* a Hebrew name, translates as "servant of Yahweh" or "worshiper of Yahweh."[3] Thus *Obadiah* could be an appellation such as *Malachi* ("messenger") or *Theophilus* ("friend of God") instead of a personal name. If *Obadiah* is just an appellation, then almost any righteous servant of God could have been inspired to write this prophecy. This is possible, but it is more likely that a prophet named Obadiah wrote the text.

The twenty-one verses of Obadiah fall neatly into three main parts. In verses 1 through 9 Obadiah prophesies of Edom's judgment and destruction. The following five verses, 10 through 14, give the reasons for this judgment and the fate of both Edom and Jerusalem. The final verses, 15 through 21, speak of the day of the Lord, which brings both judgment and salvation as well as the restoration of Israel. Although Obadiah's prophecy represents the smallest book in the Old Testament, interpretation raises some difficult questions. Various Judeo-Christian commentaries on Obadiah present a microcosm of the many ways in which commentators of various denominations interpret Old Testament prophecies: fundamentalist versus mainstream, conservative versus liberal, higher criticism versus literary style. Many journal articles, as well as two recent book-length commentaries about the vision of Obadiah,[4] contain a rich store of theological, historical, and literary[5] studies; however, a spiritual assessment of the text is missing from all commentaries. This is a significant part of the message; the economy of scripture insists that it be so. Why else would Obadiah be included as part of the Old Testament, particularly when so much of the first portion of it is repeated almost word for word in Jeremiah 49:7–22? As the Reverend Ray C. Stedman noted, "The Scriptures have that beautiful faculty of appearing to be one thing on the surface, but on a deeper level, yielding rich and mighty treasures. That is certainly true of this amazing book of Obadiah."[6]

Christian Perspectives

Obadiah's use of the term *savior* has interested Christian scholars. Methodist reformer John Wesley identified the Saviors-Deliverers with Jesus Christ, his apostles, and other preachers of the gospel, both past and present.[7] Etymologically, the Hebrew word *yâsha* is the root word from which the words *Jesus* and *salvation* are derived. They denote the saving power of God, which brings to the world salvation that "properly belongs to the divine sphere."[8] Saviors are those who preserve or deliver from danger and destruction. In Nehemiah 9:27, saviors are probably judges. But saviors can also be wise men and women of spiritual insight and faith. The definition—along with work for the dead—that is closest to Latter-day Saint doctrine is that saviors are "the chosen instruments [of God] which go forth to teach all nations and make known the glory of the King in their midst."[9] Raabe's 1996 translation of Obadiah renders *saviors* as *deliverers,* giving a little more of the sense of "rescuer" or "liberator," very similar to the deliverers raised up by the Lord in Judges 3:9. The meaning of Obadiah is related to a message of "faith in God's moral government and hope in the eventual triumph of His just will"—a pastoral message to aching hearts that God is on the throne and cares for his own.[10]

Reverend Stedman discussed a spiritual teaching of Obadiah by examining the description of pride among the descendants of Esau, the Edomites. Stedman's perspective parallels remarkably President Ezra Taft Benson's oft-quoted talk on pride.[11] The proud look, self-sufficiency (to a fault), violence, indifference, gloating, and exploitation are all mentioned. Adding to that impressive list, Stedman further explains how this "pride of their heart" has deceived the Edomites and kept them from knowing the truth.[12]

Another perspective from Christian scholars relates to Obadiah's themes of "judgment and salvation, of justice and restoration with a vision of history's consummation."[13] In this context, "the 'holiness' of Mount Zion . . . [v. 17] means its freedom from the violation of heathen invaders and from any "abomination of desolation."[14] Reformer John Calvin interprets this to mean that God would be mindful of His covenants. Concerning verse 17, Calvin states: "Obadiah clearly promises that there would be a restoration of the Church."[15] A temple will once again be consecrated. Others interpret this verse as signifying "the conversion and restoration of the Jews, and that under Jesus Christ the original *theocracy* shall be restored."[16]

Jewish Perspectives

Many Jews consider Obadiah one of the important "minor" prophets. The Babylonian Talmud insists that the prophet Obadiah was the same versatile man who somehow served both King Ahab and Elijah in the mid-800s B.C. and who hid one hundred righteous prophets (or believers in God) from Ahab[17] (1 Kings 18). Louis Ginzberg comments on Ahab's Obadiah and the connection all of this has to a savior or deliverer on Mount Zion: "By birth an Edomite, Obadiah had been inspired by God to utter the prophecy against Edom. In his own person he embodied the accusation against Esau, who had lived with his pious parents without following their example, while Obadiah, on the contrary, lived in constant intercourse with the iniquitous King Ahab and his still more iniquitous spouse Jezebel without yielding to the baneful influence they exercised."[18]

According to *The Legends of the Jews,* the Aggadat Bereshit 14, 32, relates that Isaiah and Obadiah "uttered their prophecies in seventy-one languages."[19] This number is interesting, for the same source says that Obadiah was forced to prophesy against Edom "by the seventy-one members of the 'heavenly Synedrion' [sanhedrin]."[20] From this legend one may even imply that saviors on Mount

Zion are not alone in doing their saving work: They are assisted by angelic messengers.

Although members of The Church of Jesus Christ of Latter-day Saints and many other Christians look at the broader perspective of Esau and the Edomites, one Jewish perspective accepts Obadiah's narrow nationalism as he condemned Israel's enemy, Edom, and the other pagan nations and looked forward to the exaltation of his own people, Israel. This anti-Edom sentiment is part of a continuum that runs all the way from the womb where Esau and Jacob wrestled (Genesis 25:21–23), to the refusal of the Edomites to allow the Israelites of the Exodus to pass through their land (Numbers 20:14–21), to the present-day political and religious difficulties. A Jewish apocryphal work, 1 Esdras 4:45, even insists that the Edomites not only helped the Babylonians conquer the Israelites but specifically destroyed the temple in Jerusalem.[21]

Latter-day Saint Perspectives

Like the prophetic messages of other minor prophets, Obadiah's message becomes for Latter-day Saints both a literal scripture as well as an allegory of good versus evil—Mount Esau versus Mount Zion. Because of its wickedness and lasting hatred for Israel, Edom, like Babylon, becomes a symbol for the world and worldliness (D&C 1:36). Latter-day Saints typically ignore the first twenty verses of Obadiah and his harangues against the Edomites, perhaps because other prophets, namely Jeremiah, wrote in like manner, or most likely because the exciting prospects in verse 21 outshine the negativity of the preceding verses. Latter-day Saint prophets and other General Authorities almost unanimously interpret verse 21 in a completely different manner from that of any other church. "Saviors on Mount Zion" are those who perform work for our kindred dead. The Lord counseled Joseph Smith on this matter in these words: "The keys are to be delivered, the spirit of Elijah is to come, the Gospel to be established, the Saints of God gathered, Zion built up, and the Saints to come up as saviors on Mount Zion. But how are they to become saviors on Mount Zion? By building their temples, erecting their baptismal fonts, and going forth and receiving all the ordinances, baptisms, confirmations, washings, anointings, ordinations and sealing powers upon their heads, *in behalf of all their progenitors who are dead,* and redeem them that they may come forth in the first resurrection and be exalted to thrones of glory with them; and herein is the chain that binds the hearts of the fathers to the children, and the children to the fathers, which fulfills the mission of Elijah."[22] Joseph Smith elaborated further: "A view of these things reconciles the Scriptures of truth, justifies the ways of God to man, places the human family upon an equal footing, and harmonizes with every principle of righteousness, justice and truth."[23]

Matthias Cowley gave another definition of saviors that was a direct result of missionary work: "The man who forsakes his father and mother for the Gospel's sake has accepted something in the Gospel that will bring his father and mother, his sister and brother to him, and they will fulfill the words of the prophet Obadiah that 'saviors shall come up on mount Zion.'"[24]

Finally, Charles W. Penrose talked about saviors from the perspective of individual families: "Now, brethren, what I am after is this: Let us Latter-day Saints, called to be saviors of men, called to be saviors of this world, called to be saviors to introduce that which will save mankind and bring them up from their lowest state into a condition where they will be fit to hold converse with Deity, let us be careful that we plant in the minds of our children the truth and nothing but the truth so far as we can understand it. . . . The boundless universe is before us all to learn and to live and to come up to the standard occupied by our Eternal Father and to be fit for his society."[25]

A Personal Perspective

Early in the morning on Wednesday, 19 February 1997, I had an extraordinarily vivid dream of a dilapidated truck full of eight abused and sad children, pleading with their eyes that I could rescue them from their pain and sorrow. The haunting details were seared in my memory deeply enough that I can still remember one teenager with a torn, checkered blouse, muddy skirt, and stringy, matted hair. I did not know the significance of this dream until I was in my office a couple of hours later, wondering whether I should work on this paper or turn to more pressing needs in the library. It was then that I noticed a new title from the book cart, by Carlfred Broderick: *My Parents Married on a Dare*. I thumbed through the book, and my eyes stopped on page 119, where the words "Saviors on Mount Zion" fairly leaped out at me. I quote from his chapter "Children Being Born into Abusive Families": "In suffering innocently that others might not suffer, such persons, in some degree, become as 'saviors on Mount Zion' by helping to bring salvation to a lineage."[26]

I immediately realized one of the chief reasons for my own passion for the gospel. Again, in the words of Dr. Broderick: "God actively intervenes in some destructive lineages, assigning a valiant spirit to break the chain of destructiveness in such families. Although these children may suffer innocently as victims of violence, neglect, and exploitation, through the grace of God some find the strength to 'metabolize' the poison within themselves, refusing to pass it on to future generations."[27]

I also realized that I had fulfilled this mission four times: once by leaving my own abusive and alcoholic family; twice more by marrying first one and then another abused woman, both of whom died of cancer nine years apart; and most recently by marrying a widow who had, along with some of her eleven children, been abused before her husband died. Together, my wife and I could consider ourselves saviors on Mount Zion who have the opportunity to stop the cycle of abuse in both of our lineages.

From this perspective, I am interested in broadening the definition of saviors on Mount Zion to include that of Dr. Broderick. I discovered that compared to the perspectives of other religions, the LDS interpretation of the word *saviors* is unique. This may be related to our distinctly LDS belief that we are children of God, created in the image of our Father in Heaven, and that we are "joint-heirs with Christ" (Romans 8:17). The non-LDS perspective that is most similar to Dr. Broderick's comes from the well-known *Interpreter's Bible:* "Herein lies the painfulness of man's relationship to man. One stands aside and lets another suffer. One takes pleasure in another's distress. One capitalizes on another's misfortunes. Despite all that can be said about the amiability of human nature, this is what happens again and again all down the line of human social life. It is not always so. But we need to be asking ourselves continually about our neutralities, our inward cruelties, our ruthlessness."[28]

Conclusion

Several observations can be made concerning the book of Obadiah, its vision of the Edomites, and the saviors on Mount Zion.

In likening the scriptures to ourselves, Latter-day Saints can be saviors on Mount Zion not only for the dead but also for the living. At the very least, Latter-day Saints should spend a great deal of time repenting, forgiving, and enduring.

According to many Judeo-Christian scholars, the family of Abraham will become the saviors on Mount Zion when the Messiah finally comes. Like the tribe of Judah, we Latter-day Saints are a covenant people. Being saviors is a daunting task that we cannot do without help from above, even a pillar of fire by night and a cloud by day. Whether Latter-day Saints look at the vision of Obadiah as history, as prophecy fulfilled, or as an allegory for the victory of good over evil, the message is clear that "only the Day of the Lord, which will establish once and for all the reign of God in history, will *break this cycle of violence* and insure Judah a future of self-determination and security."[29] How remarkable it is that after twenty verses of condemnation,

Obadiah concludes his prophecy with a clear message of hope for all men and women: that we can not only be saviors but will be judged by saviors as well and not by tyrants of the soul.

Latter-day Saints know from the Bible as well as the Book of Mormon that the Lord sometimes intervenes in human lives to set us straight (Alma the Younger), redirect our purposes for a greater good (the apostle Paul), change the course of our lives (President Gordon B. Hinckley), or rescue a lineage (those who have been converted to the gospel). In discovering Obadiah's message, I thus found another reason not only for my own conversion but for my wife's as well: to deliver our families from the cycle of abuse and to save our lineages. Saviors on Mount Zion, among others, are those "who refuse to pass on the destructive, toxic parenting they received. . . . It gives meaning to the sacrifice and recognition to the courage of those who have committed their lives to purifying a lineage."[30]

More than one hundred years ago, President Woodruff said that "saviors upon Mount Zion have been raised up, while the kingdom is the Lord's, as the Prophet Obadiah said they would be."[31] These saviors are not only ordained missionaries but are also the many saints who labor to help break the cycle of spiritual, emotional, or physical abuse and restore Zion and the purity of the gospel to individuals and families. Every Latter-day Saint, man or woman, young or old, should feel alive and awake to a duty to teach and live correct principles that prevent the miniholocausts that can and do exist at the family level.

Finally, by using and magnifying our spiritual gifts, Latter-day Saints can act as saviors on Mount Zion by helping the world overcome and eliminate the barbarisms of abuse, war, torture, force, genocide, poverty, ignorance, exclusion, bigotry, and hatred. That is the larger legacy of Latter-day Saints and children of Abraham: saviors on Mount Zion.

NOTES

1. Joseph Smith, *Teachings of the Prophet Joseph Smith,* sel. Joseph Fielding Smith (Salt Lake City: Deseret Book, 1972), 330. Other LDS comments on Obadiah: Ellis T. Rasmussen, "Zephaniah, Obadiah, and Micah: Prophets during Times of Crises," *Instructor,* July 1963, between pages 248 and 249; *Church News,* 14 July 1973, 15. The Scripture Citation Index on the Gospel Infobases *Collector's Edition 1997 CD-ROM* lists Obadiah as quoted by four general authorities in general conferences: F. Arthur Kay, April 1985; LeGrand Richards, October 1975; Theodore M. Burton, October 1970 and October 1972; and Russell M. Nelson, October 1994. Many additional uses are listed, including citations in the *Times and Seasons* and in Bruce R. McConkie, *Mormon Doctrine,* 2d ed. (Salt Lake City: Bookcraft, 1962), 678. A teacher's supplement by Archibald F. Bennett called *Saviors on Mount Zion* (Salt Lake City: Deseret Sunday School Union Board, 1950) was used for Sunday School course 21. Unfortunately, there is no reference to Obadiah in it.

2. The restoration of the gospel is not just an event called the First Vision but an ongoing process in the dispensation of the fullness of times, both in the Church generally and for its members individually.

3. James P. Boyd, *The Self-Pronouncing Bible Dictionary* (Philadelphia: A. J. Holman, 1924), 209.

4. Paul R. Raabe, *Obadiah,* vol. 24D of *The Anchor Bible,* ed. William Foxwell Albright and David Noel Freedman, 44 vols. to date (New York: Doubleday, 1996). This Missouri Synod Lutheran theologian has written a very understandable and perceptive commentary of 310 pages. Original Hebrew words are transliterated. Ehud Ben Zvi, *A Historical-Critical Study of the Book of Obadiah* (Berlin: Walter de Gruyter, 1996) is a more scholarly treatment in which the author, presumably Jewish in background, uses Hebrew characters rather than Roman transliterations. Both commentaries have extensive bibliographies and scripture indexes.

5. Robert B. Robinson, "Levels of Naturalization in Obadiah," *Journal for the Study of the Old Testament* 40 (1988): 88, mentions anaphorae, chiasms, assonance, parallelism, and alliteration.

6. Ray C. Stedman, "Obadiah: Death to Edom!" in *World Wide Study Bible* on web site http://ccel.wheaton.edu/wwsb/obadiah/.

7. John Wesley, "Notes on the Book of Obadiah," on web site http://wesley.nnc.edu/wesley/notes/031obad.txt.

8. G. Johannes Botterweck and Helmer Ringgren, eds., *Theological Dictionary of the Old Testament,* 8 vols. to date (Grand Rapids, Mich.: Eerdmans, 1990), 6:462, 463.

9. Arno C. Gaebelein, *Gaebelein's Concise Commentary on the Whole Bible* (Neptune, N.J.: Loizeaux Brothers, 1985), 692.

10. Leslie C. Allen, "Obadiah," in *Holman Bible Dictionary* (Nashville: Holman Bible Publishers, 1991), 1035.

11. Ezra Taft Benson, *Ensign,* May 1989, 4–7.

12. Stedman, "Obadiah."

13. William P. Brown, *Obadiah through Malachi* (Louisville, Ky.: Westminster John Knox Press, 1996), 7.

14. Carl F. Henry, ed., *The Biblical Expositor,* 3 vols. (Grand Rapids, Mich.: Baker Book House, 1985), 2:316.

15. John Calvin, *Commentaries on the Twelve Minor Prophets* (Grand Rapids, Mich.: Eerdmans, 1950). Printed from the Internet: http://www.iclnet.org/pub/resources/text/ipb-e/epl-04/cvobd-04.txt.

16. Adam Clarke, *The Holy Bible . . . with a Commentary and Critical Notes* (Nashville, Tenn.: Abingdon, 1977), 696.

17. Rabbi Dr I. Epstein, *The Babylonian Talmud: Seder Nezikin* III (London: Soncino Press, 1935), 253.

18. Louis Ginzberg, *The Legends of the Jews,* 7 vols. (Philadelphia: Jewish Publication Society of America, 1937), 4:240, 241. Epstein, *Babylonian Talmud,* reports the following on page 253: "Let Obadiah, who has lived with two wicked persons [Ahab and Jezebel] and yet has not taken example by their deeds, come and prophesy against the wicked Esau, who lived with two righteous persons [Isaac and Rebekah] and yet did not learn from their good deeds."

19. Ginzberg, *Legends of the Jews,* 5:195.

20. Ginzberg, *Legends of the Jews,* 6:344.

21. David W. Baker, *Obadiah* (London: Inter-Varsity Press, 1988), 22.

22. Smith, *Teachings of the Prophet Joseph Smith,* 330; emphasis added.

23. Joseph Smith, *History of The Church of Jesus Christ of Latter-day Saints,* ed. B. H. Roberts, 2d ed. rev., 7 vols. (Salt Lake City: Deseret Book, 1973), 4:599.

24. Matthias Cowley, in Conference Report, October 1903, 55.

25. Charles W. Penrose, in Conference Report, April 1918, 22.

26. Carlfred Broderick, *My Parents Married on a Dare* (Salt Lake City: Deseret Book, 1996), 119; chapter originally published in "I Have a Question," *Ensign,* August 1986.

27. Broderick, *My Parents Married on a Dare,* 119.

28. *The Interpreter's Bible,* ed. George A. Buttrick, 12 vols. (New York: Abingdon Press, 1953), 6:863–64.

29. Kathleen Nash, "Obadiah: Past Promises, Future Hope," *Bible Today* 25 (January 1987): 281; emphasis added.

30. Broderick, *My Parents Married on a Dare,* 117.

31. Wilford Woodruff, in *Collected Discourses, 1894–1896,* comp. and ed. Brian H. Stuy, 5 vols. (B. H. S. Publishing, 1991), 4:10.

CHAPTER NINE

The Habakkuk Principle: Abigail and the Minor Prophet

CAROLYN GREEN OWEN

The prophet Habakkuk is recognized for two things. The first, paradoxically, is for being little recognized at all. His is an obscure voice even for a minor prophet, this Omni of the Old Testament, with his tiny contribution of three chapters totaling fifty-six verses of scripture. His name itself is a puzzle: it may come from a Hebrew root (*h-b-q*) signifying either an "embracer" (of the law of God? of righteousness?) or "the one embraced" (by God? by joy in the revelation of God's goodness?).[1] But it is just as likely to refer to an Akkadian fruit tree, delightfully named the *habbaququ*.[2] The prophet does not tell us who his parents were or whether they were goodly. We know nothing of his history; we cannot be certain of his time. There is an apocryphal story that an angel intercepted him in the field and commissioned him to deliver a pot of stew to Daniel in the lions' den: "Habakkuk said, 'Sir, I have never seen Babylon, and I know nothing about the den.' Then the angel of the Lord took him by the crown of his head and carried him by his hair; with the speed of the wind he set him down in Babylon, right over the den. Then Habakkuk shouted, 'Daniel, Daniel! Take the food that God has sent you.' . . .

Carolyn Green Owen is a graduate student in literary biblical criticism (English) at Brigham Young University.

And the angel of God immediately returned Habakkuk to his own place."[3] This is unconvincing biography, but it has an authentic note: Daniel clearly understands divine providence, for he thanks God and not Habakkuk for remembering to feed him. Daniel thanks the Lord for bringing food and Habakkuk thanks the Lord for bringing justice in virtually the same words: *You have remembered me, O God, and have not forsaken those who love you.*[4] Both prophets hold the same confident hope, which becomes through prayer and rough experience Habakkuk's working Principle: The Lord God of Israel will never abandon those who do not abandon him in their sorrow or danger or need but who call to him in faith.

According to his record, Habakkuk wrestled this testimony from two rounds of dialogue with the Lord about the unrighteousness of the Jews (possibly the same Jews who were persecuting the prophet Lehi, ca. 640–598 B.C.). Briefly but memorably put, it is a basic creed for both Jews and Christians and the second, stouter pillar of Habakkuk's reputation: "The just shall live by his faith" (KJV Habakkuk 2:4[5]). An early rabbi noticed the economy of this line and praised the author for cleverly loading all 613 commandments of the Torah into only three Hebrew words.[6] Paul the apostle quoted the verse to underwrite the Christian doctrine of justification by faith (see Romans 1:17; Galatians 3:11). Later the scripture became a favorite axiom of Martin Luther and hence "the touchstone of the Protestant Reformation."[7] It is the climax of Habakkuk's theodicy—his defense of the reliable goodness of God in an unjust world—and a complication of his Principle: the righteous in Israel not only must believe that the Lord will not abandon them but are called to live in faith that he will not. At times that faith may be tested.

Habakkuk lives when the "everlasting arms" of God supporting Israel seem less palpable than they did in the days of Moses and the Exodus (see Moses' psalm, Deuteronomy 33:26–29). Like most prophets, he feels the evils of his people personally and pulls on God's sleeve to do something about it. Their exchange consists of Habakkuk's first, testy complaint (Habakkuk 1:2–4) and God's response to it (1:5–11) and then a second, longer complaint (1:12–17) and God's second, shorter, more enigmatic reply (2:2–3), resulting in a prophecy (2:4–20). Habakkuk wants to know who will discipline the Jews for their "slack" law and their slow, "bent" justice (AT 1:4). He protests that he is weary of looking at such mischief and the suffering it causes, yet it continues—and worsens. Why does the Lord not intervene? Why not now? Habakkuk seems uneasy about God's relaxed style of crisis management.

The Lord replies that he is planning a solution of international scale. He is bringing the Chaldeans, or Babylonians, to possess the land as a judgment against the people (1:6). In case Habakkuk is not familiar with the Chaldeans, who destroyed the Assyrian capital of Nineveh in 612 B.C., defeated the Egyptians three years later at Carchemish, and are now looking at Judah, the Lord includes a description: they are a "fierce and impetuous nation" (AT 1:6), "dreadful and fearful" (AT 1:7); their horses are "sharper than wolves" (AT 1:8); they "come entirely for violence" (AT 1:9), laughing at kings and their fortifications (1:10); they "heap up the dust" of a land which is not theirs and cruelly "seize it" (AT 1:10). Habakkuk "wonder[s] marvelously" (KJV 1:5) at the Lord's faultless plan for judging and correcting the people—but then he seems to fault it (see KJV 1:13–17). He is nervous about the rudeness of the invading army. When the Jews are reproved, who will discipline the Chaldeans?

The Lord returns to Habakkuk on his watchtower and commands him to write a vision, in plain large letters, for readers on the run (the kind of readers we are today; see 2:2). The vision is first of all a prophecy against both temporal and spiritual Babylon, which appears as the image of an unjust man. Through a series of five scathing pronouncements, or "taunt songs" ("Woe to him . . ."; see KJV 2:6–20), Habakkuk verbally burns the image in effigy. Later, in his prayer (3:1–16), the prophet shares his hopeful vision of justice (3:12) and salvation (3:13), comprehending all that he desires for himself and his people. But there is an unexpected qualification: the vision is for a *future* "appointed time," not for today. The time of fulfillment is vague and unspecified, but the prophet is advised to "wait for it, for it will surely come; it will not delay" (AT 2:3). He is invited to realize that, while waiting, "the righteous man will live in his faithfulness" (AT 2:4), for as long as he must. In *steadfast* faithfulness he must endure, trusting in the Lord. Habakkuk, surprised and pleased to learn that proper happiness is not a circumstantial nicety but the sure reward of faith, writes a poem—a miniature psalm—exclaiming that even though his gardens may produce no blossoms or fruit (no grapes, no olives) and the flocks and herds die, and there is no meat, yet he will rejoice in the secure blessing of the Lord. He realizes that even when all appearances indicate otherwise—when wrongs seem to persist indefinitely, when catastrophe is at the door, and it looks as if there is nothing God can do or will do—yet God does keep faith, to punish evil and to reward good (3:17–19).

This "Habakkuk Principle" is not merely a folk tradition or the endemic optimism of the Israelite people. The Lord, as represented in the Old Testament, is distinguished by his *chesed,* a word most often translated into English as "mercy" or "lovingkindness" but perhaps more precisely the quality of "doing what is expected."[8] Man expects that God will keep his covenant promises, and God reliably keeps them. "With *everlasting faithfulness* I will have mercy on you, says the Lord your Redeemer" (AT Isaiah 54:8). To the just man living in his faith (the *chasid,* "saint," who is like God in his attribute of *chesed*), sure *deliverance* from affliction is promised by divine covenant with Israel and guaranteed by the Lord's fidelity. The Lord personally declares through Isaiah his firm nurturing purpose respecting Jacob's posterity:

> Listen to me, house of Jacob,
> and all the remnant of the house of Israel,

who are carried as a load by me from birth,
    who are carried by me from the womb;
till your old age I am he [who bears you],
    till you are hoary with age I will bear [you] as a heavy load;
I have made [you], and I will carry [you];
    and I will bear [you] as a heavy load, and I will deliver [you].
(AT Isaiah 46:3–4; compare D&C 133:52–53)

Before that, Moses's final words had celebrated this truth: "O your happiness, Israel! Who is like you—a people *delivered by the Lord . . . !*" (AT Deuteronomy 33:29). A third prophet, Jeremiah, who himself was caught in the Chaldean captivity, recognizes the same ancient, auspicious promise and mixes this veteran advice with his laments:

The Lord is good to those who wait for him,
to the soul that seeks him.
It is good to hope and be still
for the *deliverance* of the Lord.
(AT Lamentations 3:25–26)

This enduring belief in the steadfastness or trustworthiness of God is perhaps the root faith of Hebrew scripture and the centerpiece of Israelite piety.[9]

It will surprise no one familiar with the ironic transformations of biblical scripture if the textbook case of a just man living by his faith turns out to be a just woman, namely Abigail, first the wife of Nabal and then of David. Although she lived in the final days of king Saul, as much as four hundred years before Habakkuk, her story is thematically related to his Principle and clearly demonstrates its validity—not simply for the "house of Israel" as a people but for the privately troubled Israelite. We meet her in 1 Samuel 25, in an episode that is ostensibly the story of a random confrontation and its timely resolution but which then becomes something more consequential, both for Abigail and for the united kingdom of Israel.

As the text relates, the fugitive David and his six hundred men are subsisting in the wilderness of Paran, secluded and momentarily safe from Saul. While camped in the pasturelands, they extend their protection to the herdsmen of nearby wealthy sheep rancher, Nabal of Carmel; but when David asks Nabal for provisions in return, Nabal insults him, refusing to give him even bread and water.[10] David then straps on his sword and marches forth with four hundred men, swearing to exterminate Nabal's male household before morning. A concerned servant reports to Nabal's wife, Abigail, who hastily placates David with food for his men and, in the servile and self-effacing language of extreme courtesy, takes the blame for the offense herself ("Please forgive your maidservant's transgression"; AT 25:28), although she had in fact known nothing about it. To everyone's relief she restrains David "from coming into bloodguilt and from delivering yourself with your own hand" (AT 25:26)—that is, from killing innocent people (a violation of the law of Moses) and from arranging his own revenge (a violation of the ancient view of God's justice that undergirds the Habakkuk Principle). David blesses Abigail for her prudence and courage in meeting him (25:33). He bows to her judgment, accepts the supplies, and sends her home in peace (25:35). The situation is defused.

Meanwhile, Nabal is feasting roisterously in his house. Because he is "very drunk," Abigail does not "tell him anything, either a little or a lot, until the light of morning" (AT 25:36). When he eventually hears, his merry heart "die[s] within him," and he becomes "like a stone" (AT 25:37). Ten days later, the Lord "strikes" Nabal in some undisclosed manner, and he dies (AT 25:38). Precipitately, in the telling, David sends messengers to negotiate with Abigail ("David sent us to you to take you to him for a wife"; AT 25:40). Once again, Abigail considers quickly, responding submissively ("Behold, your maidservant will be a menial to wash the feet of the servants of my lord"; AT 25:41). She rises in a hurry, collects the five maids "who went at her heels" (AT), rides after David's proxies, and becomes his wife—all in verse 42. So we will know that this is the Deuteronomist speaking and not a Hollywood screenwriter, it must be added that "David also took Ahinoam of Jezreel, and the *two of them* became his wives" (AT 25:43).

The clear opposition between the good wife Abigail and the surly husband Nabal that is apparent in this summary of the chapter becomes explicit for the reader in the language of verse 3 (AT):

> And the name of the man was Nabal
> and the name of his wife was Abigail
> and the woman was good of understanding
> and beautiful of form
> but the man was harsh
> and wicked in his dealings
> and he was a Calebite.

It advertises to the reader that this story will be another narrative realization of the primal conflict between good and evil, wisdom and foolishness, righteousness and wickedness. These last two are Habakkuk's terms. The full text of Habakkuk 2:4 (AT) reads: "Behold the puffed-up man; his soul is not *right* [just, straight] within him. But the *righteous* [just] man will live in his faithfulness." In the precise structural design of a proverb, Habakkuk sets up an antithesis between just and unjust types, as prophets, psalmists, and proverbialists typically do. And just as precisely, he might have cast Abigail and Nabal, who audition for the roles and fill them as well as anyone in scripture.

But here, where these two major characters are first introduced, the Israelite reader or listener might have begun to pick up clues that the English-speaking reader does not. Looking speculatively at what the Israelite heard in the Hebrew vocabulary of 1 Samuel 25, it is possible to discover in this generic mismarriage of good and bad a more specific polarity between spiritual intelligence and spiritual obtuseness. For the Hebrew ear, in this one verse the narrator establishes Abigail as a righteous, spiritually mature woman who may credibly expect favorable divine attention (the "deliverance" of the faithful) and Nabal as an impious, spiritually inexperienced fool who will inevitably receive divine judgment (the "punishment" or "annihilation" of the wicked). The story then plays out as a real-life demonstration of the practical effects of spiritual assets and liabilities, as portended by the Habakkuk Principle. The foundation for this interpretation is poured at the level of language, too methodically to be merely an accident of vocabulary.

In her archetypal character, Abigail represents the proverbial *eshet hayil,* the worthy woman, like Ruth or Esther, or the "virtuous woman" of Proverbs 31. Nabal, however, plays the fool rather than the corresponding *gibbor hayil,* or mighty man of valor. But not quite the proverbial fool. *Nabal* is one Hebrew word for "fool," but it is not the typical choice of Hebrew wisdom literature. The authors of Proverbs, for example, who constantly pit the wise man against the fool do not generally pit him against the *nebalim* but against the *kesilim* (the dullards) or the *petaim* (the simple or uninstructed). A *nabal* is not merely a dull or senseless fellow but a villain committing disgraceful crimes: he may be self-promoting (Proverbs 30:32), arrogant (Proverbs 17:7), given to abusive language (including profanity, contumely, and blasphemy; see Micah 7:6, Deuteronomy 32:15), evil-thinking and speaking (Isaiah 32:6), sexually immoral (Judges 19:23), irreligious (Psalm 74:22), and even atheistic (Psalm 14:1; 53:1). In sum, he is a pocket of spiritual and moral deficiency in the fabric of the community—close to being outcast from it (see Job 30:3–8); it seems almost trivial that he is also gluttonous (Proverbs 30:21–22) and miserly (Jeremiah 17:11).

This family of meanings associated with the Hebrew root for Nabal's name (*n-b-l*) is evoked, more or less, by the word itself, so that when the narrator tells us "the name of the man was Nabal" (AT 1 Samuel 25:3), we may promptly infer (if we are Hebrew-speaking) his complete profile. Even so, there is some evidence that the arm of this well-lettered writer is stretched out still in the direction of further subtleties. We may imagine him looking beyond the basic meanings of "foolish" (*nabal*) and "foolishness" (*nebalah*) to catch every nuance of the root and work it into his narration. What he might find is this: A *nebel* could be the skin-bottle of wine that Nabal dips into often; alternatively, it is a clay jar or pitcher, cheap, common, and easily destroyed. A different *nebel* is a musical instrument, commonly played at feasts, sometimes as a "mark of luxury [or] revelry" (the trademarks of Nabal's feasting in the story); it was a member of the guitar family with, aptly, a "bulging resonance body at [the] lower end." *Nebalah* is senselessness, "as shown in disregard of moral and religious claims, especially of disgraceful sins." *Nabelut* might refer to the "immodesty" of Nabal's language, or the "shamelessness" of his drunkenness. The associated verb *nabel* means to "languish," to "wither and fall" or "fade," to "sink or drop down" from exhaustion or discouragement (or perhaps from a strike of the divine hand?). A *nebelah* is a corpse, which Nabal becomes. The point is this: if a clever narrator had somehow anticipated and included every relevant entry in the current standard biblical Hebrew-English lexicon,[11] the text need not be different from the way it appears. Nabal's name was therefore his index, as Abigail informs David: "Do not pay attention to this useless man, to Nabal; for as his name is so is he. His name is 'Fool,' and folly is with him" (AT 25:25).[12] He is the living embodiment of the lexicon—at least in Hebrew, the definitive impious fool.[13]

Abigail, on the other hand, is by local reputation precisely the proverbial helpmate.[14] One can believe that she has worked responsibly and long, her candle going not out by night, to prepare the two hundred loaves, two bottles of wine, five dressed sheep, five measures of parched grain, one hundred clusters of raisins, and two hundred cakes of pressed figs intended for her household but presented to David instead as an improvised "blessing," or gift. Her Hebrew epithets are *tobat sekhel* (prudent, sensible, perceptive, understanding) and *yephat toar* (beautiful of face or form). The related verbal form *sakhal* has the expected sense of "being prudent" or "acting circumspectly" but also of "giving insight" or "teaching," and even "prospering" or "causing to prosper."[15] The elements of her reputation are precisely the elements of her interaction with David. Her particular experiences in smoothing over other quarrels have trained her to respond to this emergency—no doubt the reason the servant comes to her.

The author, however, does not wish to present Abigail as merely a shrewd and beautiful woman—Delilah was likely as much. The index to Abigail's character, and to her ultimate good fortune, lies in the expression *tobat sekhel,* which in 1 Samuel 25:3 is variously translated into English as "clever" (NRSV), "of good understanding" (KJV), but perhaps most aptly as "intelligent" (NIV, REB, AB). More than simply clever, Abigail is prudent; more than simply prudent, she is intelligent. It is important, however, to discriminate between intelligences. In the text we see active evidence that Abigail is a provident home economist and arbiter of volatile situations. She is *capably* intelligent. More significantly, the narrator suggests that she is wise with the particular sort of wisdom that comes from the tree of knowledge in Eden: "a tree to be desired to make one wise [*sekhel*]" (Genesis 3:6). He implies through his diction that Abigail has that endowment of intelligence that constitutes *enlightenment*—another possible meaning of *sekhel*—which is perhaps not wrongly understood as the familiar dispensation of revealed light and knowledge communicated from divine to human spirit. Such enlightened intelligence is the due comfort of a just man or woman in Israel, the confirmation of faithfulness and the chief help to sustain faithful lives. On Abigail's receptiveness to this gift, her recognition of it, and her trust in its reliability hinge the fates of all the principals in the story.

With the presentation of these two severely contrasted characters, expectations—that the good will be happy and the bad will not—are set up and are then disappointed. Because Abigail appears to possess the full spectrum of womanly virtues (from physical beauty to spiritual intelligence), we might expect, according to Israelite views of justice, that she will be living in well-deserved peace and prosperity; but in fact she is sorely tried. She has made a bad marriage, a contract that was likely arranged for her out of concern for her community status and material security. Perhaps the alliance with wealthy Nabal was celebrated as a brilliant settlement by parents who were somewhat "foolish" themselves. We may suppose too that Abigail, in the tradition of Hannah but without the mediation of a priest, has prayed often to be relieved in some appropriate way from the stress of the mismatch. Perhaps, like Hannah (whose biographer—the author of 1 Samuel—may also be Abigail's), "her soul was bitter, and she prayed to the Lord and wept grievously" (AT 1 Samuel 1:10). She may have prayed as the prophets pray: *How long, O lord, will I cry out for help?* (AT Habakkuk 1:2; see also Isaiah 6:11; D&C 121:1–3). She may even have added, in desperate impatience, as Habakkuk will cry centuries later in his own distress: *And you will not hear! I cry out to you of violence, and you will not deliver me!* (AT Habakkuk 1:2).

If Abigail has faithfully prayed, why has not the Lord, who brought up the house of Israel from bondage in Egypt, delivered *her*—a less spectacular feat? For that matter, why has he not interposed himself between Abigail and this unfortunate marriage, fulminating with indignant judgment and an injunction? Is not the Lord also, preeminently, *tobat sekhel?* He is, and so we hear him asking, "Unfortunate for whom?" Abigail's marriage is also—in ancient Israel, predominantly—Nabal's marriage. It was not unfortunate for him. Before the Lord God of Israel, Nabal and Abigail "at the altar" are types of Jacob and Rachel, of Abraham and Sarah, even of Adam and Eve. Their union is potentially an enduring, beneficent, and fruitful relationship that might replenish the earth. Like Cain, if Nabal does well he will be accepted (see Genesis 4:7). The Lord has not prevented the marriage nor does he end it precipitately but generously keeps faith with Nabal during his "preparatory state," granting him wealth and influence and a divinely favored wife. Throughout, the Lord does not rush his own judgment nor bias his interest but regards

Nabal's needs equally with Abigail's. The Lord waits to see whether Nabal will "turn and be healed," and he requires Abigail to wait with him. He is measuring the worth of Nabal, but he is measuring Abigail as well. Though the Lord may regret Abigail's distress, it appears that he does not release her from her commitment until Nabal has had full opportunity to repent of his *nebalah*—his foolishness. Meanwhile, she must abide her marriage, creditably managing her household and herself, avoiding provocations that might tempt Nabal to spiteful decisions rather than to repentance; for the elective ending of a marriage, like the elective ending of a life, removes all possibility for further repentance in that sphere, a final and consequential decision that the Lord has reserved for himself (see Deuteronomy 32:35; Hebrews 10:30–31; D&C 64:10; 98:23–48). So as David waits for Saul to remember his faith, Abigail waits for Nabal to develop his, and God waits for them all. The consistent hope is that Abigail or some other compelling influence will overcome Nabal's resistance and convert his irreligious nature to faithful observance of basic commandments. In that case, her joy would be great with him in the kingdom of their Father. That outcome, as ambitious (or repellent) as it may seem, is the Lord's first concern for Nabal or any like him.

Let us assume that the Lord has heard Abigail—for according to the root ethic of Hebrew scripture, he does not fail to hear the cries of the faithful—and he has told her, as he will later tell Habakkuk, of an "appointed time" that was surely coming and for which she must faithfully wait. But the trial that is of unknown length or exact outcome is particularly anguishing. Will Abigail remain like Habakkuk a "watchman on the tower," waiting for the Lord to speak, trusting that he will act; or will she decide to manipulate the givens of the situation "with her own hand"? We do not *see* Abigail doing the latter: The narrator does not record that Abigail has attempted to "deliver" herself from the disagreeable but legitimate contract that binds her. As far as we know, she does not wander the neighborhood, indiscreetly crying on available shoulders; she does not console herself through extramarital intrigues. She has not abandoned her home to support herself through harlotry. She has poisoned neither herself nor Nabal. Without actually knowing, we trust that she was indeed and not just reputedly *tobat sekhel* and therefore has not taken any of the few, disagreeable alternatives available to her but has remained self-respectfully in her house, attending to her offices as the matron of a large estate, catering her husband's banquets on call, pressing figs, necessarily trusting that the Lord will prove to be "the God of my deliverance" (AT Habakkuk 3:18). Though a difficult marriage may have curbed personal growth, Abigail's life is evidence that even in poor marital circumstances it may yet be possible to keep every commandment and develop every attribute necessary for eternal life. If Abigail has ever supposed that her uncongenial marriage excuses her from making that effort, there is no evidence for it in the story.

At some point in her ordeal David arrives at Carmel, a crisis arises, and Nabal's servant hurries to warn Abigail of inevitable doom upon her household, despite her years of prudent homemaking and peacekeeping. When he asks her to "consider what to do," surely she sees her opportunity to be delivered—to be "free." David's action will leave her a widow. Moreover, her personal condition might even be improved by her coming, through the fortunes of war, into David's possession, perhaps as a member of his house. She has only to remain at home, keep still, and Nabal (and many others) will be dead before morning. But would the Lord approve such a plan? Is this how divine providence appears? Could this awful instrument of massacre serving pride and revenge be the convenient shape of her promised salvation? Rather, it looks to Abigail as the Chaldeans must have looked to Habakkuk: David may chasten Nabal, but who will chasten David? But then again, if Abigail rescues Nabal, who will rescue Abigail? Presumably, everything will return to the relentless status quo—or worse, assuming reprisals from Nabal. What if she attempts to stop David—

and fails? Will it be her fault? David's fault? Nabal's fate? The will of the Lord? One of the telling constraints of the story is that there is little time to consider alternatives or design her approach, hence the great opportunity for a fatal mistake. It is already too late to reach David's camp in time to stop his departure; by this time David has mustered his army and started toward Nabal.

Directly, Abigail makes her decision, makes preparations, and then "makes haste." She meets David's company in the course of their assault—one housewife on her donkey confronting four hundred armed and angry men in a ravine somewhere short of Carmel, her own "valley of the shadow." What she says and does here, though quickly determined, is wholly effective. She absorbs David's debasement by abasing herself (note her energetic tumble through seven verbs): "And Abigail saw David, and she hurried and she got down off the donkey, and she fell before David on her face and she bowed to the ground, and she fell at his feet and she said . . ." (AT 1 Samuel 25:23–24). She apologizes; she assumes the blame, diverting David's attention from her husband: "Upon *me,* my lord, [be] the punishment" (AT 25:24). She asks for an audience, repeating herself in her excitement (a cameo-sized chiasm): "Please let your maidservant speak in your ears, and hear the words of your maidservant" (AT 25:24). Without disloyalty to Nabal, she is all on David's side. She does not argue her case. Her technique is to portray the contested point—Will David smite Nabal?—as already having been decided in Nabal's favor, as if she has come only to congratulate David for sparing him. She begins by dropping this foregone conclusion into an introductory phrase: "*since* the Lord has restrained you . . ." (AT 25:26). Again, she reasons: "It *will come to pass* that *when* the Lord does for my lord all the good that he has spoken concerning you . . . this *will not be* a stumbling block for you or a stumbling of conscience for my lord, either to shed blood without cause or to deliver yourself" (AT 25:30–31)—another slipped-in conclusion, for David has not yet made up his mind about the blood.

Superficially, her remarks are simply good rhetorical strategy; and David seems to accept her assumptions at face value. He is not as much persuaded as deflected.

Granted that Abigail is experienced and perceptive, how is she able spontaneously to prevent the catastrophe—to *deliver* her household—and not only subdue her "enemy" with a few words but receive his blessing? What factor makes the critical difference? Is it her submissiveness? To a modern reader Abigail appears more than conciliatory; she is abject and servile. We do not hear her claiming mistreatment, defending her turf, or even tearfully pleading for mercy—just meekly making amends for a wrong she did not commit. *That* seems underplayed. Is it her flattery? She compliments David's military skill and implies his favor with the Lord. Men like to hear those things. Is it her beauty? Abigail is *yephat toar*—very pretty. Does confidence in her attractive appearance enable her to proceed with courage and accuracy to the targeted reorganization of her life? Perhaps it is the material "blessing" that Abigail presents to David. Though it cannot be an extravagant food supply when divided among six hundred men, it was a generous and salving gesture—particularly as the original plea was for "whatever comes to hand" (AT 25:8).

No final answer is reported in the verses of text, but a good possibility is suggested by the Habakkuk Principle: Abigail does not in fact rescue her household but cooperates with the Lord as a means to bring about a small, domestic miracle, as Esther cooperates to bring about a larger, national one. In Israel it is God who delivers, not the plausible "arm of flesh." The responsibility of the anxious human helper is rather to "be silent before [be resigned to] the Lord, and wait longingly for him" (AT Psalm 37:7). This has been Abigail's wisdom. When she averts the destruction of her household she certainly does live, and deserves to remain alive, on account of her faith. This is one legitimate sense of Habakkuk 2:4 (and an ever-present theme of Hebrew scripture, especially of Psalms and Proverbs). But Abigail does more than prevent death *because* she is faithful. Her reputation suggests that she has routinely met adversity, and will quash this present attack as well, by means of her faith.[16] She lives—meets life and moves from moment into moment—in the faith that she will receive divine direction. As it opens a conduit for divine intelligence, her faith is both the *justification* for receiving such guidance and the *means* of taking consistently right action. We do not see the Lord or his angel in this passage, or even hear his voice; but we might believe that we are watching his agent. Frequently in scripture the deepest footprint of God's active presence is left not in the fresh cement of the text itself but in the loose gravel at the margin of the page. Biblical text as we have it does not always explicitly tell us when a private conduit has opened between God and man, and that "over the line" is being relayed the intelligence that is the privilege and mainstay of the just man or woman. The narrator does not introduce it here. But in a biblical story with this particular kind of narrative gap, where the speech or the actions of a character seem unaccountably to display inordinate intelligence (Abigail meeting David, Rebekah meeting Eliezer), or when they seem oddly uncharacteristic, unexpected, or inexplicable (Eve eating the apple, Abraham sacrificing Isaac, Sarah expelling Hagar, Rebekah coaching Jacob, Rachel stealing the *teraphim*), or elliptical (Cain failing an acceptable sacrifice, Jacob wrestling with the angel), it may be that the actor is simply following—or rejecting—a program of divine guidance that is not in the text. Respecting the adventures of the righteous in ancient Israel, it is a hypothesis that is always relevant and might be tried.

Accordingly, under the threat of imminent ruin created by David and Nabal, when Nabal's servant drops the outcome of the affair into her apron, it seems likely that Abigail, knowing and trusting the sacred protocols, "thinks to pray"; and in response she receives the long-promised divine visitation, in the form of inspired intelligence to interpret her situation, to comprehend her role in it, and to take prompt, effective action. At the moment of her appeal, she might then have several unexpected faith-rewarding realizations: (1) that the "appointed time" for her deliverance has come, (2) that the Lord will deal personally with Nabal, and (3) that she must intervene to teach David the same principle of forebearing faith that has preserved her. She might also receive practical intelligence to teach her specifically what she must do from moment to moment—how to comport herself, manage her emotions, speak compellingly—to avert disaster and gain a promising reward. It is principally the Lord who "remembers" Abigail rather than David (see 1 Samuel 2:9); and Abigail finds, as does Hannah, that "the Lord is a God of knowledge" (AT 2:3). According to this scenario, from this moment she is a woman acting under instructions, following meticulously the program of inspiration that guides her, checking each thought and action against the Spirit for approval. She is willing to let go of her own cleverness—even her own disgust and terror—to preserve an attitude of *listening.*

Hence, having accomplished the immediate purpose of her dialogue with David—forestalling disaster—Abigail unaccountably goes on, still begging forgiveness, her speech becoming more audacious and more difficult to explain. She accesses two inaccessible pieces of information and relays them confidently to David. First she alludes to his future kingship as an excellent reason to show forbearance: "The Lord will surely make for my lord an established house, for my lord has fought the battles of the Lord; and let evil not be found in you in [all] your days" (AT 25:28). Officially, David's anointing had been a private affair, "among his brothers" (AT 16:13). What they knew, others might of course have been told by family or family servants or by Samuel himself. Abigail could thus have heard rumors of the ordination. In that case her knowledge would have been on the level of gossip, but the authoritative and peremptory language of her speech suggests confirmed testimony.[17] Next she foretells David's escape from Saul's persecution, as well as any other intentional harm, because "the soul of my lord has been bound in the bundle of the living with the Lord your God" (AT 25:29). In the immediate context, Abigail's statement is a subtle reminder to David that if he sheds innocent blood he will be "blotted out of the book of the living, and not be written with the righteous" (Psalm 69:28; see also Exodus 32:32–33); ultimately, it is a promise of eternal life (see Revelation 20:12–15). When she volunteers this message, she reveals the fate that David has wished to know, regarding both his temporal safety and his status with the Lord—but which surely only God can secure.[18] How can she be certain that Saul will not surprise David tomorrow? How can she frankly promise David the favor of the Lord? How does she know that the Lord will legitimate her promise?

Carried away by the momentum of these plainspoken remarks, Abigail forgets to edit out her obvious premonitions. Boldly, she swears a shocking oath to David: "As the Lord lives and as your soul lives . . . may your enemies, and those who seek to harm my lord, *be as Nabal*" (AT 1 Samuel 25:26). Her oath is serious business, gravely blasphemous unless fulfilled, demonstrating her absolute confidence in the outcome—she is not guessing. At this very moment, however, as both David and Abigail know, wealthy Nabal is at home with friends enjoying a lavish post-shearing banquet "like the feast of a king" (AT 25:36). It is a true Hebrew *mishteh,* an "occasion for drinking"—hardly due payoff for an enemy. Where is her logic? This discrepancy has led some scholars to propose that verse 26 should be relocated to her second and final speech, between verses 41 and 42, after Nabal has died.[19] More likely, the verse is not misplaced but simply reflects Abigail's foreknowledge of the action. Unless the possibility of personal revelation is real, her final remark is similarly perplexing: "When the Lord has done well for my lord, then remember your maidservant" (AT 25:31). The maidservant is of course Abigail herself. But what does she mean by "remember"? She is acting to prevent David from incidentally canceling her marriage in the process of taking his revenge. From David's own charged point of view, how better could he "remember" (*zakhar*, "remember, protect, deliver") her? What more could she expect him to do—and when? (At this point, does even *she* know what she expects him to do? Does she know only that Nabal will be judged, or that he will die?) Following this second, unexpected installment of her speech, with its excursion into blessing and prophecy, David must have been astonished—but impressed.

In phrase after phrase, Abigail publishes what she cannot know except by inspiration. Is it possible that she has been endowed as were Helaman's sons Nephi and Lehi, who "had power and authority given unto them that they might speak, and *they also had what they should speak given unto them*"? (Helaman 5:18; emphasis added). Perhaps the "conversation" between the Lord and Abigail was like an earlier one between the Lord and Samuel. The Lord gave Samuel instructions to anoint David king of Israel: "Fill your horn with oil [pack your asses with groceries] and go" (AT 1 Samuel 16:1). Noting the dangers, Samuel protested: "How can I go? If Saul [Nabal] hears, he will kill me" (AT 16:2). The Lord outlined an opening strategy and then promised, "I will make you know what to do" (AT 16:3).[20] Although Abigail is neither prophetess, priestess, nor matriarch in Israel, for this moment she is a suitable mouthpiece for the mission to recall David to his better judgment, in effect to rescue *him* even before he rescues *her.* David, whose corresponding spiritual gifts were established at his ordination (see 16:13), is not offended by her language but acknowledges its source and its capability: "Blessed is the Lord God of Israel, who sent you today to meet me. And blessed is your judgment and blessed are you who have restrained me today from committing the sin of bloodshed and from delivering myself with my [own] hand" (AT 25:32–33).

David and Abigail part in mutual respect, and Abigail returns home to Nabal (see 25:36) to play their single scene together (following what is perhaps the custom of their marriage, it has little dialogue). After the resolution of the crisis, Nabal has to be told about the aftermath of his quarrel. From his perspective it will be news of mutiny—a large consignment of goods is missing from his larder, and his rejection order has been overturned. Despite his being "so ill-natured that no one can speak to him" (NIV 25:17), Abigail elects to tell him herself about the rapprochement with David—not when he is too drunk from feasting to comprehend the details, or too merry to respond (or too mean and unrestrained not to kill her outright), but the next morning "when the wine is gone out of him" (AT 25:37) and he is sober enough to hear the story clearly and to catch the point that the deed has saved his life. But not for long. Apparently while Abigail is speaking to him (perhaps as a result of it—shocked by her disobedience? shocked by her loyalty?) Nabal collides with the end of his mortal probation. As he later deals with Saul, and much later with Habakkuk's unrighteous Jews, the Lord "returns the wickedness of Nabal upon his [own] head" (25:39). David does not lift his hand; Abigail does not lift hers. There is no bloodguilt; there is divine rather than self-deliverance. Nabal dies by the hand and will of the Lord in an obscure manner suggesting the inscrutability of divine ways.[21]

After Nabal's death, as David prepares to move his household to the Philistine city of Gath, he and Abigail agree to marry. It is a remarriage for David as well, to an intelligent woman who has extensive property and useful political connections[22] but who is not, like his first wife, the daughter of a king (an early gratuity that had recently been annulled by Saul; see 25:44). But for Abigail her new marriage represents deliverance of a splendid sort. We see that, freed from Nabal, she does not then find happiness with Amos the baker, a local and decent fellow who has pitied her for years, but rides off with David, a popular military hero, who is her proper counterpart—the *gibbor hayil* (see 16:18)—and one of the few men in Old Testament scripture who, like herself, is *yepheh toar*, the narrative formula for physical beauty.[23] Like the heroine of a folktale she marries the future king, presumably the paragon of the realm. In the context of the Old Testament, this may be a figure of the superabundance of God's blessings: they rise to the limit of what man can imagine (to ancient Israel this was the luxury of royalty). The Lord himself calls our current attention to it: "the blessings which I give unto you are above all things" (D&C 18:45).

Some readers may be uncomfortable with the resemblance of Abigail's life—or God's justice—to fairy tale motifs. They may ask why Abigail would "haste" after David's servants to marry a man with whom she has spoken only once and who woos by committee. Is it hasty (like the mourning and the marriage) to conclude that the Lord intends and approves, if he does not require, David's offer of marriage to Abigail? Quite likely she herself perceives it as the—not unattractive—will of the Lord. When the offer comes, perhaps she realizes through the intelligence that is her gift (according to a precocious understanding of marriage that is currently stated only in modern revelation) that the Lord is here intending not only a temporal dynasty but an eternal companionship, constituting the perfect union of equals that God desires for all his children. On his part, David is certain to recollect the popular proverb that "a wife who behaves prudently is from the Lord" (AT Proverbs 19:14). Although there was no general "temple marriage" in David's Israel (and as yet no temple), prophets of the Lord held the Melchizedek Priesthood and had the power to seal such ordinances. David, as the Lord's anointed, was married in this way, as the Lord explained to Joseph Smith: "David's wives and concubines were given unto him of me, by the hand of Nathan, my servant, and others of the prophets who had the keys of this power" (D&C 132:39). Abigail, as one of these "given" wives, consents to it willingly. But here, as all along, her submissiveness seems not primarily to David but to the Lord. "Behold," she says, ostensibly to David's men, "your handmaid will be a menial to wash the feet of my lord's servants" (AT 1 Samuel 25:41). With the removal of the comma (which does not exist in biblical Hebrew) we have, conceivably, the familiar *Behold your handmaid.* This phrasing might represent the proper feminine reply to the Lord's call, similar to the faithful man's *Hinenni* ("Here I am"). And then we may have, in the spirit of Hannah's hymn of praise (2:1–10) or Mary's "Magnificat" (Luke 1:46–55): *I will be a menial to wash the feet of my Lord's servants.* Like Rebekah suffusively watering Eliezer's camels and then "hasting" to meet the unknown Isaac—and for the same intelligent reason—Abigail does not dally.

This auspicious business is concluded under heavy dramatic irony, for we know that later David will indeed kill a man to obtain his wife and thereby lose his anticipated inheritance. The above scripture continues: "And in none of these things [i.e., David's marriages] did he sin against me save in the case of Uriah and his wife; and, therefore he hath fallen from his exaltation, and received his portion; and he shall not inherit them out of the world, for I gave them unto another, saith the Lord" (D&C 132:39). Those so given likely include Abigail. As readers of scripture and subscribers to the Habakkuk Principle, we are concerned that the just who have suffered long in faith should receive justice—and not merely poetic justice but a cup running over. But here is David, the deliverer, looking very much like one of Habakkuk's Chaldeans after all. Is it "just" that faithful Abigail should be given to one man, and then to another, and then to another again? Legalities aside, are human feelings so flexible and so resilient? Is this a rescue, or a wrench?

Though we may be comforted that the Lord's interest in righteous, prudent living and his intention to bless just and faithful lives are genuine and secure, we might note that he has seemed less interested in romance. What looks like indifference, however, may be simply his firm, omniscient opinion that any persons who actually inherit eternal life in the celestial kingdom of God will find each other interesting and adequate. In particular, any man and woman who have determinedly loved and served the Lord, who have deserved and gratefully accepted his blessing, and who present themselves together at the gate of the New Jerusalem, are going to recognize in each other, as in all of that present company, the embodiment of everything they love best and desire most. They could have no objection to each other. It is perhaps a "hard saying" rather than a romantic notion that if Abigail were to meet a repentant Nabal on the porch of that august City, she would find him *yepheh toar*—beautiful.

Thus the world is not decisively righted for Abigail when David arrives—or for Habakkuk when the Chaldeans come to Jerusalem. At this point of apparent deliverance in both their lives, neither has yet endured to the end; other agencies will assert themselves precariously before the story closes. There is more living to do, in spiritually intelligent faith, until the appointed time comes for Habakkuk's "vision" and for the sealing of Abigail's blessings. These promises will in fact be ultimately realized in the same event. The clue to this truth emerges, unlikely enough, in Hebrews 10:32–39, which not only includes a reference to Habakkuk 2:4 but also seems curiously reminiscent of Abigail's very situation. In this passage Paul is speaking to fellow "second generation" Christians, some of whom are disappointed (as Habakkuk was) that the true kingdom has not yet come. Recommending perseverance, Paul asks them to "recall those earlier days when, after you had been *enlightened,* you endured a hard struggle with sufferings. . . . Do not, therefore, abandon that confidence of yours; it brings a great reward. For you need endurance, so that when you have done the will of God, you may receive what was promised" (NRSV Hebrews 10:32, 35–36). Then he quotes Habakkuk—from the Septuagint, a Greek translation of Hebrew scripture:

> For yet "in a very little while,
> the one who is coming will come and will not delay;
> but my righteous one will live by faith.
> My soul takes no pleasure in anyone who shrinks back."
> But we are not among those who shrink back and so are lost, but among those who have faith and so are saved.
>
> (NSRV 10:37–39)

This version suggests that it is not some anonymous "vision" but Christ himself who is "surely coming" and "will not delay." In fact, Habakkuk's prophecy includes a brief theophany in which the Lord appears in apocalyptic imagery as a mighty warrior, more cosmically terrible than the Chaldeans. Pulling the Old and New Testament strands together, then, it is at Christ's advent that "those who have faith" will at last "receive what was promised," the "great reward" of eternal life. Habakkuk will receive his reward, the Lord will make for Abigail a "sure house," and "God himself . . . will wipe every tear from their eyes" (Revelation 21:4) and fully justify the steadfast faith which they have placed—at no risk—in him.

The Habakkuk Principle necessarily includes this conviction of the providence of God—of God himself as the means of justice and the object of trust. It is not the same thing as ordinary "hopemongering,"[24] which, though optimistic and well-intended, is without a reliable agent. The faith of the just man is an unconditional trust in the willingness and ability of the Lord himself to rectify and avenge injustice. It must be accompanied by a firm acceptance of whatever it is that the Lord is willing and able to do. The stories of Habakkuk and Abigail convince us that the Lord is trustworthy; but they also startle us with the companion realization that he will deliver us in his own way, requiring our courage and endurance. This world is for the proving and the judgment of all. Before the end, the wheat and the tares will grow together for a long time. In that crucible of agency we cannot reasonably trust the Lord to save *our* people, or *our* marriage, or *our* mortal life. Rather, we can trust him to do what is right—a manifold and comprehensive act too large for us to easily see.

Notes

1. Carl Friedrich Keil, *Biblical Commentary on the Old Testament,* vol. 2, *The Twelve Minor Prophets,* trans. James Martin (Grand Rapids, Mich.: Eerdmans, 1949), 49.

2. David Baker, *Nahum, Habakkuk, and Zephaniah: An Introduction and Commentary* (Leicester, England: Inter-Varsity Press, 1988), 43.

3. From the apocryphal Old Testament book Bel and the Dragon 35–37, 39, in *The Harper Collins Study Bible: New Revised Standard Version* (New York: HarperCollins Publishers, 1993), 1643; hereafter NRSV.

4. Bel and the Dragon 38. Compare Habakkuk 1:12: "Are you not from everlasting, Lord, my God, my Holy One? We will not die." Some relieved surprise at the Lord's providence seems common to both.

5. All translations from the Hebrew are the author's (AT), except where otherwise noted. Other translations quoted are the King James Version (KJV), the New Revised Standard Version (NRSV), the Revised English Bible (REB), the New International Version (NIV), and the Anchor Bible (AB). All italics in quotations of scripture are the author's.

6. The Talmudic Rabbi Simlai, as cited in *The Anchor Bible Dictionary,* ed. David Noel Freedman, 6 vols. (New York: Doubleday, 1992), 3:5.

7. Walter A. Elwell, *Baker Encyclopedia of the Bible,* 2 vols. (Grand Rapids, Mich.: Baker Book House, 1988), 1:908.

8. See Katharine Doob Sakenfeld, *The Meaning of Hesed in the Hebrew Bible: A New Inquiry,* Harvard Semitic Monographs, no. 17 (Missoula, Mont.: Scholars Press, 1978).

9. The New Testament describes the millennial Lord in the same terms. When Christ appears as a warrior-king, wearing blood-red garments and riding a white horse at the head of an army of saints, one of his names will be "Faithful and True" (see Revelation 19:11).

10. Regina Schwartz suggests that in so doing "Nabal has violated the covenant agreement by which David protects him and in turn has earned protection." See Regina Schwartz, "The Histories of David: Biblical Scholarship and Biblical Stories," in *"Not in Heaven": Coherence and Complexity in Biblical Narrative,* ed. Jason P. Rosenblatt and Joseph C. Sitterson Jr. (Bloomington and Indianapolis: Indiana University Press, 1991), 209. According to Isaiah, Nabal is behaving like a typical "fool," "leaving the hungry empty and depriving the thirsty of drink" (Isaiah 32:6).

11. See related entries in Francis Brown, S. R. Driver, and Charles A. Briggs, *The Brown-Driver-Briggs Hebrew and English Lexicon* (Peabody, Mass.: Hendrickson Publishers, 1996), 614–15.

12. Readers have wondered why parents would name their child "Fool." (For that matter, why would Adam and Eve name their son "Ephemeral," the meaning of Abel, *Hevel,* in Hebrew?) Perhaps it was a later nickname or epithet. It is possible, too, that the name of Abigail's husband was not given in the narrator's sources, so that his true name was not known to the writer (Nabal is first introduced in

the text as an anonymous "man in Maon"; v. 2). Needing a name for the character to complete the parallel structure of verse 3, perhaps he took his cue from a line of dialogue traditionally attributed to Abigail ("'Fool' is his name . . . "; v. 25) and adopted it as an apt designation.

13. Verse 3 includes other "concealed" information which expands the negative force of Nabal's Hebrew name. The narrator tells us that Nabal is "harsh in his dealings," but instead of using the more neutral word *maasim* to signify "dealings," he chooses *maalalim,* which generally (with important exceptions) refers to "bad practices." The noun comes from the verb *alal,* which means not only "to act or deal" but specifically to deal "harshly" or "severely" and is used in the Hebrew Bible to refer to "abusing a woman" (see Judges 19:25; see also Brown, Driver, and Briggs, *Hebrew and English Lexicon,* 759). *Qasheh,* the word for "harsh," "rude," or "ruthless," is also the "stiff" in "stiff-necked" (*quesheh oreph*) and the "hard" in "hard of heart" (*qeshey lev*)—another linguistic means of locating Nabal among the unrighteous (unspiritual) in Israel (see Brown, Driver, and Briggs, *Hebrew and English Lexicon,* 904, 525). The indication that Nabal is a Calebite seems auspicious, since Caleb was a hero of the conquest of Canaan; but the man was a Kenizzite, a non-native Israelite, whose name signifies "dog" in Hebrew, perhaps a reference to Nabal's doglike ferocity in a quarrel.

14. Abigail's name may mean in Hebrew "my father rejoices." If "a wise son makes a father rejoice" (Proverbs 10:1), apparently a prudent daughter such as Abigail might do the same. But see Proverbs 17:21: "The father of a fool has no joy."

15. For definitions and scriptural references, see Brown, Driver, and Briggs, *Hebrew and English Lexicon,* 968.

16. The difference is between the *causal* and the *instrumental.* The current Jewish Bible opts for the first sense: "But the righteous man is rewarded with life/For his fidelity." Their amended version does also: "Lo there is a reward for the upright—/the life breath within him—." The Jewish Publication Society, *Tanakh: The Holy Scriptures: The New JPS Translation according to the Traditional Hebrew Text* (Philadelphia: Jewish Publication Society, 1985), 1065 (Habakkuk 2:4); see also footnote d-d, 1065. Brown, Driver, and Briggs, *Hebrew and English Lexicon,* adopts this sense, while the KJV, the NRSV, and the NIV allow the second meaning.

17. According to Jon D. Levenson, Abigail's prediction is an "undeniable adumbration of Nathan's prophecy which utilizes the identical language (2 Samuel 7:16). It is this element which led the rabbis, according to David Kimchi, to count Abigail among the seven women who they believed had been graced with the holy spirit." See Jon D. Levenson, "1 Samuel 25 as Literature and as History," *Catholic*

Biblical Quarterly 40 (January 1978): 20. Besides presaging Nathan, it is possible that Abigail was repeating Samuel's exact words to David at his ordination (the words are not given in the text; see 1 Samuel 16:13). The mere recognition of these words might have arrested David in his course.

18. In scripture, the transfer of information "which no man knoweth save me and thee alone" often functions as evidence of the divine signature (see D&C 15:3; 16:3).

19. See P. Kyle McCarter Jr., *I Samuel*, vol. 8 of *The Anchor Bible*, ed. William Foxwell Albright and David Noel Freedman, 40 vols. to date (Garden City, N.Y.: Doubleday, 1980), 394: "Verse 26 is clearly out of place. It assumes (1) that David has already been restrained from assaulting Nabal personally, and (2) that Nabal has already met his downfall. It fits most comfortably between vv 41 and 42 below and is tentatively restored there. Perhaps it was displaced from there because Abigail is addressing David directly though he is not present; but such is already the case in v 41!"

20. It may be that Abigail did not know in advance what she would say to David, only that she must speak to him (see D&C 24:6: "And it shall be given thee in the very moment what thou shalt speak").

21. Is it possible that during the ten days that Nabal lay stricken (paralyzed?) he was taught the gospel and repented? Consider the experiences of Alma (Mosiah 27:19–20, 24, 28–30), King Lamoni (Alma 18:40–42; 19:6, 12–13), and Lamoni's father (Alma 22:18). Or perhaps Nabal was taught and did not repent, *and so* he died.

22. See McCarter, *1 Samuel*, 402: "The partnership of such a wife bodes well for David's future, not only because of her 'good intelligence' (v 3) and counseling skills but also because she is the widow of a very rich Calebite landowner. . . . The last point is an important one. David has lost his newly acquired base of power in consequence not only of his exile from Gibeah, where he had become a popular hero, but also, as we learn in v 44, the loss of his royal-blooded wife, Michal. He has been required to return to his homeland. Now we find him marrying the widow of a high-ranking member of the class that controlled Hebron . . . as well as another woman from nearby Jezreel (v 43). He is becoming a prominent figure in the heartland of Judah. To be sure, the narrative does not suggest that he is deliberately building a base of power—all of this is the working out of a divine plan in which he, too, is caught up—but when the time comes—that is, when Saul falls—David will be ready. And he will become king first at Hebron (2 Samuel 2:1–4)." Footnote 3 on the same page refers to Jon D. Levenson's speculation "that Nabal may

have been the leader of the Calebite clan and that David thus laid claim to the position by marriage to Abigail."

23. The list includes Joseph (Genesis 39:6), David (1 Samuel 16:12, 18), and David's son Absalom (2 Samuel 14:25).

24. Herbert Kohl defines "hopemongering" as "the affirmation of hope and the dream of a just and equitable future despite all the contrary evidence provided by experience." Herbert Kohl, *"I Won't Learn from You" and Other Thoughts on Creative Maladjustment* (New York: New Press, 1994), xiii. Hopemongering, so defined, is the secular, humanly caring and resourceful version of the Habakkuk Principle—faith in what man can and will do for man.

CHAPTER TEN

THE PROPHETIC MINISTRY OF HAGGAI: THE BLESSINGS OF THE TEMPLE

RAY L. HUNTINGTON

As is true of many of the prophets in the Old Testament, we have little information detailing the life of Haggai. Despite his being mentioned in two books of the Old Testament (Haggai and Ezra), nothing is known of his birthplace, family background, or the events surrounding his prophetic calling.

The name *Haggai* probably means "festal" or "feast" and may indicate that Haggai was born during one of the three important Jewish feasts of Unleavened Bread, Pentecost (or Weeks), or Tabernacles.[1] Textural information from the book of Haggai reveals that Haggai began his Jerusalem ministry during the second year of Darius, king of Persia, in 520 B.C., approximately eighteen years after the Jews returned from Babylonian captivity to rebuild the temple in Jerusalem (Haggai 1:1). Dating from the book of Haggai shows that Haggai prophesied in Jerusalem for three and one-half months—beginning in late August and ending in early December of 520 B.C. It is reasonable to assume, however, that his ministry continued beyond this period.

Jewish tradition suggests that Haggai saw the temple of Solomon before its destruction in 586 B.C. and was

---

Ray L. Huntington is assistant professor of ancient scripture at Brigham Young University.

therefore an elderly man at the beginning of his ministry in 520 B.C. Others, such as Augustine, suggest that both Haggai and Zechariah prophesied in Babylon before the return of the Jewish exiles in 538 B.C.[2]

Historical Setting of the Book of Haggai

After Judah's unsuccessful rebellion against Babylonian overlords in 586 B.C., the city of Jerusalem, together with the magnificent temple of Solomon, was destroyed. The destruction of the temple, like no other event, symbolized the decline of the kingdom of Judah and the withdrawal of God's blessings and divine protection.[3]

After the fall of Babylon to the Medes and Persians in 538 B.C., Cyrus, king of Persia, issued a decree authorizing the Jews to return to Jerusalem to rebuild their temple (Ezra 1:2–4; 6:3–5). A significant number of Jews remained in Babylon, but, the book of Ezra records, close to fifty thousand exiles returned to Jerusalem under the leadership of Zerubbabel of the royal house of David (Ezra 2). In 536 B.C., two years after the Jews' return to Jerusalem, the altar of sacrifice and foundation of the temple had been rebuilt (Ezra 3:3–11). Despite that work, for the next sixteen years the Jews discontinued their efforts to rebuild the temple. This stoppage was due to the extreme opposition generated by the Samaritans and to apathy among the Jewish exiles (Ezra 4:1–5, 24). Not until the inspired ministry of Haggai in 520 B.C. was work on the temple resumed.

Haggai's Prophetic Message

Though information about the prophet's personal background is lacking, the central focus of Haggai's message is clear: Now is the time to build God's holy temple. Haggai began his prophetic message by declaring: "Thus speaketh the Lord of hosts, saying, This people say, The time is not come, the time that the Lord's house should be built" (Haggai 1:2). The foundation of the temple had been completed in 536 B.C., but no additional progress on the temple's reconstruction had been made for sixteen years, and according to the Lord in verse 3, the Jews were rationalizing that it was not the time to resume their efforts. The book of Haggai records, "Is it time for you, O ye, to dwell in your cieled houses, and this house lie waste?" (Haggai 1:4). The phrase "cieled houses" may refer to the costly cedar paneling many of the wealthy Jews were using to decorate the interior of their homes. If so, it is clear from the Lord's question that He is displeased with the efforts of those who have used their energies and wealth to lavishly adorn their own homes while neglecting the Lord's house.

Haggai's message in verse 4 provides an important insight regarding the significance the Lord has placed upon temples and the work associated with these sacred buildings. According to Joseph Smith, one of the primary reasons for the gathering of God's children, whether in Haggai's day or in our dispensation, is to: "build unto the Lord a house whereby He could reveal unto His people the ordinances of His house and the glories of His kingdom, and teach the people the way of salvation: for there are certain ordinances and principles that, when they are taught and practiced, must be done in a place or house built for that purpose."[4]

Without the ordinances obtained in the temple, the Jews were lacking a vital ingredient to their spiritual welfare. Moreover, their efforts to beautify their homes while failing to rebuild the Lord's house clearly demonstrated that their worldly endeavors had taken precedence over the Lord's commandments.

The book of Haggai is especially relevant for the day in which we live, for many of our worldly endeavors, such as work, civic involvement, schooling, or recreation, may influence us to procrastinate or abandon the important work that takes place in the Lord's holy temples. Regarding this issue, President Marion G. Romney counseled the Saints by quoting President Spencer W. Kimball: "Many people spend most of their time working in the service of a self-image that includes sufficient money, stocks, bonds, investment portfolios, property, credit cards, furnishings, automobiles, and the like to *guarantee* carnal security throughout, it is hoped, a long and happy life. Forgotten is the fact that our assignment is to use these many resources in our families and quorums to build up the kingdom of God—to further the missionary effort and the genealogical and temple work. . . . Instead, we expend these blessings on our own desires."[5]

In contrast, those who are burdened with life's demands and challenges will find increased peace and joy as a result of their labors in the temple. In support of this idea, Elder John A. Widtsoe wrote: "I believe that the busy person on the farm, in the shop, in the office, or in the household, who has his worries and troubles, can solve his problems better and more quickly in the house of the Lord than anywhere else. If he will . . . [do] the temple work for himself and for his dead, he will confer a mighty blessing upon those who have gone before, and . . . a blessing will come to him, for at the most unexpected moments, in or out of the temple will come to him, as a revelation, the solution of the problems that vex his life. That is the gift that comes to those who enter the temple properly."[6]

Haggai continued the Lord's message by asking the Jews to consider their ways (Haggai 1:5). The word *consider* is used to translate the Hebrew word *soom,* which means "to attend to" and is used five times in the book of Haggai.[7] In this case the prophet was asking the Jews to carefully "attend to," or "assess," their neglect of the temple, because the Lord had not been obligated to bless their lives. Haggai wrote:

"Ye have sown much, and bring in little; ye eat, but ye have not enough; ye drink, but ye are not filled with drink; ye clothe you, but there is none warm; and he that earneth wages earneth wages to put it into a bag with holes.

"Thus saith the Lord of hosts; Consider your ways. . . .

"Ye looked for much, and, lo, it came to little; and when ye brought it home, I did blow upon it. Why? saith the Lord of hosts. Because of mine house that is waste, and ye run every man unto his own house.

"Therefore the heaven over you is stayed from dew, and the earth is stayed from her fruit.

"And I called for a drought upon the land, and upon the mountains, and upon the corn, and upon the new wine, and upon the oil, and upon that which the ground bringeth forth, and upon men, and upon cattle, and upon all the labour of the hands" (Haggai 1:6–11).

The writings of Haggai leave little doubt that both temporal and spiritual blessings are withheld from the Saints when they neglect the work performed in the Lord's temples. In contrast, if the Jews resumed their labors to rebuild the temple, the Lord promised them his help and support: "I am with you" (Haggai 1:13; 2:4).

I believe the Lord's statement, "I am with you," can be understood in two equally important ways. The first is the Lord's promise to render divine help and strength to those who were involved in the rebuilding of the temple in Haggai's day. The second, and the broader of the two meanings, is that the Lord will be with us through the bestowal of profound blessings resulting from our faithful temple attendance (Haggai 2:18–19). For example, the following statements demonstrate how the Lord is with us through the bestowal of significant blessings reserved for those who attend the temple faithfully where possible:

"Many parents, in and out of the Church, are concerned about protection against a cascading avalanche of wickedness which threatens to engulf [the world]. . . . There is a power associated with ordinances of heaven—even the power of godliness—which can and will thwart the forces of evil if we will but be worthy of those sacred [covenants made in the temple of the Lord]. . . . Our families will be protected, our children will be safeguarded as we live the gospel, visit the temple, and live close to the Lord."[8]

"The Lord will bless us as we attend to the sacred ordinance work of the temples. Blessings there will not be limited to our temple service. We will be blessed in all of our affairs. We will be eligible to have the Lord take an interest in our affairs both spiritual and temporal."[9]

"I am satisfied that if our people would attend the temple more, there would be less of selfishness in their lives. There would be less of absence of love in their relationships. There would be more of fidelity on the part of husbands and wives. There would be more of love and peace and happiness in the homes of our people."[10]

The Jewish people in Haggai's day undoubtedly received similar blessings as they participated in the temple ordinances available to them. It is clear that they understood the necessity of the temple in their spiritual lives, inasmuch as they readily harkened to Haggai's call to renew their labors on the temple: "And the Lord stirred up the spirit of Zerubbabel the son of Shealtiel, governor of Judah, and the spirit of Joshua the son of Josedech, the high priest, and the spirit of all the remnant of the people; and they came and did work in the house of the Lord of hosts, their God" (Haggai 1:14).

Haggai's Prophetic Message

Once work on the temple resumed, Haggai asked those who had seen the temple of Solomon to compare it with the temple they were currently building. It is apparent from the Lord's question, "Is it not in your eyes in comparison of it as nothing?" that the second temple was not as beautiful or elaborately adorned as Solomon's temple (Haggai 2:3). Nevertheless, the Lord counseled the Jews to "be strong" and "work," with the assurance that he would be with them in their labors, as he was with the Israelites in their exodus from Egypt (Haggai 2:4–5). Moreover, the Lord made it clear to the Jews why their efforts to beautify the temple were important by declaring that the "desire of all nations" would soon come to the temple in Jerusalem. Haggai records "For thus saith the Lord of hosts; Yet once, it is a little while, and I will shake the heavens, and the earth, and the sea, and the dry land; and I will shake all nations, and the desire of all nations shall come: and I will fill this house with glory, saith the Lord of hosts" (Haggai 2:6–7).

The "desire of all nations" is the Holy One of Israel—

even Jesus Christ, who would eventually come to his holy temple in Jerusalem. Haggai's prophecy in verses 6 and 7 is probably dualistic; it may refer to the Savior's numerous visits to the temple in Jerusalem during his mortal ministry as well as his visitation to the temple at the time of his second coming, in which the Lord will shake the heavens, earth, sea, and dry land, and the desire of all nations (Christ) shall come.[11] Thus, Haggai reminded the Jews that their continued efforts to build and beautify the temple would not be in vain, because Jehovah himself would personally visit the temple and fill it with his glory. In this context it is easy to understand what Haggai meant when he prophesied that the "glory of this latter house shall be greater than of the former," because the Lord's anticipated personal visits to the temple would glorify the current edifice beyond that of the temple of Solomon (Haggai 2:9). In a broader sense, all dedicated temples of the Lord are sacred edifices in which God's Spirit and glory reside. Joseph Smith taught this important concept to the Saints during the dedicatory prayer of the Kirtland Temple: "That thy glory may rest down upon thy people, and upon this thy house, . . . that it may be sanctified and consecrated to be holy, and that thy holy presence may be continually in this house; and that all people who shall enter upon the threshold of the Lord's house may feel thy power, and feel constrained to acknowledge that thou hast sanctified it, and that it is thy house, a place of holiness" (D&C 109:12–13).

As we continually visit the house of the Lord, we can also partake of the Lord's Spirit and feel his glory manifest within its interior. Moreover, we will be blessed to partake of God's peace which is found abundantly in his holy temples (Haggai 2:9). In referring to the sacred environs of the temple, Elder David B. Haight declared, "The moment we step into the house of the Lord, the atmosphere changes from the worldly to the heavenly, where respite from the normal activities of life is found, and where peace of mind and spirit is received. It is a refuge from the ills of life and a protection from the temptations that are contrary to our spiritual well-being."[12]

In Haggai 2:11–14, the prophet reminded the Jews that the consecrated meat of the animal sacrifices used in the temple made the priests' clothing holy, because it was in direct contact with the garment (Leviticus 6:27); however, the garment itself could not transmit that holiness to a third or fourth object. Moreover, anything touched by an unclean individual would become unclean (Numbers 19:11–13, 22). Thus, uncleanness is much more easily transmitted than holiness.[13] Through references to the Mosaic law regarding holiness and uncleanness, Haggai may have been alluding to the fact that the Jews' sacrifices and offerings on the rebuilt altar of the temple could not transmit holiness to them nor absolve them of their failure to continue rebuilding the temple. Furthermore, even though the Jews had returned to a promised land consecrated by the Lord, that fact alone could not make them a holy people. The only way for them to become a holy people was to rebuild the temple and participate worthily in the temple services.

Then the Lord asked the Jews to "consider from this day and upward" the consequences of failing to rebuild the temple (Haggai 2:15). Haggai lists the consequences as poor harvests (2:16); blasting, or intense heat, from the eastern winds; mildew; and hail (2:17), which would have had disastrous effects upon their crops. Conversely, Haggai promised the Jews that their obedience in rebuilding the temple would result in "seed in the barn" as well as abundant harvests from the vine, fig tree, pomegranate, and the olive tree (2:19). Indeed, the Lord would bless them.

Although many of the Old Testament prophets' messages and exhortations went unheeded by the ancient house of Israel, Haggai's ministry appears to be an exception. As a result of his work, the faithful Jews in Jerusalem resumed their work on the temple and continued until it was completed in 515 B.C. Because of their obedience to the message of a prophet of God, the temple once again stood in Jerusalem as a blessing in the lives of God's faithful Saints.

Latter-day Israel must remind itself of Haggai's message. As we participate in temple ordinances, we allow the Lord to bless us, as he did the Jews in Haggai's day, with a variety of temporal and spiritual blessings.

Notes

1. *The NIV Study Bible,* ed. Kenneth Barker (Grand Rapids, Mich.: Zondervan, 1985), 1400.

2. Sidney B. Sperry, *Old Testament Prophets* (Salt Lake City: Deseret Sunday School Union, 1965), 71.

3. "Temples through the Ages," in *Encyclopedia of Mormonism,* ed. Daniel H. Ludlow, 4 vols. (New York: Macmillan, 1992), 4:1463.

4. Joseph Smith, *Teachings of the Prophet Joseph Smith,* sel. Joseph Fielding Smith (Salt Lake City: Deseret Book, 1938), 308.

5. Quoted by Marion G. Romney, in Conference Report, April 1977, 121; emphasis in original.

6. John A. Widtsoe, "Temple Worship," *Utah Genealogical and Historical Magazine* 7 (April 1921): 63–64.

7. William Gesenius, *Gesenius' Hebrew and Chaldee Lexicon to the Old Testament Scriptures,* trans. Samuel P. Tregelles (Grand Rapids, Mich.: Eerdmans, 1949), 787.

8. Ezra Taft Benson, "Atlanta Georgia Temple Cornerstone Laying," 1 June 1983, as quoted by Dean L. Larsen, "The Importance of the Temple for Living Members," *Ensign,* April 1993, 12.

9. Boyd K. Packer, *The Holy Temple* (Salt Lake City: Bookcraft, 1980), 182.

10. Gordon B. Hinckley, as quoted by Larsen, "Importance of the Temple," 12.

11. Bruce R. McConkie, *The Millennial Messiah* (Salt Lake City: Deseret Book, 1982), 272–73.

12. David B. Haight, "The Temple: A Place of Refuge," *Ensign,* November 1990, 61.

13. Barker, *NIV Study Bible,* 1403.

CHAPTER ELEVEN

The Everlasting Gospel: A Comparison of Dispensations

CAMILLE FRONK

Any serious study of the scriptures elicits queries related to the nature of the Lord's Church before the dispensation of the meridian of time. While such language as baptism unto repentance, faith in the Lord Jesus Christ, and the gift of the Holy Ghost is abundant in the New Testament record, such familiar terms are conspicuously absent in the Old Testament account. Are we then to conclude that these fundamental principles and ordinances of the gospel were not understood and practiced before the coming of Jesus Christ? Numerous LDS scriptural sources and words of modern prophets suggest that the answer is "no." God is the same yesterday, today, and forever (1 Nephi 10:18; D&C 20:12; Hebrews 13:8) and so are the saving principles and ordinances of the gospel. The position taken in this paper is that these eternal principles and ordinances were understood and practiced at times during the Old Testament period.

The Book of Mormon teaches the value of coming to believe the truths written in one standard work by studying the teachings of another book of scripture (Mormon 7:9). The Savior also encouraged his followers to consider

Camille Fronk is assistant professor of ancient scripture at Brigham Young University.

all scripture as a whole in order to understand the gospel message. After commanding the Nephites to search the words of the prophets in order to learn "all things concerning my people" (3 Nephi 23:1–5), Christ "expounded all the scriptures in one" and commanded the Nephites that this is what they should teach (v. 14). By expounding scriptures in one, or integrating all scripture—ancient and modern—we are able to better identify the content of ancient prophets' messages and the depth of their gospel understanding.

Jacob taught that all the holy prophets before his time not only "knew of Christ" but also "believed in Christ," "had a hope of his glory," and "worshiped the Father in his name" (Jacob 4:4–5). Furthermore, Nephi the son of Helaman witnessed that many prophets, including Abraham, Zenos, Zenock, Ezias, Isaiah, and Jeremiah "did testify boldly" of Christ to the people in their day (Helaman 8:13–24). Finally, Christ himself witnessed that "all the prophets from Samuel and those that follow after, as many as have spoken, have testified of me" (3 Nephi 20:24). It appears that anyone who is or was called a prophet by God is appointed to testify of Christ.

Other scripture gives added dimension to a prophet's message, regardless of the dispensation in which he lived. Peter witnessed that "all his holy prophets since the world began" spoke of "the times of restitution of all things" (Acts 3:21). Such prophecies infer that these same prophets would have borne witness of a universal apostasy that would necessitate a restoration of all things. Christ informed the Nephites that "many" of the prophets testified of repentance and baptism as conditions for salvation (3 Nephi 23:5). From Doctrine and Covenants 138 we learn that the spirit world was organized for the preaching of the gospel to those who died "without a knowledge of the truth, or in transgression, *having rejected the prophets"* (v. 32; emphasis added). And what were those who had rejected the prophets taught there? The same truths that prophets taught them in mortality adapted to their condition as disembodied spirits—"faith in God, repentance from sin, vicarious baptism for the remission of sins, the gift of the Holy Ghost by the laying on of hands. And all other principles of the gospel that were necessary for them to know in order to qualify themselves that they might be judged according to men in the flesh, but live according to God in the spirit" (vv. 33–34).

Joseph Smith taught that the early inhabitants of this earth were as aware of the plan of salvation as those who have been instructed since the time of his coming. "We cannot believe that the ancients in all ages were so ignorant of the system of heaven as many suppose, since all that were ever saved, were saved through the power of this great plan of redemption, as much before the coming of Christ as since; if not, God has had different plans in operation . . . to bring men back to dwell with Himself; and this we cannot believe, since there has been no change in the constitution of man since he fell."[1]

The findings from these inspired sources are powerfully clear; the prophets have proclaimed the same fundamental testimony since the world began. Their witness centers on Christ and his earthly mission (Mosiah 15:11, 13) and includes the first principles and ordinances of the gospel, which are essential for salvation. In addition, all the holy prophets testified by the gift of the Holy Ghost from the beginning of this world (Moses 5:58–59; D&C 20:25–26; 2 Peter 1:21) and "had the Melchizedek Priesthood and were ordained by God himself."[2] The message and witness define a man as a prophet. One who does not testify of Christ, preach the principles of salvation by the power of the Holy Ghost, or receive his calling from God is not a prophet.

Despite evidence of consistency in a prophet's message throughout all ages, one is reminded of well-documented differences in religious practices of God's chosen people from the time of Adam to Moses, and from Moses to Jesus Christ. Much of the confusion and misconception surrounding the gospel presented by Old Testament prophets emerges as a result of misunderstandings concerning how much of the gospel the children of God knew and what ordinances they received during these two time periods. It is therefore meaningful to explore and contrast the unifying, as well as the distinguishing, characteristics among the Lord's people during the Old Testament era.[3]

The Higher Priesthood Was Always on the Earth

The Melchizedek Priesthood, or higher priesthood, is essential to administer the gospel, to hold the keys of the mysteries of the kingdom, and to manifest the power of godliness through its ordinances (D&C 84:19–22). Latter-day prophets have clearly taught that this greater priesthood and the keys of presidency have been on the earth since the beginning. "The Priesthood was first given to Adam," Joseph Smith taught, "he obtained the First Presidency, and held the keys of it from generation to generation."[4] President Joseph Fielding Smith declared that "the Lord, of necessity, has kept authorized servants on the earth bearing the priesthood from the days of Adam to the present time; in fact, there has never been a moment from the beginning that there were not men on the earth holding the Holy Priesthood. Even in the days of apostasy, and apostasy has occurred several times, the Lord never surrendered this earth and permitted Satan to have complete control."[5]

Modern scripture reiterates that the "Holy Priesthood" not only was in operation among the people, in an unbroken chain from Adam all the way down to Moses (D&C 84:6–16), but that it "continueth in the church of God in all generations" (D&C 84:17). Showing the continuing nature of this priesthood after Moses, Joseph Fielding Smith specified, "the prophets of Israel, such as Samuel, Isaiah, Jeremiah and Elijah, held the Melchizedek Priesthood."[6] While modern revelation reports unquestionably the perpetual presence of the higher priesthood, the same certainty cannot be obtained from the standard Old Testament text; however, passages from the biblical text that may affirm these modern prophets' declarations will be discussed here.

The Ordinances of the Gospel from Adam to Moses

Evidence indicates that ordinances of salvation were available to the children of God from Adam to Moses. Joseph Smith declared "that [Adam] received revelations, commandments, and ordinances at the beginning is beyond the power of controversy."[7] Those prophets who succeeded Adam knew the same gospel and ordinances. "How could Abel offer a sacrifice and look forward with faith on the Son of God for a remission of his sins, and not understand the Gospel?," the Prophet Joseph asked. "If Abel was taught of the coming of the Son of God, was he not taught also of His ordinances? We all admit that the Gospel has ordinances, and if so, had it not always ordinances, and were not its ordinances always the same?"[8]

The First Principles and Ordinances of the Gospel

Adam's baptism and reception of the gift of the Holy Ghost after leaving the Garden of Eden are well documented in Moses 6:64–65 but are not found in the Old Testament account as it has come down to us.[9]

The conditional requirements Adam followed to qualify for these blessings are the same for us today. God instructed him, "If thou wilt turn unto me, and hearken unto my voice, and believe, and repent of all thy transgressions, and be baptized, even in water, in the name of mine Only Begotten Son, who is full of grace and truth, which is Jesus Christ, the only name which shall be given under heaven, whereby salvation shall come unto the children of men, ye shall receive the gift of the Holy Ghost, asking all things in his name, and whatsoever ye shall ask, it shall be given you" (Moses 6:52).

God then charged Adam to teach these things "freely" to his children and to "all men, everywhere" (Moses 6:57–58). Later Enoch was instructed to teach his people the same gospel requirements of repentance, baptism, and receiving the Holy Ghost (Moses 7:10–11). Finally, after his ordination, Noah was commanded to teach his people the gospel "even as it was given unto Enoch" (Moses 8:19–24). Joseph Smith taught, "we have sufficient grounds to go on and prove from the [B]ible that the gospel has always been the same; and the officers to officiate, the same; and the signs and fruits resulting from the promises, the same."[10] From this he reasoned that prophets such as Noah and others would have practiced the principles and ordinances of the gospel.

These fundamental gospel principles and ordinances are strikingly similar to requirements taught and administered in the latter-day Church. "All the principles of the Gospel are eternal," declared President Joseph Fielding Smith, "the plan of salvation was given to Adam and he taught it to his children. Adam was baptized and received the gift of the Holy Ghost. So were all those who accepted the Gospel in the beginning. Faith in God the Father and in his Son Jesus Christ and in the Holy Ghost is also a celestial law. Men had to repent and be baptized in all ages when the Gospel was among them, if they sought favor in the presence of God."[11]

Temple Ordinances

That plan of salvation, which provides a way for men and women to return and dwell with God, includes temple covenants and ordinances. Temple blessings were available to many in the Church from the time of Adam. In reference to the righteousness of Abraham, Isaac, and Jacob, the Lord declared that "they have entered into their exaltation, according to the promises, and sit upon thrones, and are not angels but are gods" (D&C 132:37). Because the full blessings of exaltation are given only to a worthy husband and wife, we can assume that the great patriarchs' wives also received these celestial blessings through faithful observance of temple covenants. Elder John A. Widtsoe taught, "there are evidences that even in patriarchal days, in the days of Adam, there was the equivalent of temples, for the Priesthood was held in its fulness, as far as the people needed it; and there is every reason to believe that from

Adam to Noah, temple worship was in operation. After the flood the Holy Priesthood was continued; and we have reason to believe, in sacred places, the ordinances of the temple were given to those entitled to receive them."[12] Individuals who lived from the time of Adam to Moses and who qualified for temple blessings through their personal worthiness had the necessary ordinances available to them.

Individual Response to These Ordinances

Scripture records that at various times from Adam to Moses, many respected their covenants and remembered their obligations to the Lord. The peoples of Enoch and Melchizedek were recognized for their righteousness and the unimaginable blessings they experienced as a result. "The Lord came and dwelt with [the people of Enoch]" and "they were of one heart and one mind, and dwelt in righteousness; and there was no poor among them" (Moses 7:16, 18). "And his people [the people of Melchizedek] wrought righteousness, and obtained heaven" (JST Genesis 14:34; see also Alma 13:14–19).

On the other hand, scripture also suggests that some members of the Lord's church before Moses were not always faithful to their covenants and even sought to alter them. Noteworthy is the example of people who lived at the time the Lord made his great covenant with Abraham. "My people have gone astray from my precepts, and have not kept mine ordinances, which I gave unto their fathers; and they have not observed mine anointing, and the burial, or baptism wherewith I commanded them; but have turned from the commandment, and taken unto themselves the washing of children, and the blood of sprinkling; and have said that the blood of the righteous Abel was shed for sins; and have not known wherein they are accountable before me" (JST Genesis 17:4–7). This example confirms that many doctrines were taught accurately by holy prophets but were later misinterpreted by the people. Again we are struck by the fact that the voice of the prophets remains a constant witness and message while the reaction of the people is as varied as observed in today's society.

In summary, the Lord's people who lived upon the earth between the time of Adam and Moses enjoyed the blessings of the fullness of the gospel as we do today. This fullness included faith in Christ, repentance of sins, baptism by immersion for the remission of sins for those who were accountable, the gift of the Holy Ghost, and the temple ordinances and covenants. This same level of gospel knowledge and blessings, however, did not continue among the general membership of the Church after the time of Moses.

The Gospel in Its Fulness Withheld Generally

Numerous passages of scripture confirm that after leaving Egypt, the children of Israel not only had the opportunity to be taught the gospel in its fullness as in former generations but they also had the opportunity to accept it and receive all of its blessings. In the New Testament Paul taught concerning the Israelites of Moses' day, "for unto us was the gospel preached, as well as unto them: but the word preached did not profit them, not being mixed with faith in them that heard it" (Hebrews 4:2). From the Doctrine and Covenants we learn that Moses actually taught his people "plainly" in the wilderness "and sought diligently to sanctify his people that they might behold the face of God; but they hardened their hearts and could not endure his presence" (D&C 84:23–24). Even the Old Testament describes the unwillingness in the hearts of the children of Israel at Sinai to enjoy the greater blessings of the gospel when they pleaded with Moses, "speak thou with us, . . . but let not God speak with us lest we die" (Exodus 20:19).

Again, the same gospel was being offered. It was accessible to the Lord's people at the time of Moses, but they chose to reject it when they heard it. "If they had been sanctified and holy," said Brigham Young, "the children of Israel would not have travelled one year with Moses before they would have received their endowments and the

Melchisedec Priesthood. But they could not receive them, and never did. Moses left them, and they did not receive the fulness of that Priesthood."[13] And so, the higher priesthood and the ordinances thereof were taken "out of their midst" (JST Exodus 34:1–2; D&C 84:25).[14]

Gospel Distinctions Before and After Moses

The Old Testament record and latter-day revelation suggest two concurrent levels of Church organization functioning after the time of Moses: Worthy leaders continued to enjoy the blessings of the Melchizedek Priesthood, while the general congregation was limited to the blessings and ordinances of the lesser Levitical priesthood. For example, under the lesser priesthood, only men from the tribe of Levi were authorized to offer sacrifice to the Lord for the children of Israel or preside as High Priest of the Levitical order (a descendent of Aaron within the tribe of Levi). Yet there is record that Gideon, from the tribe of Manasseh (Judges 6:14–24); David, from the tribe of Judah (2 Samuel 6:12–18); and Samuel, from the tribe of Ephraim (1 Samuel 7:9–10) offered sacrifices at various times, a role reserved for the priestly tribe of Levi. David's sons are called *kohanim* in 2 Samuel 8:18 and 1 Chronicles 18:17, generally translated as "priests" in the Old Testament.[15] In addition, Solomon, from the tribe of Judah, dedicated the temple, obviously a priesthood duty (1 Kings 8; 1 Chronicles 6–7). An apocryphal source cites Solomon declaring himself a priest, while he is clearly not from the lineage of Levi: "I am a priest of the Lord, and to Him I serve as a priest; and to Him I offer the offering of His thought."[16] It is arguable that a second and superior priesthood was in operation at this time, one that was not dependent on lineage (Hebrews 7).[17]

More specifically, many prophets between Moses and the coming of Christ held the sealing power, a function of the higher priesthood. Elijah, a prophet in the northern kingdom about 850 B.C., held the keys of the sealing power of the Melchizedek Priesthood. He later restored those keys to

Peter, James, and John on the Mount of Transfiguration (Matthew 17:3) and again to Joseph Smith and Oliver Cowdery in the Kirtland Temple (D&C 110:13–16). Additionally, when the Lord discussed the sealing connected to eternal marriage, he stated that "David's wives and concubines were given unto him of me, by the hand of Nathan, my servant, and others of the prophets who had the keys of this power" (D&C 132:39).

John A. Widtsoe suggested that since there were those who held the higher priesthood under Moses, the tabernacle in the wilderness would have been used for higher ordinances in addition to animal sacrifice. He wrote, "When Israel was in Egypt, the Priesthood was with them, and we may believe from certain sayings of the Scriptures that Israel had in Egypt a temple or its equivalent, the mysterious 'testimony.' When Israel was in the wilderness temple worship was provided for, for the Lord said to the Prophet Joseph Smith (D&C 124:38): 'For, for this cause I commanded Moses that he should build a tabernacle, that they should bear it with them in the wilderness, and to build a house in the land of promise, that those ordinances might be revealed which had been hid from before the world was.' In the tabernacle (temple) of the wilderness, the ordinances of God's house were given to a certain extent, at least, as we give them today."[18]

Priesthood holders not of the tribe of Levi who assumed priesthood duties after the time of Moses also held positions of authority among the people as judges (such as Gideon), prophets (such as Samuel), and kings (such as David and Solomon). Through modern prophets we learn that many of these "prophets, priests, and kings" received temple ordinances and covenants while the main membership of the Church focused on the law of Moses, illustrating this additional level within the Church after Moses. More importantly, it shows us that the Lord kept his promise that the Melchizedek Priesthood would always continue in the Church of God (D&C 84:17).

More than a thousand years after Moses, Jesus Christ

himself would personally minister upon the earth. His earthly ministry included the role of *Elias as a restorer.* Jesus restored the gospel in its fullness with the accompanying Melchizedek Priesthood and its ordinances to the general congregation.[19] The gospel couldn't be "restored" to the children of God if it hadn't first existed and been known by his people earlier.

The apostle Paul tells us that the law of Moses was *"added* because of transgressions" (Galatians 3:19; emphasis added) among the children of Israel. Joseph Smith commented on the passage, "What, we ask, was this law added to, if it was not added to the Gospel?"[20] The fullness restored by Christ did not disappear under Moses and subsequent prophets, but a lesser law was *added* to support a spiritually struggling people who did not have access to the higher blessings. Since Aaron and the seventy elders of Israel already held the priesthood before the lesser priesthood was given (Exodus 24:9–11), John Taylor submitted that they originally held the same higher priesthood that Adam and those after him had enjoyed, again pointing to the "additional" lesser priesthood: "It would seem that Aaron and the seventy elders of Israel then had the Melchizedec [*sic*] Priesthood, and the Aaronic was about being combined with it, as we have them now. Moses held the keys of the Melchizedec Priesthood, and presided over the whole. Aaron was then in possession of the Melchizedec Priesthood; but another or lesser priesthood was about to be conferred upon him, which was done soon after."[21] It was the removal of the added law of Moses and the return of the fullness of the gospel to the house of Israel generally that the Savior restored at his coming.

While the law of Moses contained provisions that encouraged an ethical life, it was adapted to help the spiritually weak prepare for a fullness of the gospel. Elder Bruce R. McConkie clarified a specific difference between the gospel enjoyed by the Church before Moses and the consequences when the higher priesthood was not held by the general membership: "Whenever the Lord's people on either continent enjoyed the fulness of the everlasting gospel, this means that they had faith in Christ, repented of their sins, were baptized for the remission of sins, and had the gift of the Holy Ghost. Whenever they were restricted to the lesser law, the law of Moses, and thus had only the preparatory gospel, they still exercised faith, sought repentance, and subjected themselves to baptism in water, but were unable to obtain the right to the constant companionship of the Holy Spirit."[22] Clearly the absence of the Holy Ghost as a gift to the general Church was a marked difference from earlier times and encompassed the lack of multiple subsequent blessings. It can be seen, however, that they could continue to receive the continued blessings of the preparatory gospel, including faith in Christ, repentance from sin, baptism by immersion for the remission of sin, and the occasional influence of the Spirit.

Ordinances Available from Moses to Christ

The preparatory gospel "is the gospel of repentance and of baptism, and the remission of sins, and the law of carnal commandments, which the Lord in his wrath caused to continue with the house of Aaron among the children of Israel until John [the Baptist]" (D&C 84:26–27; see also 107:13–14, 20). With the keys for its administration comprehended in the lesser priesthood, the ordinance of baptism could continue unaltered under the law of Moses.

The Doctrine and Covenants confirms that John the Baptist received baptism "while he was yet in his childhood" (D&C 84:28),[23] obviously before he began his public ministry, but the passage does not identify who administered this ordinance, prompting some to muse that a heavenly being could have baptized him. Elder McConkie was adamant that there would be no reason to expect anyone other than one called to the priesthood then living on the earth to perform the needed ordinance—and not only for John but for countless others who qualified.[24] He stated, "Baptism is an eternal ordinance, an everlasting rite, a continuing requirement in God's kingdom, and it was practiced by the Jews before John ever came on the scene to minister for a short season among men. He was no more the originator of baptism than he was of faith or repentance or sacrifice or any of the other laws in the which he believed or the ordinances in which he participated. It is true that the Jews today no longer perform baptisms, just as they have ceased their sacrificial rites, but it was not so anciently, and it had not been so from the beginning."[25]

Reflection upon reactions to the doctrine of baptism taught and practiced among the Nephites before Christ's coming, and the Jews at the time of Christ, provide additional impetus to conclude that the knowledge and practice of baptism were common among the Israelites before the coming of Christ. When Jacob taught that all "must repent, and be baptized in his name, having perfect faith in the Holy One of Israel, or they cannot be saved in the kingdom of God" (2 Nephi 9:23), there is no indication that these principles and ordinance were new revelation to him or his people.[26] Likewise, when John the Baptist began his ministry, there is no indication that people were asking what new ordinances he was proposing; rather, they were wondering how they should be living once they had received baptism (Luke 3:2–18). Finally, when a leader and teacher of the Jews, Nicodemus, came to Jesus at night and was taught about being "born again," Jesus appeared amazed that he, being a learned Jew, would not know or understand the meaning and significance of baptism unto repentance (John 3:1–13).[27]

Potential Support from Ancient Texts

Though neither the practice of nor the term *baptism* is found within the King James Version of the Old Testament, many other religious texts and traditions infer that baptism unto repentance was known and practiced by the children of Israel. Granted, by solely using the standard Biblical text and Jewish traditions and writings as acceptable evidence, without consideration of modern revelation through living prophets, one cannot prove that baptism preceded John and the Christian era. After receiving a clear testimony of modern prophets, however, we may appreciate possible complementary insights from other sources.

Jewish tradition is not silent concerning baptism; however, it was generally received by men and women converting to Judaism (proselytes) and those identified as "Levitically defiled."[28] Under both of these circumstances three rites were required in ancient times: circumcision, baptism, and sacrifice. Some rabbinic traditions attribute *symbolic* baptism to the children of Israel as they passed through the Red Sea.[29] Others suggest that Israel could not receive the Torah unless they "first submit to the three ceremonies of circumcision, baptism, and sacrifice" the same as proselytes.[30] With this understanding, it may then be argued from the law itself that what was required for the proselyte was also originally required for lineal Israel: "One ordinance shall be both for you of the congregation, and also for the stranger that sojourneth with you, an ordinance for ever in your generations: as ye are, so shall the stranger be unto the Lord" (Numbers 15:15–16).

Nineteenth-century scholar Alfred Edersheim described baptism as it was performed for those desiring admission or readmission into Judaism by referring to Talmudic writings: "The baptism was to be performed in the presence of three witnesses. . . . The person to be baptized, having cut his hair and nails, undressed completely, made fresh profession of his faith, before what were designated 'the fathers of the baptism' and then immersed completely, so that every part of the body was touched by the water. The rite would, of course, be accompanied by exhortations and benedictions."[31] Edersheim also described the purpose and desired outcome of the rite of baptism: "As he stepped out of these waters he was considered as 'born anew'—the language of the Rabbis, as if he were 'a little child just born' as 'a child of one day.' . . . More especially was he to regard himself as a new man in reference to his past. Country, home, habits, friends, and relations were all changed. The past, with all that had belonged to it, was past, and he was a new man—the old, with its defilements, was buried in the waters of baptism."[32] These commentaries on Jewish tradition symbolize being "born again" and becoming a new creature with verbal commitments and total immersion in water.

Members of a Jewish sect who separated themselves from mainstream Jewish society and lived in a desert community near the Dead Sea from about 150 B.C. to A.D. 70 chronicled much of their religious life in what have been called the Dead Sea Scrolls. Fragments and entire scrolls, some stored in clay jars, began to be discovered in 1947 inside caves around Qumran, on the northwest shoulder of the Dead Sea. One of the main sectarian documents included in this collection of scrolls, referred to as the "Rule of the Community," reports what members of the Qumran community perceived as a necessary correlation between a repentant life and religious ablutions. "He cannot be purified by atonement, nor be cleansed by waters of purification, nor sanctify himself in streams and rivers, nor cleanse himself in any waters of ablution. Unclean, unclean is he, as long as he rejects the judgments of God. . . . It is by humbling his soul to all God's statutes, that his flesh can be cleansed, by sprinkling with waters of purification, and by sanctifying himself with waters of purity."[33] In the minds of the Qumran community, without a changed heart, purifying waters were of no avail.

It is important to understand that these passages cannot be used to claim that the Qumran community nor Jewish society before Christ were performing baptisms strictly after the manner of John the Baptist, nor can we assume they understood the importance and purpose of baptism unto repentance as a saving ordinance; however, these citations do indicate traditions that have striking parallels to the true ordinance of baptism by immersion for remission of sins. They suggest the possibility of apostate traditions derived from covenant Israel.

Conclusion

Knowledge and subsequent testimony of the Lord's gospel and the accompanying ordinances of salvation are not established by scrutiny of ancient manuscripts and archeological discoveries. It is only through revelation and the whisperings of the Spirit that we come to know gospel truths. The witness of modern prophets and scripture contribute immeasurably to our personal inspiration and understanding. Through continuing revelation we can know assuredly of the unchangeable nature of our God.

Brigham Young taught, "The doctrines of the gospel are the same now as they were in the days of Adam, or Elijah, or Jesus, when he was upon the earth."[34] There was no mysterious alternative gospel taught by prophets of God in ages past. God *is* the same yesterday, today, and forever. There is security in knowing that the rules don't change; the principles and ordinances necessary for salvation are understood and taught by prophets in all dispensations of time. When there is no record of some prophets' teachings in the Old Testament, and only portions of others' discourses, we can be assured of fundamental points that would have been included in their witness to ancient Israel (even though these elements are not represented in the received text).

The lack of prophetic teaching of the saving ordinances of the gospel preserved in the Old Testament may well qualify as a portion of the "plain and precious" scripture that was removed from the Bible (1 Nephi 13:26–40). Nephi prophesied that precious parts of the gospel were taken away to "pervert the right ways of the Lord, that they might blind the eyes and harden the hearts of the children of men" (1 Nephi 13:27). One highly successful way to pervert the ways of the Lord would be to confuse and even erase the prophetic voice concerning gospel principles and ordinances necessary for salvation.

"We are safe in saying that from the day that Adam was created and placed in the Garden of Eden to this day," Brigham Young taught, "the plan of salvation and the revelations of the will of God to man are unchanged, although mankind have not for many ages been favored therewith, in consequence of apostasy and wickedness. There is no evidence to be found in the Bible that the Gospel should be one thing in the days of the Israelites, another in the days of Christ and his Apostles, and another in the 19th Century, but, on the contrary, we are instructed that God is the same in every age, and that his plan of saving his children is the same. He has not changed his laws, ordinances and covenants pertaining to Himself and the salvation of mankind. The plan of salvation is one, from the beginning of the world to the end thereof."[35]

Notes

1. Joseph Smith, *Teachings of the Prophet Joseph Smith,* sel. Joseph Fielding Smith (Salt Lake City: Deseret Book, 1938), 59–60.

2. Smith, *Teachings of the Prophet Joseph Smith,* 181.

3. At times, the congregation of the Lord's chosen people is referred to as his "Church," as the following statement by Elder Bruce R. McConkie illustrates: "Was there a Church anciently, and if so, how was it organized and regulated? There was not so much as the twinkling of an eye during the whole so-called pre-Christian Era when the Church of Jesus Christ was not upon the earth, organized basically in the same way it now is. Melchizedek belonged to the Church; Laban was a member; so also was Lehi, long before he left Jerusalem." Supplement to *A CES Symposium on the New Testament* (Salt Lake City: The Church of Jesus Christ of Latter-day Saints, 1984), 6. *Church* in this context does not suggest a necessary chapel or other holy edifice nor specific programs and policies but reflects essential priesthood keys and ordinances that always accompany the Lord's gospel and his prophets.

4. Smith, *Teachings of the Prophet Joseph Smith,* 157.

5. Joseph Fielding Smith, *Answers to Gospel Questions,* 5 vols. (Salt Lake City: Deseret Book, 1979), 2:45.

6. Joseph Fielding Smith, *The Way to Perfection* (Salt Lake City: Deseret Book, 1970), 75.

7. Smith, *Teachings of the Prophet Joseph Smith,* 168.

8. Ibid., 59. At another time, the Prophet Joseph taught, "According to Paul (Gal. 3:8), the Gospel was preached to Abraham. We would like to be informed in what name the Gospel was then preached, whether it was in the name of Christ or some other name. If in any other name, was it the Gospel? And if it was the Gospel, and

that preached in the name of Christ, had it any ordinances? If not, was it the Gospel? And if it had ordinances what were they?" Ibid., 60.

9. While not an independently reliable source, a Jewish apocryphal text suggests knowledge of a supposed baptism for Adam and his posterity after they left the garden: "And to the north of the garden there is a sea of water, clear and pure to the taste, like unto nothing else; so that, through the clearness thereof, one may look into the depths of the earth. And when a man washes himself in it, becomes clean of the cleanness thereof, and white of its whiteness—even if he were dark. And God created that sea of his own good pleasure, for He knew what would come of the man He should make; so that after he had left the garden, on account of his transgression, men should be born in the earth, from among whom righteous ones should die, whose souls God would raise at the last day; when they should return to their flesh; should bathe in the water of the sea, and all of them repent of their sins." 1 Adam & Eve 1:2–4, in Rutherford H. Platt Jr., ed., *Forgotten Books of Eden,* trans. S. C. Malan (New York: World Publishing, 1927), 4–5.

10. Smith, *Teachings of the Prophet Joseph Smith,* 264.

11. Smith, *Way to Perfection,* 173–74.

12. John A. Widtsoe, *Temple Worship* (Brigham Young University: Presidencies of BYU Stakes, 1964), 2.

13. Brigham Young, in *Journal of Discourses,* 26 vols. (Liverpool: Latter-day Saints' Book Depot, 1854–86), 6:100.

On another occasion President Young discussed what wickedness they were guilty of that prevented them from receiving these greater blessings and increased the duration of time they would be without the higher priesthood. "This Priesthood has been on the earth at various times. Adam had it, Seth had it, Enoch had it, Noah had it, Abraham and Lot had it, and it was handed down to the days of the Prophets, long after the days of the ancients. But the people would not receive the Prophets, but persecuted them, stoned them and thrust them out of their cities, and they had to wander in the wilderness and make dens and caves their homes. The children of Israel never received the Melchisedek Priesthood; they went into bondage to enjoy it in part, but all its privileges and blessings they never would receive in full, until Jesus came, and then but a few of them would receive it." In *Journal of Discourses,* 9:87.

14. The Nephite nation provides a classic example of a "remnant" of the children of Israel after the time of Moses who received and operated under the Melchizedek Priesthood during the time it was withheld from the Israelites generally. Additional references suggest possibilities of still other groups in other areas of the world who may

have been similarly blessed (1 Nephi 17:38; 22:3–5; 2 Nephi 10:21–22).

15. The New Revised Standard Version of 2 Samuel 8:18 translates the word as "priest" but many other translations avoid the association of priesthood function with non-Levites. For example, the King James Version renders the term as "chief rulers," the Amplified Version uses "chief [confidential] assistants to the king," the New American Standard Version reads "chief ministers," and the New International Version suggests "royal advisors."

16. Odes of Solomon 20:1–2, in *The Old Testament Pseudepigrapha,* ed. and trans. James H. Charlesworth, 2 vols. (Garden City, N.Y.: Doubleday, 1983) 2:753.

17. P. Kyle McCarter Jr. claims that "almost all critics" agree that Old Testament readings that appear to indicate a possible additional priesthood "are interpretive paraphrases of the reading of M[asoretic] T[exts] by scribes who considered it impossible that there should be non-Levitical priests." He suggests that such priestly appellation to non-Levites can be explained as "special priests assigned to the royal household" and "members of the royal family." *II Samuel,* vol. 9 of *The Anchor Bible,* 40 vols. to date (New York: Doubleday, 1984), 255–57.

Other scholars concede the possibility of a second, nonlineal priesthood in operation: "That Samuel functioned as a priest, at least on occasion, seems clear. Therefore one must either reckon with a non-Levitic priesthood during this time; or the term 'Levite' was used more as an appellative meaning priest than as an ethnic title." Merlin D. Rehm, "Levites and Priests," in David Noel Freedman, ed., *The Anchor Bible Dictionary,* 6 vols. (New York: Doubleday, 1992), 4:302.

18. Widtsoe, *Temple Worship,* 2.

19. See JST John 1:20–28; and LDS Bible Dictionary, s.v. "Elias," 663.

20. Smith, *Teachings of the Prophet Joseph Smith,* 60.

21. John Taylor, *Items on Priesthood,* as quoted in Lee A. Palmer, *Aaronic Priesthood through the Centuries* (Salt Lake City: Deseret Book, 1964), 19.

22. Bruce R. McConkie, *The Mortal Messiah,* 4 vols. (Salt Lake City: Deseret Book, 1981), 1:396.

23. It is assumed that John was baptized at age eight, the age of accountability, the same as we are instructed today (D&C 68:27) because age eight and accountability have roots in the Abrahamic covenant given long before Moses (JST Genesis 17:11).

24. Robert J. Matthews suggested that many others living then on the earth could have baptized John. "We know that Zacharias had the

priesthood, but he would not have been the *only* one who had it. There were other priests holding the priesthood who also took their turn at the temple. The person or persons who ordained John to the Aaronic Priesthood and who also baptized him are not identified by name to us at the present." Robert J. Matthews, *A Burning Light: The Life and Ministry of John the Baptist* (n.p., 1972), 23.

Elder McConkie affirmed: "Baptism was an established way of life among faithful Jews in John's day. We do not suppose that all the Jews of that day were baptized, for apostasy was rife and rebellion was common. But among the chosen seed there certainly were many faithful people who were baptized on the same basis as they offered sacrifices. . . . It goes without saying that Zacharias and his fellow priests were baptized. We cannot do other than believe that Elisabeth, Mary, Joseph, Simeon, Anna, the shepherds who heard the heavenly choirs, and hosts of others who waited patiently for the Consolation of Israel had also partaken of this sacred ordinance, all before the ministry of John ever began." McConkie, *Mortal Messiah,* 1:396–97.

25. Ibid., 1:395.

26. Ibid., 1:396.

27. See John A. Tvedtnes, *The Old Testament Church* (Salt Lake City: Deseret Book, 1980), 7.

28. Specific parameters for infractions that would render one "levitically defiled" are difficult to identify. The entire chapter of Leviticus 15 suggests the genre of violations pertaining to sanitary issues that separated any of the children of Israel from the congregation until purification rites were performed to reinstate them into society.

29. Alfred Edersheim, *The Life and Times of Jesus the Messiah,* 2 vols. (Grand Rapids, Mich.: Eerdmans, 1962), 1:274; Louis Ginzberg, *The Legends of the Jews,* trans. Paul Radin, 7 vols. (Philadelphia: Jewish Publication Society of America, 1982), 3:88; see also 1 Corinthians 10:1–4.

30. See Ginzberg, *Legends of the Jews,* 3:88; see also Philo (ca. 20 B.C.–ca. A.D. 50), *De Decalogo,* 11.

31. Edersheim, *Life and Times of Jesus,* 2:745–46. See also 1:270–74 for Edersheim's discussion of "baptism of repentance"; Milton R. Hunter, *The Gospel through the Ages* (Salt Lake City: Stevens and Wallis, 1945), 192–96; and *The New Standard Jewish Encyclopedia,* ed. Cecil Roth and Geoffrey Wigoder (New York: Doubleday, 1970), s.v. "Baptism," 230.

32. Edersheim, 2:745–46.

33. James H. Charlesworth, ed., *The Dead Sea Scrolls,* 2 vols. (Louisville, Ky.: Westminster John Knox Press, 1994), 1:13–14 (col. 3.4–9).

34. Brigham Young, in *Journal of Discourses,* 5:229. Brigham Young also stated, "And the Gospel was among the children of men from the days of Adam until the coming of the Messiah; this Gospel of Christ is from the beginning to the end." In *Journal of Discourses,* 13:269.

35. Brigham Young, in *Journal of Discourses,* 10:324.

CHAPTER TWELVE

PROPHETS AND PRIESTHOOD IN THE OLD TESTAMENT

ROBERT L. MILLET

The prophetic voice is a voice of authority, divine authority. Those called to speak for the Lord Jehovah are empowered by Jehovah and ordained to his holy order. Thus it seems appropriate, as a part of this conference, to devote some attention to the nature of prophetic authority—the power of the holy priesthood among the prophets in ancient Israel.

Joseph Smith the Prophet wrote in 1842: "We believe in the same organization that existed in the Primitive Church, namely, apostles, prophets, pastors, teachers, evangelists, and so forth" (Article of Faith 6). When the time was right, when God the Eternal Father elected in his infinite wisdom to reestablish his kingdom on earth, he began to restore the basic priesthoods, offices, quorums, and councils that had been put in place by Jesus in the meridian of time. The "marvellous work and a wonder" foreseen by Isaiah (Isaiah 29:14) would also entail a restoration of the Church of Jesus Christ that had existed in the centuries preceding the mortal ministry of Jesus (see D&C 107:4). That restoration would consist of Old Testament truths, powers, priesthoods, covenants, and ordinances, such that "a whole and complete and perfect union, and welding together of dispensations, and keys, and powers, and glories should take

---

Robert L. Millet is dean of Religious Education at Brigham Young University.

place, and be revealed from the days of Adam even to the present time. And not only this, but those things which never have been revealed from the foundation of the world, but have been kept hid from the wise and prudent, shall be revealed unto babes and sucklings in this, the dispensation of the fulness of times." (D&C 128:18).

The Melchizedek Priesthood, that "Holy Priesthood after the order of the Son of God" (D&C 107:3), is, like its Author, infinite and eternal (Alma 13:7–9). "The Priesthood is an everlasting principle," Joseph Smith explained, "and existed with God from eternity, and will to eternity, without beginning of days or end of years."[1] It is about that Holy Priesthood that we shall speak—more specifically, the Melchizedek Priesthood, through which this divine authority operated from Adam to Malachi. Sadly, the Old Testament is almost silent in regard to the High Priesthood. Thus we must rely heavily upon the doctrinal teachings of Joseph Smith as set forth in his sermons, revelations, and translations. Further, we will turn to clarifications and expansions provided by those who knew Brother Joseph firsthand, as well as those apostolic and prophetic successors to whom is given the divine mandate to build on the doctrinal foundation he laid.

Adam and the Priesthood

Once the church of God is organized on earth with legal administrators, there is the kingdom of God. "The kingdom of God was set up on the earth from the days of Adam to the present time," the Prophet Joseph Smith explained, "whenever there has been a righteous man on earth unto whom God revealed His word and gave power and authority to administer in His name. And where there is a priest of God—a minister who has power and authority from God to administer in the ordinances of the gospel and officiate in the priesthood of God—there is the kingdom of God."[2]

From the days of Adam to the time of Moses, men and women lived under the patriarchal order of the Melchizedek Priesthood. That is, they lived in a family order presided over by a patriarch. It includes the new and everlasting covenant of marriage.[3] "Adam held the priesthood," Elder Russell M. Nelson observed, "and Eve served in matriarchal partnership with the patriarchal priesthood."[4] President Ezra Taft Benson explained that "Adam and his descendants entered into the priesthood order of God. Today we would say they went to the House of the Lord and received their blessings. The order of priesthood spoken of in the scriptures is sometimes referred to as *the patriarchal order* because it came down from father to son. But this order is otherwise described in modern revelation as an order of family government where a man and women enter into a covenant with God—just as did Adam and Eve—to be sealed for eternity, to have posterity, and to do the will and work of God throughout their mortality."[5]

Though we are uncertain as to the precise organization of the Church during the so-called pre-Christian times, the priesthood leaders among the ancients sought to follow the will of God in all matters. Such persons as Adam, Seth, Enos, Cainan, Mahalaleel, Jared, Enoch, Methuselah, Lamech, and Noah were all high priests; they governed the church and kingdom in righteousness and by virtue of their civil (kingly) and ecclesiastical (priestly) positions. Other worthy men held the higher priesthood, but these patriarchs were the presiding officers and held the keys or right of presidency.[6] "Adam, our father, the first man, is the presiding high priest over the earth for all ages," Elder McConkie observed. "The government the Lord gave him was patriarchal, and . . . the righteous portion of mankind were blessed and governed by a patriarchal theocracy.

"This theocratic system, patterned after the order and system that prevailed in heaven, was the government of God. He himself, though dwelling in heaven, was the Lawgiver, Judge, and King. He gave direction in all things both civil and ecclesiastical; there was no separation of church and state as we know it. All governmental affairs were directed, controlled, and regulated from on high. The Lord's legal administrators on earth served by virtue of their callings and ordinations in the Holy Priesthood and as they were guided by the power of the Holy Ghost."[7]

Adam was earth's first Christian. He was baptized, confirmed, born of the Spirit, quickened in the inner man, ordained, and received into the holy order of God (see Moses 6:64–68). "The priesthood was first given to Adam; he obtained the First Presidency, and held the keys of it from generation to generation."[8] In the book of Moses, Joseph Smith's inspired translation of the early chapters of Genesis, the Prophet recorded the revelation of the gospel to Adam. We read there of Adam's baptism and spiritual rebirth. "And he heard a voice out of heaven, saying: Thou art baptized with fire, and with the Holy Ghost. This is the record of the Father, and the Son, from henceforth and forever." And now note the language of the scripture: "And thou art after the order of him who was without beginning of days or end of years, from all eternity to all eternity. Behold, thou art one in me, a son of God; and thus may all become my sons. Amen" (Moses 6:66–68).

Adam was born again and became through adoption a son of Christ. President Joseph Fielding Smith wrote: "To Adam, after he was driven from the Garden of Eden, the plan of salvation was revealed, and upon him the *fulness* of the priesthood was conferred."[9] Truly, as Elder John Taylor wrote, "Adam was the natural father of his posterity, who were his family and over whom he presided as patriarch, prophet, priest, and king."[10]

The Sons of Adam

The account of Cain and Abel's offerings in Genesis 4 is brought to life and given a doctrinal context by the Prophet's inspired translation. We learn that God had commanded Adam, Eve, and their posterity to "offer the firstlings of their flocks" as an offering in "similitude of the sacrifice of the Only Begotten of the Father" (Moses 5:5–7). Cain, one who "loved Satan more than God," turned away from his parents' teachings and entered into league with the Father of Lies. At Satan's urging, and in what seems to be a defiance of the command to offer a blood sacrifice,[11] Cain "brought of the fruit of the ground an offering unto the Lord." On the other hand, Abel "hearkened unto the voice of the Lord" and "brought of the firstlings of his flock." The Lord "had respect unto Abel, and to his offering; but unto Cain, and to his offering, he had not respect." Cain then entered into an unholy alliance with Satan, plotted and carried out the death of his brother Abel, and instigated secret combinations in the land (Moses 5:18–51).

The Prophet Joseph explained that by faith in the atonement of Christ and the plan of redemption, "Abel offered to God a sacrifice that was accepted, which was the firstlings of the flock. Cain offered of the fruit of the ground, and was not accepted, because he could not do it in faith, he could have no faith, or could not exercise faith contrary to the plan of heaven. It must be shedding the blood of the Only Begotten to atone for man; for this was the plan of redemption; and without the shedding of blood was no remission [see Hebrews 9:22]; and as the sacrifice was instituted for a type, by which man was to discern the great Sacrifice which God had prepared; to offer a sacrifice contrary to that, no faith could be exercised, because redemption was not purchased in that way, nor the power of atonement instituted after that order; consequently Cain could have no faith; and whatsoever is not of faith, is sin." The Prophet went on to say that however varied may be the opinions of the learned "respecting the conduct of Abel, and the knowledge which he had on the subject of atonement, it is evident in our minds, that he was instructed more fully in the plan than what the Bible speaks of. . . .

". . . How could Abel offer a sacrifice and look forward with faith on the Son of God for a remission of his sins, and not understand the Gospel?" Now note what the Prophet asks: "And if Abel was taught of the coming of the Son of God, was he not taught also of His ordinances? We all admit that the Gospel has ordinances, and if so, had it not always ordinances, and were not its ordinances always the same?"[12]

Almost seven years later, Brother Joseph stated that God had "set the ordinances to be the same forever and ever, and set Adam to watch over them, to reveal them from heaven to man, or to send angels to reveal them." That Adam "received revelations, commandments and ordinances at the beginning is beyond the power of controversy; else how did they begin to offer sacrifices to God in an acceptable manner? And if they offered sacrifices they must be authorized by ordination." The Prophet then quotes from the apostle Paul: "By faith Abel offered unto God a more excellent sacrifice than Cain, by which he obtained witness that he was righteous, God testifying of his gifts; and by it he being dead yet speaketh" (Hebrews 11:4). "How doth he yet speak?" Joseph asked. "Why he magnified the Priesthood which was conferred upon him, and died a righteous man, and therefore has become an angel of God by receiving his body from the dead, holding still the keys of his dispensation; and was sent down from heaven unto Paul to minister consoling words, and to commit unto him a knowledge of the mysteries of godliness." And then, as a type of summary on these matters, the Prophet spoke concerning Cain and Abel: "The power, glory and blessings of the Priesthood could not continue with those who received ordination only as their righteousness continued; for Cain also being authorized to offer sacrifice, but not offering it in righteousness, was cursed. It signifies, then, that the ordinances must be kept in the very way God has appointed; otherwise their Priesthood will prove a cursing instead of a blessing."[13]

We know little concerning the keys of Abel's dispensation, spoken of above, except for the fact that a modern revelation indicates that one line of the priesthood descended "from Noah till Enoch, through the lineage of their fathers; and *from Enoch to Abel,* who was slain by the conspiracy of his brother, who received the priesthood by the commandments of God, by the hand of his father

Adam, who was the first man" (D&C 84:15–16; emphasis added). With the murder of Abel and the defection of Cain to perdition, God provided another son for Adam and Eve through which the blessings of the evangelical priesthood or patriarchal order would continue. Seth was "ordained by Adam at the age of sixty-nine years, and was blessed by him three years previous to his (Adam's) death, and received the promise of God by his father, that his posterity should be the chosen of the Lord, and that they should be preserved unto the end of the earth; because he (Seth) was a perfect man, and his likeness was the express likeness of his father, insomuch that he seemed to be like unto his father in all things, and could be distinguished from him only by his age" (D&C 107:39–43; compare Moses 6:10–11).

Enoch and His City

Enoch, the son of Jared, was the seventh from Adam. Jared "taught Enoch in all the ways of God" (Moses 6:21). "Enoch was twenty-five years old when he was ordained under the hand of Adam; and he was sixty-five and Adam blessed him" (D&C 107:48). He was called by God as a prophet and seer to declare repentance to a wicked generation. Because Enoch was obedient and submissive, Jehovah transformed a shy and hesitant young man into a mighty preacher of righteousness. The Lord put his Spirit upon Enoch, justified all his words, and walked with him (Moses 6:26–34). "And so great was the faith of Enoch, that he led the people of God, and their enemies came to battle against them; and he spake the word of the Lord, and the earth trembled, and the mountains fled, even according to his command; and the rivers of water were turned out of their course; and the roar of the lions was heard out of the wilderness; and all nations feared greatly, so powerful was the word of Enoch, and so great was the power of the language which God had given him" (Moses 7:13). That is to say, Enoch was faithful to the covenant of the Melchizedek Priesthood, which allowed God to swear an oath unto him, an oath that granted unto Enoch godlike powers

(JST Genesis 14:27–31; compare Helaman 10:4–10; D&C 84:33–44).[14]

Because of his own righteousness and the power of his witness, Enoch established a society of the pure in heart. He established Zion, a people who "were of one heart and one mind, and dwelt in righteousness; and there was no poor among them" (Moses 7:18; compare D&C 97:21). Zion represents the pinnacle of human interaction, the ideal community, or, as President Spencer W. Kimball taught, "the highest order of priesthood society."[15] Through preaching righteousness and incorporating the doctrines of the gospel into all they did, including applying the pure love of Christ into their social relations and thereby consecrating themselves completely, Enoch and his people founded a holy commonwealth and were eventually translated or taken into heaven without tasting death. The people of Enoch "walked with God, and he dwelt in the midst of Zion; and it came to pass that Zion was not, for God received it up into his own bosom; and from thence went forth the saying, Zion is fled" (Moses 7:69). "And men having this faith, coming up unto this [priesthood] order of God, were translated and taken up into heaven" (JST Genesis 14:32). "And [Enoch] saw the Lord, and he walked with him, and was before his face continually; and he walked with God three hundred and sixty-five years, making him four hundred and thirty years old when he was translated" (D&C 107:49). Enoch's society became the pattern, the prototype, for all faithful men and women who lived thereafter. The apostle Paul could therefore write of Abraham as one of many who "looked for a city which hath foundations, whose builder and maker is God" (Hebrews 11:10).

The Prophet Joseph Smith explained that translation is a power that belongs to the Melchizedek Priesthood, a dimension of the holy order of God.[16] John Taylor added that "the translated residents of Enoch's city are under the direction of Jesus, who is the Creator of worlds; and that he, holding the keys of the government of other worlds, could, in his administrations to them, select the translated people of Enoch's Zion, if he thought proper, to perform a mission to these various planets, and as death had not passed upon them, they could be prepared by him and made use of through the medium of the holy priesthood to act as ambassadors, teachers, or messengers to those worlds over which Jesus holds the authority."[17]

Noah and the Priesthood

Noah, the tenth from Adam, was ordained at the age of ten years (D&C 107:52). "God made arrangements beforehand," Elder John Taylor explained, "and told Methuselah that when the people should be destroyed, that a remnant of his seed should occupy the earth and stand foremost upon it. And Methuselah was so anxious to have it done that he ordained Noah to the priesthood when he was ten years of age. Noah then stood in his day as the representative of God."[18]

Noah was thus more, far more, than a weather prophet; he was a legal administrator, one empowered by God to call a wicked generation to repentance. "And *the Lord ordained Noah after his own order,* and commanded him that he should go forth and declare his Gospel unto the children of men, even as it was given unto Enoch. And it came to pass that Noah called upon the children of men that they should repent; but they hearkened not unto his words." Further, his call to repentance was not just a warning of impending disaster; it was a call to come unto Christ and be saved. "Believe and repent of your sins," Noah said, "and be baptized in the name of Jesus Christ, the Son of God, even as our fathers, and ye shall receive the Holy Ghost, that ye may have all things made manifest" (Moses 8:19–20, 24; emphasis added). In speaking of the patriarchal order of the Melchizedek Priesthood in the days of Noah, John Taylor stated that "every man managed his own family affairs. And prominent men among them were kings and priests unto God."[19]

The Prophet Joseph explained the position of Noah (the

angel Gabriel) in the priesthood hierarchy. Noah "stands next in authority to Adam in the Priesthood; he was called of God to this office, and was the father of all living in this day, and to him was given the dominion."[20] The Prophet also observed that "the keys of this Priesthood consisted in obtaining the voice of Jehovah that He talked with him [Noah] in a familiar and friendly manner, that He continued to him the keys, the covenants, the power and the glory, with which He blessed Adam at the beginning."[21]

Melchizedek and Abraham

Abraham, known to us as the "father of the faithful," sought for the "blessings of the fathers" and the right to administer the same (Abraham 1:1–3). He "was not only a prince on the earth but a prince in the heavens, and by right came to the earth in his time to accomplish the things given him to do. And he found by tracing his genealogy that he had a right to the priesthood, and when he ascertained that, he prayed to the Lord, and demanded an ordination."[22] His father Terah was an idolater and so Abraham's blessings could not come to him in father-to-son fashion. And so it was that he looked to Melchizedek, the great high priest of that day, for counsel, direction, and authority. In his discussion of the ancients who entered the rest of the Lord, Alma chose Melchizedek to illustrate his doctrine. "And now, my brethren," he said, "I would that ye should humble yourselves before God, and bring forth fruit meet for repentance, that ye may also enter into that rest. Yea, humble yourselves even as the people in the days of Melchizedek, who was also a high priest after this same order [the holy order of God] which I have spoken, who also took upon him the high priesthood forever" (Alma 13:13–14). God swore the same oath to Melchizedek that he had sworn to Enoch and granted him the same godlike powers. Melchizedek obtained peace in Salem, "And his people wrought righteousness, and obtained heaven, and sought for the city of Enoch which God had before taken (JST Genesis 14:25–36).

The Saints of God who lived at this time, "the church in ancient days," called the Holy Priesthood after the name of Melchizedek (D&C 107:2–4). A modern revelation informs us that "Esaias . . . lived in the days of Abraham, and was blessed of him—which Abraham received the priesthood from Melchizedek, who received it through the lineage of his fathers, even till Noah" (D&C 84:13–14). Further, it appears that Abraham received additional rights and privileges from Melchizedek. The Father of the Faithful sought for the power to administer endless lives, the fulness of the powers of the priesthood. According to Elder Franklin D. Richards, the Prophet Joseph explained that the power of Melchizedek was "not the power of a prophet, nor apostle, nor patriarch only, but of a king and priest to God, to open the windows of heaven and pour out the peace and law of endless life to man. And no man can attain to the joint heirship with Jesus Christ without being administered to by one having the same power and authority of Melchizedek."[23]

James Burgess recorded a sermon by Joseph Smith, a kind of doctrinal commentary on Hebrews 7, in which he spoke of three orders of the priesthood: the Aaronic, the patriarchal (the new and everlasting covenant of marriage, that which Abraham held), and the fulness of the priesthood (the realization of the blessings promised in the eternal marriage covenant). The Prophet is reported to have said: "Paul is here treating of three different priesthoods, namely, the priesthood of Aaron, Abraham, and Melchizedek. Abraham's priesthood was of greater power than Levi's [Aaron's], and Melchizedek's was of greater power than that of Abraham. . . . I ask, Was there any sealing power attending this [Levitical] Priesthood that would admit a man into the presence of God? Oh no, but Abraham's was a more exalted power or priesthood; he could talk and walk with God. And yet consider how great this man [Melchizedek] was when even this patriarch Abraham gave a tenth part of all his spoils and then received a blessing under the hands of Melchizedek, even the last law or a fulness of the law or priesthood, which constituted him a king and priest after the order of Melchizedek or an endless life."[24] In summary, Joseph the Prophet explained, "Abraham says to Melchizedek, I believe all that thou hast taught me concerning the priesthood and the coming of the Son of Man; so Melchizedek ordained Abraham and sent him away. Abraham rejoiced, saying, Now I have a priesthood."[25] The keys of the priesthood then continued through Isaac, Jacob, Joseph, Ephraim, and so on through the centuries, down to the time of Moses. To what degree the Melchizedek Priesthood and its powers were utilized among the people of Israel during their Egyptian bondage is unclear.

From Moses to Christ

We learn from modern revelation that Moses was ordained to the high priesthood by his father-in-law, Jethro the Midianite. That priesthood line then traces back from Jethro through such unknown ancient legal administrators as Caleb, Elihu, Jeremy, Gad, and Esaias. The revelation then speaks of the divine authority coming through Abraham, Melchizedek, Noah, Enoch, Abel, and Adam (D&C 84:6–16). That the priesthood had been given to Jethro through Midian implies—once again, as was the case with the priesthood descending through Abel, in addition to Seth (D&C 84:6–16; 107:40–52)—that there was more than one line of authority. It may be that the priesthood was transmitted through several lines but that the keys or right of presidency remained with and were passed on by the ordained patriarchs.

In speaking of the children of Israel, the Prophet stated: "Their government was a theocracy; they had God to make their laws, and men chosen by Him to administer them; He was their God, and they were His people. Moses received the word of the Lord from God Himself; he was the mouth of God to Aaron, and Aaron taught the people, in both civil and ecclesiastical affairs; they were both one, there was no distinction."[26] Moses sought diligently to bring the children of Israel to a point of spiritual maturity wherein they could enjoy the highest blessings of the priesthood—the privilege of entering into the rest of the Lord, into the divine presence. Jehovah's desire was that the Israelites become "a kingdom of priests, and an holy nation" (Exodus 19:6). "But they hardened their hearts and could not endure his presence; therefore, the Lord in his wrath, for his anger was kindled against them, swore that they should not enter into his rest while in the wilderness, which rest is the fulness of his glory. Therefore, he took Moses out of their midst, and the Holy Priesthood also; and the lesser priesthood continued" (D&C 84:19, 24–26; compare D&C 107:18–19). That is, Israel's unwillingness to enter the Lord's presence (Exodus 20:19) signaled their lack of preparation as a nation to see God and thus the need to bear the holy priesthood and enjoy its consummate privileges. For one thing, as Abinadi pointed out, many of the children of Israel did not comprehend the place of the Law of Moses as a means to a greater end. "And now," he asked, "did they understand the law? I say unto you, Nay, they did not all understand the law; and this because of the hardness of their hearts; for they understood not that there could not any man be saved except it were through the redemption of God" (Mosiah 13:32).

"And the Lord said unto Moses, Hew thee two other tables of stone, like unto the first, and I will write upon them also, the words of the law, according as they were written at the first on the tables which thou brakest; but it shall not be according to the first, for *I will take away the priesthood out of their midst;* therefore my holy order, and the ordinances thereof, shall not go before them; for my presence shall not go up in their midst, lest I destroy them. But I will give unto them the law as at the first, but it shall be after the law of a carnal commandment; for I have sworn in my wrath, that they shall not enter into my presence, into my rest, in the days of their pilgrimage" (JST Exodus 34:1–2; emphasis added; see also JST Deuteronomy 10:1–2).

When Moses was translated, the keys of the Melchizedek

Priesthood were taken from among the Israelites as a body and the patriarchal order of priesthood ceased. True, there were still men like Aaron, his sons, and the seventy elders of Israel who bore the Melchizedek Priesthood. But no longer did the Melchizedek Priesthood pass from father to son. Thereafter, the priesthood of administration among the people generally was the Aaronic Priesthood. The ordination of men to the Melchizedek Priesthood and the bestowal of its keys came by special dispensation.[27]

President Joseph Fielding Smith therefore pointed out: "In Israel, the common people, the people generally, did not exercise the functions of priesthood in its fulness, but were confined in their labors and ministrations very largely to the Aaronic Priesthood. The withdrawal of the higher priesthood was from the people as a body, but the Lord still left among them men holding the Melchizedek Priesthood, with power to officiate in all its ordinances, so far as he determined that these ordinances should be granted unto the people. Therefore Samuel, Isaiah, Jeremiah, Daniel, Ezekiel, Elijah, and others of the prophets held the Melchizedek Priesthood, and their prophesying and their instructions to the people were directed by the Spirit of the Lord and made potent by virtue of that priesthood which was not made manifest generally among the people of Israel during all these years."

President Smith adds this detail: "We may presume, with good reason, that never was there a time when there was not at least one man in Israel who held this higher priesthood (receiving it by special dispensation) and who was authorized to officiate in the ordinances."[28] Or, as he wrote on another occasion, "The Lord, of necessity, has kept authorized servants on the earth bearing the priesthood from the days of Adam to the present time; in fact, there has never been a moment from the beginning that there were not men on the earth holding the Holy Priesthood. Even in the days of apostasy, . . . our Father in heaven held control and had duly authorized servants on the earth to direct his work and to check, to some extent at least, the ravages and corruption of the evil powers. These servants were not permitted to organize the Church nor to officiate in the ordinances of the gospel, but they did check the advances of evil as far as the Lord deemed it necessary."[29]

Joseph Smith was asked: "Was the Priesthood of Melchizedek taken away when Moses died?" The Prophet stated—and this principle guides our understanding of who held the High Priesthood from the translation of Moses to the days of Christ—that "all Priesthood is Melchizedek, but there are different portions or degrees of it. That portion which brought Moses to speak with God face to face was taken away; but that which brought the ministry of angels remained." Now note this important clarification: "All the prophets had the Melchizedek Priesthood and were ordained by God himself,"[30] meaning that God himself performed the ordination or sent a divine messenger to do so. In a meeting of the First Presidency and Quorum of the Twelve on 22 April 1849, John Taylor asked Brigham Young, "If Elijah, David, Solomon and the Prophets had the High Priesthood, how it was," inasmuch as "the Lord took it away with Moses." After much discussion, President Young "said he did not know, but wished he did." Elder Taylor, who had not been with the Prophet Joseph when the answer was first given in 1841 (he was in England), "thought perhaps the Lord conferred it himself upon some at times whom he had considered worthy, but not with permission for them to continue it down upon others."[31]

And so we operate from a perspective that all the Old Testament prophets held the Melchizedek Priesthood. Exactly how Isaiah and Micah, who were contemporaries, related to one another or who supervised whom, we cannot tell. Who was in charge when Jeremiah, Ezekiel, Habakkuk, Obadiah, or Lehi ministered in the prophetic office, we do not know. It is inconceivable to me that they went about their prophetic labors independent of one another. That Lord who called and empowered them is a God of order and not of confusion (D&C 132:8), and we would suppose that their labors were coordinated and directed by one holding the appropriate keys of the kingdom—the right of presidency, the directing power (D&C 107:8). These principles are, unfortunately, nowhere to be found in the Old Testament record.

It is from modern revelation that we learn that the ordinances of the house of the Lord have been delivered from the beginning. The book of Abraham (p. 37) speaks of "the grand Key-words of the Holy Priesthood, as revealed to Adam in the Garden of Eden, as also to Seth, Noah, Melchizedek, Abraham, and all to whom the Priesthood was revealed" (Fascimile No. 2, Explanation, Fig. 3). Modern revelation tells us, further, that sacred ordinances such as washings and anointings were carried out in ancient temples, which, the Lord said, "my people are always commanded to build unto my holy name" (D&C 124:39) and that "Nathan, my servant, and others of the prophets" held the keys of the sealing power associated with eternal marriage and the everlasting union of families (D&C 132:39). Surely if and when God elected to make available the ordinances of the priesthood to certain individuals—including the endowment and sealing blessings—he could do so in the wilderness or on mountaintops.

The scriptural passages quoted also seem to imply that the ancient tabernacle and temples allowed for more than Aaronic Priesthood sacrificial rites. The exact relationship between the prophet (who held the Melchizedek Priesthood) and the literal descendants of Aaron (who held the keys of the Levitical ordinances) is unclear. Elder Bruce R. McConkie has, however, made the following clarification: "Do not let the fact that the performances of the Mosaic law were administered by the Aaronic Priesthood confuse you. . . . Where the Melchizedek Priesthood is, there is the fulness of the gospel; and all of the prophets held the Melchizedek Priesthood." He continues: "The Melchizedek Priesthood always directed the course of the Aaronic Priesthood. All of the prophets held a position in the hierarchy of the day."[32] In short, "in all ages of the world, whenever the Lord has given a dispensation of the priesthood to any man by actual revelation, or any set of men, this power has always been given" (D&C 128:9).

The Lehite colony, a branch of ancient Israel that was brought by God to the Americas, took the priesthood to the New World. Lehi was a prophet, and, as we have seen, would have held the Melchizedek Priesthood. The Nephites enjoyed the blessings of the fulness of the everlasting gospel, a gospel that is administered by the higher priesthood. There were no Levites among the Nephites, and so we would assume that they offered sacrifice and carried out the ordinances and ministerial duties as priests and teachers by virtue of the Melchizedek Priesthood.[33] John Taylor explained that the higher priesthood was held by "Moroni, one of the prophets of God on this continent. Nephi, another of the servants of God on this continent, had the gospel with its keys and powers revealed unto him."[34]

Elijah and the Keys of the Priesthood

There is a statement from Joseph Smith that seems, to some extent at least, to contradict what has been said heretofore in regard to the keys of the priesthood in ancient Israel. Brother Joseph stated: "Elijah was the last Prophet that held the keys of the Priesthood, and who will, before the last dispensation, restore the authority and deliver the keys of the Priesthood, in order that all the ordinances may be attended to in righteousness."[35] Elijah lived about 850 B.C. If this statement were taken at face value, then no prophet after Elijah, at least in the Old Testament or Book of Mormon, would have held the keys of the Holy Priesthood. That would include such men as Elisha, Joel, Hosea, Jonah, Amos, Isaiah, Micah, Nahum, Jeremiah, Zephaniah, Obadiah, Daniel, Habakkuk, and Ezekiel, as well as Lehi and the American branch of Israel. Are we to understand that none of these men held keys? Was there no right of presidency, no directing power in regard to the covenants and ordinances of the gospel?

The troublesome statement is from a discourse on

priesthood delivered at a conference of the Church held in Nauvoo in October 1840. The Prophet Joseph began by defining the priesthood and then observed that the Melchizedek Priesthood "is the grand head, and holds the highest authority which pertains to the priesthood, and the keys of the Kingdom of God in all ages of the world to the latest posterity on the earth; and is the channel through which all knowledge, doctrine, the plan of salvation and every important matter is revealed from heaven." He went on the say that "all other Priesthoods are only parts, ramifications, powers and blessings belonging to the same, and are held, controlled, and directed by it. It is the channel through which the Almighty commenced revealing His glory at the beginning of the creation of this earth, and through which He has continued to reveal Himself to the children of men to the present time, and through which He will make known His purposes to the end of time."[36]

The Prophet then discussed the role of Michael or Adam as the one designated to oversee the revelations and ordinances of God to his people, stressing, as Joseph did so often, that the ordinances of the gospel are forever the same.[37] He went on to describe the descent of priesthood powers and rites to Abel, Cain, Enoch, Lamech, and Noah. The Prophet provided very important information regarding Enoch and the doctrine of translation. "Now the doctrine of translation," he taught, "is a power which belongs to this Priesthood. There are many things which belong to the powers of the Priesthood and the keys thereof, that have been kept hid from before the foundation of the world; they are hid from the wise and prudent to be revealed in the last times."[38]

Joseph Smith then began to discuss at length the restoration of sacrificial offerings as a part of the restitution of all things, for "all the ordinances and duties that ever have been required by the Priesthood . . . at any former period, shall be had again, bringing to pass the restoration spoken of by the mouth of all the Holy Prophets. . . . The offering of sacrifice has ever been connected and forms a part of the duties of the Priesthood. It began with the Priesthood, and will be continued until after the coming of Christ, from generation to generation. We frequently have mention made of the offering of sacrifice by the servants of the Most High in ancient days, prior to the law of Moses; which ordinances will be continued when the Priesthood is restored with all its authority, power and blessings." Then came the statement: "Elijah was the last Prophet that held the keys of the Priesthood, and who will, before the last dispensation, restore the authority and deliver the keys of the Priesthood, in order that all the ordinances may be attended to in righteousness. It is true," the Prophet continued, "that the Savior had authority and power to bestow this blessing; but the sons of Levi were too prejudiced. 'And I will send Elijah the Prophet before the great and terrible day of the Lord,' etc., etc. Why send Elijah? Because he holds the keys of the authority to administer in all the ordinances of the Priesthood." He added once again that "These sacrifices, as well as every ordinance belonging to the Priesthood, will, when the Temple of the Lord shall be built, and the sons of Levi be purified, be fully restored and attended to in all their powers, ramifications, and blessings. This ever did and ever will exist when the powers of the Melchizedek Priesthood are sufficiently manifest; else how can the restitution of all things spoken of by the Holy Prophets be brought to pass?"[39]

Remember, this sermon was delivered in October 1840, more than four years after Elijah had come to the Kirtland Temple (D&C 110). But Joseph Smith stated that Elijah "will, before the last dispensation"—meaning, presumably, before the dispensation is complete—"restore the authority and deliver the keys of the Priesthood, in order that all the ordinances may be attended to in righteousness." It could well be that the Prophet was referring to a past event as though it was yet to come. On the other hand, the context of the sermon may suggest that a part of Elijah's role as one who would restore the "fulness of the priesthood"[40] is to restore the keys associated with all the ordinances, including animal sacrifice, an event prophesied by Malachi (4:5–6), quoted by Jesus to the Nephites (3 Nephi 25:5–6), rendered differently by Moroni (D&C 2), and described in modern revelation (D&C 84:31–32). One wonders whether Elijah will not deliver those particular keys at the Council of Adam-ondi-Ahman, that grand gathering of priesthood leaders—those who have held keys of authority in all ages—just before the coming of the Lord in glory.[41]

I am grateful to my friend and colleague, Robert J. Matthews, for suggesting the following principles, each of which adds somewhat to our understanding of this matter of the keys of the priesthood:

1. It is evident that a person who holds the keys can "give" them to another without losing them himself.

2. There is a difference between holding the keys sufficiently to function and being the person designated to convey those keys to others. Both Moses and Elijah gave keys to Peter, James, and John on the Mount of Transfiguration,[42] yet it was still Moses and Elijah who brought them to Joseph Smith and Oliver Cowdery in 1836. No doubt Peter had sufficient of "Elijah's keys" to operate the Church during the meridian dispensation, yet the Lord did not use Peter to convey those sealing keys to Joseph and Oliver.

3. It is clearly stated in the Book of Mormon, more than once, that the Twelve in the Western Hemisphere were subject and would be subject to the Twelve in Jerusalem (1 Nephi 12:9; Mormon 3:18–19). This suggests, again, that a people may have sufficient keys of the priesthood to operate the Church without having the right to pass those keys to future dispensations.

4. Truly, all of the keys and powers of the priesthood have not yet been delivered to us in our day; much lies in futurity, including the keys of creation, translation, and resurrection.[43]

In summary, the keys of the kingdom of God have always been on earth when the higher priesthood was on earth; there must be order in the house of God. Those keys would have been held by the Lord's anointed after the time of Elijah. Elijah was not the last man to hold keys in the Old Testament period, since many did after him, but he was the last one in the Old Testament commissioned to return in the dispensation of the fullness of times to see to it that "all the ordinances may be attended to in righteousness."[44]

Conclusion

Ammon explained to King Limhi that "a seer is a revelator and a prophet also; and a gift which is greater can no man have, except he should possess the power of God, which no man can; yet a man may have great power given him from God. But a seer can know of things which are past, and also of things which are to come, and by them shall all things be revealed, or, rather, shall secret things be made manifest, and hidden things shall come to light. . . . Thus God has provided a means that man, through faith, might work mighty miracles; therefore he becometh a great benefit to his fellow beings" (Mosiah 8:16–18).

As Latter-day Saints we love the Old Testament. We cherish the lessons and language of its sacred pages. We know, however, that it has not come down to us in its pristine purity. Many plain and precious truths and many covenants of the Lord have been taken away and kept back by designing persons (1 Nephi 13:20–32). The understanding that the fulness of the gospel of Jesus Christ was once among the ancients is missing. The insight that prophets in the Old Testament were Christians who taught Christian doctrine and administered Christian covenants and ordinances is lacking. But thanks be to God that a seer has been raised up, even a "choice seer" (2 Nephi 3:6–7), Joseph Smith, who began the work of restoring many of those plain and precious truths to the Bible. Jehovah instructed Moses to write the things that would be spoken to him. "And in a day when the children of men shall esteem my words as naught and take many of them from the book which thou shalt write, behold, I will raise up another like unto thee; and they shall be had again among the children of men—among as many as shall believe" (Moses 1:40–41).

A study of the Old Testament by the lamp of the restored gospel ties the Latter-day Saints to the Former-day Saints. Such a study becomes far more than a lesson in history, for as the revelation declares, "Now this same Priesthood, which was in the beginning, shall be in the end of the world also" (Moses 6:7). What was true for the ancients is true for us. What inspired and motivated them can and should entice us to continuing fidelity and devotion to our covenants. The same authority by which they were baptized, confirmed, endowed, washed, anointed, married, and sealed unto eternal life—that same authority has been delivered to Joseph Smith by heavenly messengers. That we will believe, accept, and rejoice in the treasure house of doctrinal understanding delivered to us through modern revelation is my sincere prayer.

Notes

1. Joseph Smith, *Teachings of the Prophet Joseph Smith,* sel. Joseph Fielding Smith (Salt Lake City: Deseret Book, 1976), 157.

2. Smith, *Teachings of the Prophet Joseph Smith,* 271.

3. See D&C 131:1–4; Bruce R. McConkie, in Conference Report, October 1977, 50.

4. Russell M. Nelson, *The Power within Us* (Salt Lake City: Deseret Book, 1988), 109.

5. Ezra Taft Benson, "What I Hope You Will Teach Your Children about the Temple," *Ensign,* August 1985, 9; emphasis added.

6. See Joseph Fielding Smith, *The Way to Perfection* (Salt Lake City: Deseret Book, 1970), 73.

7. Bruce R. McConkie, *A New Witness for the Articles of Faith* (Salt Lake City: Deseret Book, 1985), 35.

8. Smith, *Teachings of the Prophet Joseph Smith,* 157.

9. Joseph Fielding Smith, *Doctrines of Salvation,* comp. Bruce R. McConkie, 3 vols. (Salt Lake City: Bookcraft, 1954–56), 3:81.

10. John Taylor, "Patriarchal," *Times and Seasons* 6 (1 June 1845): 921–22.

11. See John Taylor, in *Journal of Discourses,* 26 vols. (Liverpool: Latter-day Saints' Book Depot, 1854–86), 22:301; Charles W. Penrose, in *Journal of Discourses,* 25:47–48, 339.

12. Smith, *Teachings of the Prophet Joseph Smith,* 58–59.

13. Ibid., 168–69.

14. Joseph Fielding Smith, in Conference Report, April 1970, 59; Boyd K. Packer, *The Things of the Soul* (Salt Lake City: Bookcraft, 1996), 153.

15. Spencer W. Kimball, in Conference Report, October 1977, 125.

16. Smith, *Teachings of the Prophet Joseph Smith,* 170–71.

17. John Taylor, *The Gospel Kingdom,* sel. G. Homer Durham (Salt Lake City: Bookcraft, 1964), 103; see also Smith, *Teachings of the Prophet Joseph Smith,* 170–71.

18. Taylor, *Gospel Kingdom,* 103–4.

19. Ibid., 139.

20. Smith, *Teachings of the Prophet Joseph Smith,* 157.

21. Ibid., 171.

22. John Taylor, *Gospel Kingdom,* 104.

23. Andrew F. Ehat and Lyndon W. Cook, eds., *Words of Joseph Smith* (Provo: BYU Religious Studies Center, 1980), 245.

24. Ibid., 245–46; spelling and punctuation standardized.

25. Smith, *Teachings of the Prophet Joseph Smith,* 322–23.

26. Ibid., 252.

27. See Bruce R. McConkie, *The Mortal Messiah,* 4 vols. (Salt Lake City: Deseret Book, 1979–81), 1:60.

28. Smith, *Doctrines of Salvation,* 3:85.

29. Joseph Fielding Smith, *Answers to Gospel Questions,* 5 vols. (Salt Lake City: Deseret Book, 1957–66), 2:45.

30. Smith, *Teachings of the Prophet Joseph Smith,* 180–81.

31. In Ehat and Cook, *Words of Joseph Smith,* 82–83.

32. Bruce R. McConkie, "The Bible: A Sealed Book," in *Church Educational System Religious Educators' Symposium* (Salt Lake City: The Church of Jesus Christ of Latter-day Saints, 1985), 6.

33. See Smith, *Doctrines of Salvation,* 3:87; Bruce R. McConkie, *The Promised Messiah* (Salt Lake City: Deseret Book, 1978), 412, 421, 427.

34. Taylor, *Gospel Kingdom,* 140.

35. Smith, *Teachings of the Prophet Joseph Smith,* 172.

36. Ibid., 166–67.

37. Ibid., 59–60, 264, 308.

38. Ibid., 168–71.

39. Ibid., 171–73.

40. Ibid., 337.

41. Ibid., 157; Joseph Fielding Smith, *The Progress of Man* (Salt Lake

City: Deseret Book, 1964), 479–82; Bruce R. McConkie, *The Millennial Messiah* (Salt Lake City: Deseret Book, 1982), 578–88.

42. Smith, *Teachings of the Prophet Joseph Smith,* 158.

43. Spencer W. Kimball, in Conference Report, April 1977, 69–72; see also John Taylor, in *Journal of Discourses,* 23:32.

44. Smith, *Teachings of the Prophet Joseph Smith,* 172.

Index